Import/Export

How to Get Started in International Trade

2nd Edition

Carl A. Nelson

McGraw-Hill, Inc.

New York San Francisco Washington, D.C. Auckland Bogotá
Caracas Lisbon London Madrid Mexico City Milan
Montreal New Delhi San Juan Singapore
Sydney Tokyo Toronto

To those who dare:
the entrepreneurs of the world

"Fortune befriends the bold."
—Virgil

©1995 by Carl A. Nelson.
Published by McGraw-Hill, Inc.

Printed in the United States of America. All rights reserved. The publisher
takes no responsibility for the use of any materials or methods described in this book,
nor for the products thereof.

pbk   1 2 3 4 5 6 7 8 9 DOC/DOC 9 9 8 7 6 5

Library of Congress Cataloging-in-Publication Data
Nelson, Carl A. 1930–
    Import/export : how to get started in international trade / by
Carl A. Nelson. — 2nd ed.
      p. cm.
    Includes index.
    ISBN 0-07-046276-3 (pbk.)
    1. Trading companies—Handbooks, manuals, etc. 2. International
trade—Handbooks, manuals, etc. 3. Exports—Handbooks, manuals,
etc. 4. Imports—Handbooks, manuals, etc. 5. New business
enterprises—Handbooks, manuals, etc. I. Title.
HF1416.N45   1995
658.8'48—dc20   95-16132
                                                        CIP

Acquisitions editor: David J. Conti
Editorial team: Joanne Slike, Executive Editor
               Lori Flaherty, Managing Editor
               Barbara Minich, Book Editor
               Jodi Tyler and Joann Woy, Indexers
Production team: Katherine G. Brown, Director
               Ollie Harmon, Coding
               Toya Warner, Computer Artist
               Wanda S. Ditch, Desktop Operator
Design team: Jaclyn J. Boone, Designer   LHP
             Katherine Stefanski, Associate Designer   0462763

Contents

Success Stories

Introduction

GLOBAL TRADE HAS EXPLODED. WORLD EXPORTS HAVE GROWN FROM less than $100 million shortly after World War II to well over $5 trillion today. It has become the engine of global wealth pushing worldwide incomes to previously unthinkable levels.

Import/Export: How to Get Started in International Trade— Second Edition can open the mysteries of international trade, so you too can become part of the action. It is written for the owner of a small manufacturing or service firm, the person in search of a second career, or the entrepreneurial man or woman who wants to know how to get into this $5 trillion worldwide market.

Doing business across national borders is not difficult and can be very profitable, and *Import/Export* explains the basics of the international trade transactions from A to Z in terms anyone can understand. It deals with every aspect of exporting and importing, citing helpful details and examples.

Import/Export was hatched from my import/export seminars. Many students wanted the greater depth of written material for future reference. Over the years, the first edition had many printings and has been a proven success, as have the thousands of people who have read it and put it to work.

Nothing about my approach to international trade has changed, and its basic treatment is as applicable today as it was when first written. It is not enough to understand just exporting or importing. In order to be a successful trader, you must grasp your trading partner's problems; therefore, you must understand both.

My approach from the beginning was to write a professional "how-to" book that offers a small amount of theory with large portions of practical information in a tight, logical format that shows the details of the import/export *transaction*. This approach explains the process differently than anyone else in that I deal with the "commonalities" and the "differences." Most books take the government approach of dealing only with exporting. I take the private sector approach, which focuses on the profitable business. The commonalities of my book are not country specific; that is, they work in any country. Only two chapters (Chapters 6 and 7) are specific to the United States and even these chapters are generic in the sense that the general process is the same for all nations.

Unlike any previous book on international trade, this book presents the basics of import/export in terms that compare and contrast import and export. Other books on this subject separate importing from exporting, implying the two are distinctly different.

In fact, the mechanics of importing and exporting are basically the same. Importing is the mirror image (commonality) of exporting. For example, the terminology and communication for exporting and for importing across borders is identical.

This new edition takes you to the brink of the new century and beyond. The basic material has been updated and new "hot buttons" of international trade, such as how to do business in the North America Free Trade Area (NAFTA), the European Union (EU), and Asia, have been included.

WHO IS THE BOOK FOR?

The audience for this book continues to be managers of firms who wish to expand internationally as well as students and entrepreneurs who see opportunity in the expanding global marketplace.

Because this book is written by an American does not mean it is just for Americans. In every country of the world, businesses make and sell goods across borders. The methods they use, except for a few differences in national rules, are exactly the same. This book describes that universal process and is a valuable tool for anyone who wishes to profit from global trade.

This book is valuable for managers and staffs of any size firm, but it is especially valuable for the small- to medium-size manufacturing and service firms that lack practical hands-on experience and wish to learn the mechanics of importing and exporting. After all, less than 10% of manufacturing and service companies worldwide are involved in international trade. Yet to survive as globalism sweeps across the land, more must get into the game.

Many people are intrigued and challenged by the thought of starting their own profitable business where they can market their products and those of others across international borders. They see untapped markets and profits and want to know how to get into the growing business of international trade. An import/export business offers great opportunity to travel and enjoy the prestige of working with clients all over the world.

Many students (even those who have degrees in business) who wanted to enter and pursue a career in one or more phases of international trade, read the first edition of this book to learn the practical application of their theoretical work. Many teachers and professors found it suitable as a classroom text because it provided needed perspective on international trade, as well as helped students gain an appreciation of the total process and how their future fit into the big import/export picture.

Finally, it would be dishonest to suggest that the business of international trade is not still overwhelmingly male-dominated. However, importing and exporting is not only for males. The truth is, the battle of the sexes has been fought, and women have won their rightful place to participate as equals in global trade. From mailrooms to boardrooms, American women have become as commonplace as pinstripes and button-down collars, and there's more opportunity and freedom for women in world business today than at any other time.

In the United States, there are more than 5 million women-owned businesses—23% of all smaller firms—grossing more than $100 billion annually. As the total number has increased, so have those proportionately involved in international trade.

For new citizens of any country and so-called minority groups, many of the expected obstacles turn into advantages. For instance, in most of Africa, it is an advantage to be a person of color. Most newcomers to any country have the advantage of speaking and understanding another language and culture. Getting off the ground in international trade is often easier because contacts are already in place.

WHAT'S IN THE BOOK

Import/Export cites 16 concepts common to both import and export—six in Chapter 2, six in Chapter 3, and four in Chapter 4. Each fundamental concept is presented in this order to facilitate your understanding of them and because it is the order in which real-world transactions generally happen. Please don't, however, mistakenly assume that the order represents a hierarchy of importance or that each concept can truly stand alone. Each fundamental integrates with the other concepts in the process of international trade and each is equally necessary. Successful importers and/or exporters grasp the importance of these concepts and put them to work.

Some aspects of importing and exporting differ or are country specific. For example, "controls" apply only to exporting, whereas tariffs (duties) relate only to importing. The distinguishing features of importing and exporting are offered in Chapters 6 through 10. This treatment should clarify any differences and enable you to easily understand them.

This edition enlarges the explanation of the import/export transaction process in many ways:

- New chapters on doing business in specific regions in the world
- All new success stories
- Hot tips
- Tips and traps of culture
- Implications of the Internet
- Tricks using letters of credit
- Using NAFTA to do business in the Americas

Regionalism is a concept whose day has come. International trade doors are opening among neighbors. For instance, Chapter 8 explains how to take advantage of NAFTA and offers insights about its enlargement to include certain countries in South America. Chapter 9 explains the basics of how to do business in the single market of the European Union. Of course, the book would be incomplete if it did not include a discussion of how to do business in Asia (Chapter 10).

HOW TO USE THIS BOOK

Whether you enter international trade through imports or exports, you must understand the basics of both. Therefore, the best way to use this book is first to master the concepts presented in Chapters 1 through 4. But it is unlikely that you will be ready to begin trading until you organize a business to do so. Therefore, Chapter 5 shows you how to start and manage your company and put the fundamentals to work profitably in the import/export business setting. This is where the fun really begins.

The final chapter of the book, Chapter 11, provides 20 secrets to import/export success. Obey these and make big profits.

If you want to travel to exotic places, meet interesting people, make new international friends, and win great untapped profits, then *Import/Export* can change your life! This book offers a dynamic opportunity—the rewards are excitement, a touch of the exotic, and great profit potential. Don't wait! The time to get into the import/export market is now. This book answers these questions plus hundreds more.

- How do you choose a product for import or export?
- How do you make overseas sourcing contacts?
- How do you make marketing contacts?
- How do you price a product for profit?
- How do you prepare a market plan?
- How do you negotiate a transaction?
- How do you protect your patents and trade marks?
- How do you communicate with overseas businesses?
- What are the secrets of overseas travel?
- How do you finance an import or export transaction?
- How do you avoid risk?
- What is a letter of credit?
- To whom do you go for an export license?
- What are the tax incentives for exporting?
- How do you get through the customs maze?
- How to use the Harmonized Tariff Schedule?
- How do you figure import duties?
- What about import quotas?
- Where do you go for a business license?
- What does it cost to start your own import-export business?
- How do you write a business plan for an import-export business?
- What are the benefits of NAFTA?
- How can I trade in Europe's single market?
- Where do I go for information to do business in Asia?

1

Winning the Trade Game

TRADE MEANS THAT ONE PARTY PRODUCES AND EXCHANGES GOODS AND services for currency or for the goods and services offered by another party. When this exchange takes place across national boundaries, it is called *international trade*.

International trade is not a zero sum game of winners and losers. It is a game where everyone wins.

INTERNATIONAL TRADE

Exports are the goods and services *sold* by individuals or nations. Imports are the goods and services *purchased*. By these methods, products valued at more than U.S. $5 trillion worldwide are exchanged every year. When we, as consumers, enjoy fresh flowers from Latin America, tropical fruits in the middle of winter, or a foreign car, we are participants in, and beneficiaries of, international trade.

WHAT IS AN IMPORT/EXPORT BUSINESS?

I'm most frequently asked, "What is an import/export business?" "What organizational methods do traders use?" Briefly, the answer depends on whether you work for a manufacturer or are an inde-

1

pendent businessperson. A more detailed answer is given in Chapter 5.

Any manufacturer that has an exportable product can organize its own export department. Or, like many manufacturers, a company may out-source its export function to an independent import/export company.

An independent import/export company is an individual or company that acts as an international middleman (a unisex term). It sells foreign-made products (import), and/or domestic (home country) products in other countries (export). Every manufacturer not already exporting is a potential client for your independent import/export company. All over the world there are many businesses that do not export. According to the U.S. Department of Commerce, less than 10% of all American manufacturers currently sell their products overseas.

Whether you run your business part-time or full-time, from your home or as an expansion of an existing domestic manufacturing firm, an import/export business often requires little capital investment for startup. And it can grow into a giant business with billions of dollars in annual sales. The largest, like the Japanese trading companies (called Sogo Shoshas) Mitsubishi and Mitsui, do more than $60 billion a year. An import/export business also offers great opportunities to travel and enjoy the prestige of working with clients around the world.

WHERE DO IMPORTERS AND EXPORTERS TRADE?

The opportunity to conduct import/export business is everywhere because the world market has become more interdependent, and trade conditions among nations are changing rapidly. Today, conditions might favor importing with a given country, while tomorrow they might favor exporting. Realistically, international trade involves both importing and exporting, not one to the exclusion of the other.

Novices to international trade, whether companies or individuals, can get started by either importing or exporting. Once trade begins, opportunities spring out of nowhere. A person who successfully starts importing very soon learns of exporting opportunities and vice versa. In any case, a whole lot of money can be made. More than $5 trillion wouldn't be traded worldwide if the import/export business wasn't profitable.

GLOBAL OPPORTUNITIES

We are living in the era of greatest change in international trade. Called the age of globalism and interdependence, it is a time of increasing expectations brought about by the worldwide distribution of Hollywood movies, satellite communications, and speedy transportation systems. People all over the world want the same luxuries and standards. They see things and naturally want them.

Globalization is no longer a buzzword—it is a reality. National governments have a stake in the outcome of global trade because the change affects their societies. Therefore, international trade is not a static process. All over the world, businesses that make things and then attempt to sell them across borders must constantly adjust.

Globalism is a reality driven by changes in the marketplace as well as government policy. As the globalization process goes forward, the need for harmonizing interstate laws becomes more serious. Major changes took place in the late 1980s and early 1990s, which will have a significant effect on international trade into the new century and provide unprecedented opportunities.

General Agreement on Tarriffs and Trade and the New World Trade Organization

The results of the Uruguay round of negotiations on the General Agreement on Tariffs and Trade (GATT) became effective in 1995 and resulted in a major reduction in global tariffs and a concomitant stimulation of global business opportunities. One of the outcomes of the Uruguay round was the creation of a new World Trade Organization (WTO) with equal status alongside the World Bank and International Monetary Fund (IMF). This organization, with more than 120 national members, will make it easier to do business across borders by reducing tariffs and harmonizing laws and practices that are barriers to trade.

The Former Soviet Union

The most significant change during the the last quarter of the twentieth century was the breakup of the Soviet Union and the movement toward market economies in Eastern Europe. The fall of the Berlin Wall represents an excellent opportunity for traders around the globe to market goods into a major area of the world that had been shut off from progress for the greater part of the twentieth century.

Mexico

During the last decades of the twentieth century, Mexico underwent significant change when it joined GATT and became a part of the global trading community. This means a movement toward more open markets and a greater opportunity for traders from around the world to sell into that country, as well as for Mexican businesses to expand their markets.

North America

Another change from the late 1980s to the mid-1990s was the formation of a regional trade alliance between the three nations of North America. Effective January 1, 1989, Canada and the United States formed a free trade area. Then on January 1, 1994, a trade agreement went into effect that also included Mexico, thus expanding the earlier arrangement into the North American Free Trade Area (NAFTA)—the world's largest trading bloc.

New Europe

The European Union (EU) formed a single internal market (discussed more fully in Chapter 9) where the harmonization of more than 300 rules of doing business and trade have been molded into a workable system. It resulted in the substantial removal of all physical, technical, and fiscal barriers to the exchange of goods and services within the common market. The EU is now considering enlarging to include some of the newly independent states of Middle and Eastern Europe. Some of the changes agreed to are:

- A common value-added tax
- Deregulation of transportation
- Establishment of minimum industrial and safety standards
- Broadening of the EUwide bidding process for government procurement

Pacific Basin

Importing and exporting from and to the Pacific Basin nations of Australia, New Zealand, China, Japan, and the Tigers (South

Korea, Taiwan, Hong Kong, Singapore, and Thailand) has expanded faster than in any other part of the world. This is the region of greatest trade opportunity.

WHY GET INTO *TRADE*?

Three reasons exist for people to get into the trade game—imports, exports, and global community.

Imports. Everyone is buying foreign—it's in vogue. Imports are bringing big profits.

Exports. Some experts say that exports have been so far out of balance that the tide must turn. These people believe that now is the time to make profits on exports.

Global Community. People are awakening to realize that the world is interdependent—people of each nation rely on people of other nations to exchange goods, services, and ideas, and that free trade creates jobs.

IS THE TIME RIGHT TO GET INTO THE MARKET?

Many people are making big profits in international trade. Millions of others are asking, "Is the time right for me to get into the import/export game?"

The optimistic importer might say, "In my country there are more imports than exports. I'm making a whole lot of money. I better stay in imports." An optimistic exporter might say, "What goes down must come up—the rate of decline is reversing. I'm staying in exports to make big profits!"

A pessimistic importer might say, "The deficits can't go on forever. It's time to begin exporting." Whereas a pessimistic exporter might say, "Overall, things look really bad for exporting. Maybe I should start importing."

Those who are winning the trade game know that regardless of national deficits or surpluses, the time is always right for an import/export business to make profits. The winners simply swing with political and economic changes over which they have little or no control.

Chapter 2 will launch you into the first steps of an import/export transaction and speed you on your way to international trade success and profits.

2

Launching a Profitable Transaction

THE NEXT FOUR CHAPTERS EXPLAIN THE BASICS OF THE IMPORT/EXPORT transaction. They apply to manufactured products as well as the growing service industries such as computer software, construction engineering, and insurance.

These basics are "the bridge" from producer to buyer and have been in place for many years and tested over time. Nevertheless, it is possible to perceive the import/export transaction process as an obstacle. Don't let it deter you. Anyone can grasp the nuts and bolts of international trade. Invest time and money in yourself by learning as much as you can about the process before you commit to an import/export project.

This chapter addresses the first six commonalities of the importing/exporting transaction. If you understand these steps, your import/export business will get off to an excellent start.

1. Terminology
2. Homework
3. Product selection
4. Making contacts
5. Market research
6. Pricing for the bottom line

Don't mistakenly assume that the order presented in this book represents a hierarchy of importance, or that these steps are in a precise order for every import/export project. In reality, sometimes things happen simultaneously.

TERMINOLOGY

Because of increasing international interdependency, trade literacy has become as important as computer literacy in modern business. As you progress in your reading, frequently refer to the extensive glossary of terms found at the end of this book. Many of these terms are also defined wherever they first appear in the text. Don't be frightened off by the new terminology—learn it!!

HOMEWORK

Research is one of the keys to winning the trade game! Even if you have some experience in international trade, it's unwise to jump into an unresearched project. In fact, it's not unusual to spend several weeks learning about a product and its profit potential before you get serious. Think of it as an investment to lessen the number of your inevitable mistakes.

Before you start an import/export project, get answers to four preliminary questions. The answers will help you decide if the project merits further commitment of your time and funds.

Select the Product. In what product or service are you interested? With what product or service do you have some expertise? For the prospective importer/exporter, this decision is personal as well as technical. For the manufacturer of a product or the provider of a service, this step is moot—you sell your own product or service.

Make Contacts. To whom will you sell the product or service? And from whom will you obtain the product or service? Who are your contacts? Do you have more than one source for the product you intend to import or export? Carefully choose the country where you intend to sell your product.

Research the Market. Are people and/or firms willing to buy the product or service? Although products and services that carry the label "Made in 'Country X'" continue to be popular, they no longer sell themselves. If a local product has a mature market, however, it very likely has a market in other parts of the world. On the other hand, many foreign goods cost less, which increases sales potential. Generally, if the product is unique to a given culture or the quality is cheap, many people will not buy it.

Price for the Bottom Line. Do the rough calculations of price and quantity warrant undertaking the project? Determine whether the margin of profit makes the project worthwhile. What changes must you make to the product to ensure a profitable export or import? Bear in mind that just as much work goes into importing or exporting an unprofitable product or service as trading a profitable one. Don't waste time with losers.

CHOOSE THE PRODUCT

The question asked most often is, "What product should I select to import or export? Should it be rugs or machinery?"

Of course, if your firm already manufactures merchandise or provides a service, that product or service is what you sell. As an independent import/export businessperson you will have to sell someone else's product or service. In other words, you will be the middleman.

The Personal Decision

Most people begin their import/export business with a single product or service they know and understand or with which they have experience. Others begin with a line of products, or define their products in terms of an industry with which they are familiar. Above all, product selection should be a personal decision, made with common sense. For example, if you aren't an engineer, don't begin by exporting gas turbine engines. Or, if you are an electronics engineer, don't start with fashion textiles.

A good example is the American house painter who began making excellent profits exporting a line of automated painting equipment to Europe. He knew the equipment before he began.

Start your business with a product or service with which you have an advantage. You can gain that advantage from prior knowledge, by doing library research about a product, by making or using contacts, or by understanding a language or culture.

HOT TIP: Keep it simple in the beginning.

Technical Marketing Decisions

Keep in mind that the product you select might have to adapt to the cultures of other countries.

Product Standards. Although there is a movement toward harmonizing world product standards, many countries continue to have their own standards in such areas as flammability, labeling, pollution, food and drug laws, safety, etc.

Technical Specifications and Codes. Most of the world uses 220 V and 50 Hz, but products used in the United States are 120 V and 60 Hz. Similarly, most of the world uses the metric system of weights and measures. Determine how you might convert your product to meet these specifications and codes.

Quality and Product Life Cycle. In the life cycle of product innovation, new products are typically introduced first to developed countries (DCs). This leaves an opportunity for sales of earlier models to less developed countries (LDCs). Assess the life-cycle stage in which you find your export/import product.

Other Uses. Different countries use some products for different purposes. For example, motorcycles and bicycles are largely recreational vehicles in the United States, but in many countries they are the primary means of transportation.

Developed Countries. The DCs distinguish the more industrialized nations—including all member countries of the Organization for Economic Cooperation and Development (OECD) from *developing*—or LDCs.

Least Developed Countries. Some 36 of the world's poorest countries are considered by the United Nations to be the least developed of the LDCs. Most of them are small in terms of both area and population, and some are land-locked or small island countries. They are generally characterized by low per capita incomes, literacy levels, and medical standards. They often have subsistence agriculture and lack exploitable minerals and competitive industries.

Most LDCs are in Africa, but a few, such as Bangladesh, Afghanistan, Laos, and Nepal, are in Asia. Haiti is the only country in the Western Hemisphere classified by the United Nations as least developed.

MAKING CONTACTS

Importers and exporters need contacts to get started. The exporter must convince a domestic manufacturer of his or her ability to sell the manufacturer's product or service internationally. The importer, on the other hand, must find an overseas manufacturer or middleman from whom to buy the product or service.

Contacts are classified into two categories—sourcing and marketing. There are two ways to make contacts overlap, both of which could be used to expand your import/export network. *Sourcing*, or finding, means identifying a manufacturer or provider of the product or service you wish to import or export. *Marketing* simply means selling that product or service.

Sourcing Contacts

If you are an exporter, any product or service you select falls into an industry classification. And that industry very likely has an association. Almost every industry has a publication, usually a magazine or a newsletter. A good place to begin your search for product manufacturers or service companies is in the appropriate industry publication. Under "Export Information" in Chapter 5, you will find other sources of information that might help you make contacts for exportable products.

Contacts for importers are only slightly more difficult to obtain. Assuming you know in which country your product is manufactured, you need a contact in that industry in that country. Start with the nearest consulate office. Next, contact that foreign country's international chamber of commerce (COC). You might also make contacts through your embassy or through a corresponding industry association. Furthermore, you might make direct contact with the government of the country in which you are interested.

HOT TIP: Don't be baffled by foreign business organizations. See Appendix A to learn their names and how they are commonly organized.

Next, establish communications with the contact to seek further information or to ask for product samples and prices. You can make contact by letter or by electrical means such as fax, telex, or cable. (See "Communications" in Chapter 3.)

Eventually, take a trip to the country in which you intend to trade; it will make a big difference. (Travel is also explained in Chapter 3.)

SUCCESS STORY: Observing the growth and popularity of golf, his favorite game, a young soils professional targeted a combination of agricultural products and services to serve the golf course industry throughout the world. The products he exported were bioengineered organic fertilizers, pregerminated seed, and soil conditioners designed to maintain turf using ecologically responsible methods. The service he offered was management and counseling for the most effective, cost-efficient, and environmentally sensitive golf courses.

Marketing Contacts

Marketing methods and channels of distribution are the same in most countries. Agents, distributors, wholesalers, and retailers exist everywhere. These are channels through which you can make marketing contacts.

Domestic marketing contacts use direct sales, direct mail, and manufacturer's representatives; attend trade shows, swap meets, flea markets, home parties; or meet with wholesalers. Most governments can also help you find contacts.

A *Foreign sales representative* is a representative or agent residing in a foreign country who acts as a salesperson for a U.S. manufacturer, usually for a commission. Sometimes referred to as a *salesagent* or *commission agent*.

A *Distributor* is a firm that: (a) sells directly for a manufacturer, usually on an exclusive basis for a specified territory, and (b) maintains an inventory of the manufacturer's goods.

As an international marketeer (trader) you also can make contacts through World Trade Centers (WTC), trade shows, direct sales, a distributor, or an agent who is the equivalent of a manufacturer's representative. Trade fairs or shows are often the single most effective place to make contacts and to learn about products, markets, competition, potential customers, and distributors, because exhibitors offer literature and samples of their products. The terms *trade show* or *trade fair* include everything from catalog shows and local exhibits to major specialized international industry shows.

WORLD TRADE CENTERS

A WTC is an apolitical and unaligned shopping center that puts all the services associated with international trade under one roof. It is the first stop for your import/export venture. WTCs complement and support the existing services of private and government agencies. Some of the services you find at a WTC are trade information, communications services, WTC clubs, trade education programs, trade mission assistance, and display facilities.

WTCs are located in more than 170 cities with about 100 more in the planning stages. In other words, they are in virtually every major trading city in the world. The WTC NETWORK links, by electronic trading, the WTCs and their clients and affiliates worldwide. Offers to buy or sell can be advertised on the network's bulletin board.

To find out more about WTCs, contact the World Trade Centers Association (WTCA), One World Trade Center, Suite 7701, New York, NY 10048, USA; telephone: (212) 432-2626; fax: (212) 488-0064.

Lists of worldwide trade shows and international conferences are available from most large airlines such as Lufthansa and Pan American, as well as from the U.S. Department of Commerce and COCs. Your industry association also will know when and where the appropriate trade shows take place. Table 2-1 offers a range of ideas that can help you make either sourcing or marketing contacts.

MARKET RESEARCH

Market research is vital to the success of your import/export business. Will your product sell? Does anyone need your service? You must be able to sell enough of your product or service to justify undertaking it as an import/export project. If you are presenting a new product, you might have to create a market. But a good rule of thumb for the new import/export business is: "If the market isn't there, get out of the project and find another product."

International market research saves money and time. Unfortunately, too many newcomers plunge into import/export *without* determining whether they might sell the product at a profit. Answer the research items on the following checklists to help you determine the market for your product.

Table 2-1. Making Contacts.

	Source	*Market*
Import	Consulate offices International COC Industrial organizations Foreign governments WTCA	Swap meets Direct mailers Mail orders Home parties Trade shows Wholesalers Associations Representatives Retailers U.S. government WTCA
Export	*Thomas Register* *Contacts Influential* *Yellow Pages* U.S. Dept. of Commerce Trade journals Trade associations WTCA	Distributors Trade shows Retailers Foreign governments U.S. Dept. of Commerce Direct mailers United Nations U.S.A.I.D. Sell Overseas America *Business America* State Trade Promotion Offices *Journal of Commerce* WTCA

Exporter Checklist

☑ Is there already a market for the product?

☑ What is the market price?

☑ What is the sales volume for the product?

☑ Who has market share, and what are the shares?

☑ What is the location of the market, what's its size and population? People in major urban areas generally have more money than people elsewhere.

☑ What is the climate, geography, and terrain of the market country?

☑ What are the economics of the country, its gross national product (GNP), major industries, and sources of income?

☑ What is the country's currency? How stable is it? Is barter commonplace?

☑ Who are the country's employees? How much do they earn? Where do they live?

☑ Is the government stable? Do they like Americans? Does the country have a good credit record?

☑ What are the tariffs, restrictions, and quotas?

☑ What are the other barriers to market entry, such as taxation and repatriation of income?

☑ What language(s) do they speak? Are there dialects? Does the business community speak English?

☑ How modern is the country? Do they have electric power?

☑ How do they move their goods? How good is the hard infrastructure (roads, trains, etc.)? What about the soft infrastructure (schools, etc.)?

☑ Does the country manufacture your product? How much do they produce? How much is sold there?

☑ What kind and how much advertising is generally used? Are there local advertising firms? Are there trade fairs and exhibitions?

☑ What distribution channels are being used? What levels of inventory are carried? Are adequate storage facilities available?

☑ Who are the customers? Where do they live? What influences the customers' buying decisions—price, convenience, or habit?

☑ What kinds of services are expected? Do they throw away or repair? Can repair services be set up?

☑ What about competition? Do they have sales organizations? How do they price?

☑ What are the property right implications?

Importer Checklist

☑ Is there already a market for the product?

☑ What is the market price?

☑ What is the sales volume for that product?

☑ Who has market share, and what are the shares?

☑ What is the location of the market, what's its size and population? People in major American urban areas generally have more money than people who live elsewhere.

☑ Who are the wholesalers?

☑ What sort and how much advertising is generally used? Are there local advertising firms? Are there trade fairs and exhibitions?

☑ What distribution channels are being used? What levels of inventory are carried? Are there adequate storage facilities available?

☑ Who are the customers? Where do they live? What influences the customers' buying decisions? Is it price, convenience, or habit?

☑ What kinds of services are expected? Do they throw away or repair? Can repair services be set up?

☑ What about competition? Do they have sales organizations? How do they price?

☑ What are the property right implications?

The answers to these questions can be researched at most good libraries, the Department of Commerce, your COC, or you might want to employ the services of a private market research company. (See Chapters 6 and 7 for a list of export and import information sources.)

SUCCESS STORY: Market research showed Japanese imports of Western boots was growing at a 4.6% per year rate. After answering the four preliminary questions of this chapter, Robert Nielsen obtained $350,000 in capital and successfully started Old West Exports, selling such products as Tony Lama boots into a very lucrative market.

PRICE FOR THE BOTTOM LINE

Profit is an internal, individual decision that varies from product to product, industry to industry, and within the market channel. Desirable profit relates to the goals you have for your import/export business. For instance, one person's goal might be to cover their expenses, take a small salary, and be pleased if the business supports their travels to exotic places. Another's goal might be to expand his business to eventually become a major trading company. Yet another might set her goal to work for only five or six years, sell the business at a profit, and retire on the capital gain.

This segment of the chapter discusses the profit aspects of international trade, beginning with initial quotations, terms of sale, the market channel, and pricing.

Initial Quotations

Initial quotes begin either with a *request for quotation* (RFQ) sent by the importer to the exporter or with an unsolicited offer from the exporter. A simple letter or fax can be an RFQ. Figure 2-1 shows a sample letter of inquiry.

The pro forma invoice, a normal invoice document visibly marked "Pro Forma," is the method most often used to initiate negotiations. This provisional invoice is forwarded by the seller of goods prior to a contemplated shipment to advise the buyer of the type and quantity of goods to be sent, their value, and important specifications (weight, size, etc.). The purpose of the pro forma invoice is to describe in advance certain items and details. This type of invoice contains the major elements of a contract that is used later in shipping and collection documents such as letters of credit (discussed in Chapter 4).

Keep in mind that everything in a pro forma invoice is negotiable, so carefully think through any terms entered on this document. Once accepted by the purchaser, the pro forma invoice becomes a binding sales agreement or legal contract, and the seller is bound to the terms

Our Company, Inc.
Hometown, U.S.A.

Ref:
Date:

Your Company, Ltd.
2A1 Moon River
Yokohama, Japan

Our company is a medium-sized manufacturing company. We are interested in your products.

Please send us a pro forma invoice for five of your machines, C.I.F. Los Angeles. Please indicate your payment terms and estimated time of delivery after receipt of our firm order.

Sincerely,

W.T. Door

President

Fig. 2-1. Typical letter of inquiry

stated. Figure 2-2 is an example of a pro forma invoice that shows the key elements of the contract and are listed as follows:

- Product description and specifications
- Material costs
- Price
- Quantity
- Shipping costs
- Delivery terms
- Procedures

XYZ Foreign, Co.
2A1 Moon River
Yokohama, Japan

Our Company, Inc.
Hometown, U.S.A.

Purchase Order Date:
Invoice Date:
Invoice Ref. No.: PRO FORMA 00012

Terms of Payment: Confirmed
Irrevocable Letter of Credit
Payable in U.S. dollars

Invoice To:
Ship To:
Forwarding Agent:

Via: Country of Origin:

QUANTITY	PART NO.	DESCRIPTION	PRICE EACH	TOTAL PRICE
10	A2Z	Machines	$100.00	$1,000.00

Inland freight, export packing & forwarding fees $ 100.00

Free alongside (F.A.S.) Yokohama $1,100.00
Estimated ocean freight $ 100.00
Estimated marine insurance $ 50.00

C.I.F. Long Beach $1,250.00
Packed in 10 crates, 100 cubic feet
Gross weight 1000 lbs.
Net   weight   900 lbs.
Payment terms: Irrevocable letter of credit confirmed by a U.S. bank.
Shipment to be made two (2) weeks after receipt of firm order.
Country of Origin: Japan.
We certify this pro forma invoice is true and correct.

Issu A. Towa
President

Fig. 2-2. Typical pro forma invoice

Terms of Sale

In international business, suppliers use pricing terms called *terms of sale*. These pricing terms define the geographical point where the *risks* and *costs* of the exporter and importer *begin* and *end*.

International Chamber of Commerce Terms (INCOTERMS) are most widely used and if, when drawing up the contract, both buyer and seller specifically refer to INCOTERMS, they must define their respective responsibilities. In so doing, buyer and seller eliminate any possibility of misunderstanding and subsequent dispute. A copy of INCOTERMS can be had for about $25 from the ICC Publishing Corporation, Inc., 125 East 23rd St., Suite 300, New York, NY 10010; telephone: (212) 206-1150.

There are many terms of sale, but the four most commonly used are listed as follows. Figure 2-3 graphically shows examples of these terms.

- *C.I.F.* (*cost, marine insurance, freight*) is used with a named overseas port of import. The seller is responsible for charges up to the port of final destination.
- *F.A.S.* (*free alongside a ship*) is usually followed by a named port of export. A seller quotes this term for the price of goods that includes charges for delivery alongside a vessel at the port. The buyer is responsible thereafter.
- *F.O.B.* (*free on board*) is the quote that, unlike F.A.S., includes the cost of loading the product aboard the vessel at the named point, either port or inland point of origin.
- *EX* (*named point of origin, e.g., EX-factory, EX-warehouse, EX-destination*) means the seller agrees to cover all charges to place the goods at a specified delivery point. From that point on, all other costs are for the buyer.

Marine Insurance is an insurance that will compensate the owner of goods transported on the seas in the event of loss, if such loss would not be legally recovered from the carrier. It also covers overseas air shipments.

Specific Delivery Point is a point in sales quotations that designates specifically where and within what geographical locale the goods will be delivered at the expense and responsibility of the seller (e.g., F.A.S. named vessel at named port of export).

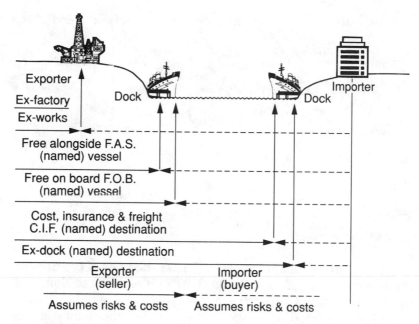

Fig. 2-3. Where the risks and costs begin and end

The Market Channel

The international market channel generally includes the manufacturer, the foreign import/export agent, any distributors (wholesalers), retailers, and buyers or customers. Figure 2-4 shows how this might look.

Price for Profit

The price of your product should be high enough to generate a suitable profit but low enough to be competitive. Ideally, as an importer or exporter you should strive to buy at or below factory prices. This can be done by eliminating from the overseas price the manufacturer's cost of domestic sales and advertising expenses.

Each step along the market channel has a cost. If a product is entirely new to the market or has unique features, you might be able to command higher prices. On the other hand, in a very competitive market, you might need to use marginal cost pricing in order to gain a foothold. *Marginal cost pricing* is the technique of setting the market entry price at or just above the threshold at

Fig. 2-4. Market channel

which the firm would incur a loss. (Under the rules of the General Agreement on Tariffs and Trade (GATT) it is illegal to dump, or gain market share by incurring a loss.)

Most new importers/exporters simply use the domestic factory price plus freight, packing, insurance, etc. Prices can be quoted in U.S. currency or in the currency of the buyer. Generally, pricing should be based on long-term, profit-maximizing objectives, and market share and volumes targeted for long-term export commitment.

It is important that you understand not only the elements that make up your price, but also those of your overseas trading associate. There are no free lunches—everything has a cost.

Figure 2-5 illustrates how a product could be moved from one country to another by an importer or exporter. In particular, it shows how the selling price in one country becomes the buying price in the other. Typical commission percentages are between 7% and 20% for an export middleman and between 5% and 20% for an import middleman (foreign distributor or agent), although commissions can be as low as 1% and as high as 40%. The key issues are the price of the product and the number of units (sales volume) that you might sell. If, for instance, the product is a *big ticket item* with a high salesprice, the commission percentage might be quite low, but a small percentage of a million-dollar sale can be very good business.

Figure 2-6 shows fictitious cost elements associated with a C.I.F. quotation that corresponds to the steps shown in Fig. 2-5.

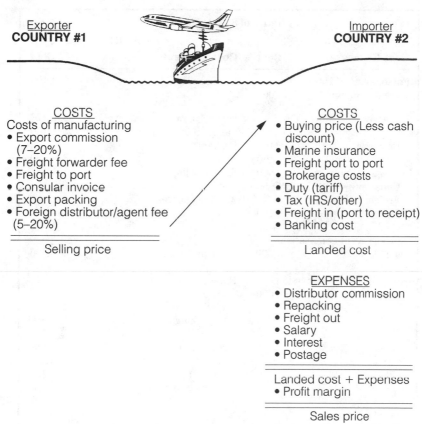

Fig. 2-5. Pricing model

Figures 2-7 and 2-8 are offered as work lists to aid you in accurately costing your product.

Is there sufficient profit at the *volume* (number of units) you might sell to make it worth your while and meet your personal profit goals? Recall that the same amount of work goes into importing or exporting a product that makes no profit as one that makes a good profit.

HOT TIP: A word of caution for manufacturers: If at first exporting doesn't appear profitable, check your manufacturing costs. It might be necessary to import less costly components in order to compete internationally.

Terms of Sale: C.I.F.

EXPORT		IMPORT	
Cost Elements	**Cost**	**Cost Elements**	**Cost**
Factory cost of 100 units @ $100/unit	$10,000	Landed cost C.I.F.	$14,105
Expenses:		Duty @ 5.5%	$ 776
		Tax (IRS or other)	$ 150
Brokerage costs	$ 100	Brokerage	
Export packing	$ 150	clearance fees	$ 50
Freight to port	$ 500	Reforwarding	
Consular invoice	$ 50	from broker	$ 100
Freight forwarder		Banking charges	$ 50
fee	$ 150	Letter of credit	
		¼%	$ 75
*Export agent commission			
@ 15% of cost	$ 1,500	Total landed cost	$15,306
*Foreign agent commission		Expenses	
@ 5% of cost	$ 500		
		Warehouse	$ —
		Repacking	$ 100
		Freight out	$ 100
		Advertising	$ 500
		+Salary	$ 1,410
		Interest	$ —
		Postage	$ 100
Marine insurance (12,950 @ $1.20 per $100 value	$ 155	Total landed plus expenses	$17,516
Transportation (Ocean)	$ 1,000	Unit cost	= $175.16
Landed cost (C.I.F.)	$14,105	Suggested selling price @ 100% markup	= $350.32
		Profit	= $17,516

*Only if an export middleman or import agent is used

+Calculated at a commission of 10% of buying price

$$\text{Markup (\%)} = \frac{\text{Sell-cost}}{\text{cost}} \times 100$$

Fig. 2-6. Examples of cost elements

Reference Information
Our Ref. _____   Customer Reference _____

Customer Information
Name _____   Cable Address _____
Address _____
_____   Telex No. _____

Product Information
Product _____   Dimensions ___ × ___ × ___
No. of Units _____   Cubic Measure _____ (sq. in.)
Net Weight _____   Total Measure_____
Gross Weight _____

Product Charges
Price (or cost) per unit _____ × units _____ Total _____
Profit (or Markup)   _____
Sales Commissions   _____
F.O.B. Factory   _____

Fees—Packing, Marking, Inland Freight
Freight Forwarder   _____
Financing costs   _____
Other charges   _____
Export Packing   _____
Labeling/Marking   _____
Inland Freight to   _____
F.O.B., Port City (export packed)   _____

Port Charges
Unloading (Heavy Lift)   _____
Loading (aboard ship)   _____
Terminal   _____
    Consular Document (check if required) _____
    Certificate of Origin (check if required) _____
    Export License (check if required) _____
F.A.S. Vessel (or airplane)   _____

Freight
Based on _____ weight _____ measure
Ocean _____ air _____
Rate _____ Minimum _____ Amount _____

Insurance
Coverage required _____
Basis _____ Rate _____ Amount _____
C.I.F., Port of destination

Fig. 2-7. Export costing worksheet

Reference Information
Our Ref. _____   Customer Reference _____

Customer Information
Name _____   Cable Address _____
Address _____   _____
_____   Telex No. _____

Product Information
Product _____   Dimensions ____ × ____ × ____
No. of Units _____   Cubic Measure _____ (sq. in.)
Net Weight _____   Total Measure _____
Gross Weight _____

NOTE: IF QUOTE IS F.O.B. FACTORY USE EXPORT
COSTING SHEET TO DETERMINE PRICE AT
C.I.F., PORT OF DESTINATION

Landed Cost (C.I.F., Port of destination)   _____
Customs duty   _____
Customs House Broker Fees   _____
Banking Charges   _____
Taxes: Federal   _____
       State   _____
       Other   _____

Total landed   _____

EXPENSES:
Inland Freight (from port city)   _____
Warehouse costs   _____
Repacking   _____
Inland Freight (from warehouse)   _____
Advertising/promotion   _____
Overhead (% of annual)   _____
Salary (% of annual)   _____
Loans (Principle/Interest)   _____

Total landed plus expenses   _____

Unit cost   _____

Selling price   _____
Margin _____ %   _____

Profit   _____

Fig. 2-8. Import costing worksheet

Now that you are satisfied that you have a viable project, the next step is to create a written, long-range market plan. Chapter 3 explains how to develop that plan, then how to put it into action to make a transaction.

3

Planning and
Negotiating to Win

IN THIS CHAPTER YOU'LL LEARN HOW TO TAKE THE NEXT STEPS IN YOUR import/export transaction. At this point, you have answered the following questions about your import/export project:

- What product or service is to be imported or exported?
- To whom will you sell the product or service? And from whom will you obtain the product?
- Who are your contacts?
- In what countries and/or regions will you market the product?
- Are people and/or firms willing to buy this product or service?
- Do the rough calculations of price and quantity warrant undertaking the project?

If the result of your homework shows you have a marketable and profitable product that will sell in sufficient volume, you are ready to commit resources (time and money) to the project. In this chapter, you'll learn how to take the next steps in your chosen import or export transaction. The six commonalities presented are:

1. The market plan
2. Negotiations

3. Tips and traps of culture

4. Intellectual property rights

5. Communications

6. Travel

THE MARKETING PLAN

Once you have determined that your project is viable, write a long-range marketing plan. A marketing plan is simply a process recorded on paper that allows you to think through the many logical ways you might convince buyers to say "yes" to a sale. It is important to integrate the international market plan with your firm's overall strategic business plan. (See Chapter 5, "Setting Up Your Own Import/Export Business" for details about how to write a business plan.)

Use the following logical, step-by-step process to write your marketing plan:

1. *Objectives* (Sales of $XXX,XXX by the end of the second year. Expansion into countries A and B by the end of the third year.)

2. *Specific tactics* (Radio advertising in two cities. Three direct mailings to each company/person on a specific list.)

3. *Schedule of activities or action plan* (A list of trade shows indicating which you will attend, including dates and the duration of trips to visit overseas distributors, with their names, addresses, and phone numbers. Specific assignments of responsibility—an essential feature of an action plan.)

4. *Budget for accomplishing the action plan*

Include every conceivable cost associated with marketing your product or service; don't scrimp. This is where most start-up firms underestimate their needs. Initial marketing costs will be high.

Segment Your Market

Market segmentation enables an import/export organization to choose its customers and fashion its marketing strategy based on identified customer wants and requirements and on the firm's specific desires and needs. Visualize segmentation on both a macro and a micro level.

The word *macro* comes from the Greek word *makros*, meaning long. It is a combining form meaning large. The word *micro* comes from the Greek word *mikros*, meaning small. A combining term meaning little, small, and microscopic.

Macro Segmentation. Divides a market by such broad characteristics as industry, shipments, location, firm size, etc. An import macro segment might divide a city into market segments. On a larger scale, it might involve dividing the United States into regions, prioritizing those regions, then developing a microplan for each region. An export macro segment might include prioritizing continents or countries within a continent. Further, export macro segments might sort by language, purchasing power, or cultural preference.

Micro Segmentation. Micro segmentation identifies the homogeneous customer groups within macro segments by finding out who makes the decisions for each homogeneous group. Micro segmentation pinpoints where (by address) and who (by name) can say "yes" to a buying decision. From this analysis, a promotional strategy is designed to target the decision-making units (DMUs).

An import micro segmentation might take the data from your market research effort and identify the location of the wholesalers. If you list and prioritize these decision-makers by name and address, you will have a logical, specific plan of attack for your marketing effort.

Your marketing plan and schedule should cover a three- to five-year period depending on the type of product(s) you market, your competitor(s), and your target market(s). Be sure to write this plan no matter how small the import/export project. Only when your marketing plan is in writing will it receive proper attention and adequate allocation of funds.

Execute Your Marketing Plan

Now comes the fun of putting your marketing plan into action. Actively market your product through trade shows, advertisements, television promotions, and direct mail, all in accordance with your budgeted plan. Remember, nothing happens in a business until something is sold.

Personal Sales

The two basic approaches to selling internationally for both imports and exports, are direct and indirect sales. Using the *direct sales method*, a domestic manufacturing firm has its own marketing department that sells to a foreign distributor or retailing firm and is responsible for shipping the goods overseas. The *indirect sales* method uses a middleman who usually assumes the responsibility for moving the goods. This is where your import/export business fits into the picture. You might sell directly to retailers or to distributors/wholesalers.

Regardless of where your targeted DMU is in the market channel, keep in mind that international sales are just like domestic sales: someone makes personal contact and presents a portfolio, brochures, price lists, and/or samples to decision-makers (potential buyers) who can say "yes."

HOT TIP: Making sales requires persistence and determination. Follow-up, and then follow-up again.

Trade Shows (Fairs). Consider using a trade show or trade fair as the keystone of your sales trip. Allow time afterward to visit companies you meet at the fair. The international trader attends trade shows to:

- Make contacts
- Identify products for import or export
- Evaluate the competition (often done without exhibiting)
- Find customers and distributors for import or export
- Build sales for existing distributors

Trade Missions. Trade missions are trips made for the express purpose of promoting and participating in international trade. State and local governments organize several types of trade missions for exporters.

Special Missions. These are organized and led by government officials with itineraries designed to bring you into contact with potential buyers and agents. You pay your own expenses and a share of the cost of the mission.

HOT TIPS ON TRADE FAIRS:

- If exhibiting to sell, don't overcommit. You could get more business than you can handle reasonably.
- If searching for products to import, don't buy until you have done your homework!
- Take more business cards to the trade show than you think you will need. Have your fax number on your card.
- Obtain language translation/interpreter help from a local university or college.
- If you are exhibiting to sell, consider advertising prior to the show to encourage potential customers to find you.

Seminar Missions. Similar to the specialized trade mission, seminar missions add several one- or two-day technical presentations to the trip by a team of industry representatives.

Industry-Organized, Government-Approved Trade Missions. Though these missions are organized by chambers of commerce (COC), trade associations, or other industry groups, government officials often provide assistance prior to and during the trip.

Catalog Shows and Video/Catalog Exhibitions. These are the least expensive ways to develop leads, to test markets, and to locate agents because you don't have to be there. You simply send product catalogs, brochures, and other sales aids to be displayed at exhibitions organized by governments and consultants. Video/catalog exhibitions are ideal for promoting large equipment and machinery that are costly to ship.

Advertising

All companies advertise to communicate with customers. As an exporter or importer, you must ask yourself whether advertising is both important to sales and whether it is affordable. The assistance of an advertising agency familiar with the market environment you wish to target could be crucial to the success of your advertising campaign. Some countries do not carry television and radio advertising. In addition, cultural differences often require more than a simple translation of promotional messages.

In countries where illiteracy is high, you might prefer to avoid written advertisements such as magazines and concentrate instead on outdoor advertising such as billboards, posters, electric signs, and streetcar/bus signs. Outdoor advertising reaches wide audiences in most countries.

> **SUCCESS STORY:** A young Japanese businessman studying in the United States took on the additional task of importing APT, a new Japanese product that is supposedly better and safer than turpentine for cleaning oil or water-based paint. He successfully introduced APT by focusing on a micro segment of 40 art stores in San Diego and 70 in Los Angeles.

Distributors

A *distributor* is a merchant who purchases merchandise from a manufacturer at the greatest possible discount and resells it to retailers for profit. The distributor carries a supply of parts and maintains an adequate facility for servicing. The distributor buys the product in its own name, and payment terms are often arranged on a credit basis. A written contract usually defines the territory to be covered by the distributor, the terms of sale, and the method of compensation (see "Avoiding Risk" in Chapter 4). The work is usually performed on a commission basis, without assumption of risk, and the representative can operate on either an exclusive or a nonexclusive basis. The contract is established for a specific time frame so that it becomes renewable based on satisfactory performance.

As with domestic sales, foreign retailers usually buy from the distributor's traveling sales force, but many buy through catalogs, brochures, or other literature.

Importers and exporters seldom sell directly to the end user. It is not recommended because: (a) it is time-consuming, and (b) it leads to goods being impounded or sold at auction when the buyer doesn't know his or her own trade regulations. Use the following checklist to determine what you want from a foreign representative:

- ☑ A solid reputation with suppliers and banks
- ☑ Financial strength
- ☑ Experience with the product or a similar product
- ☑ A sales organization
- ☑ A sales record of growth

☑ Customers

☑ Warehouse capacity

☑ After-sales service capability

☑ Understanding of business practices

☑ Knowledge of both English and the language of the country

☑ Knowledge of marketing techniques (promotion, advertisement, etc.)

Use the following checklist to understand what the foreign representative wants from you:

☑ Excellent products

☑ Exclusive territories

☑ Training

☑ Parts availability

☑ Good warranties

☑ Advertising and merchandising support

☑ Credit terms, discounts and deals

☑ Commissions on direct sales by the manufacturer in his/her territory

☑ Minimum control and/or visits

☑ Freedom to price

☑ Deal with one person

☑ Security that the product will not be taken away once it is established in the territory

☑ The right to terminate the agreement when he or she pleases

NEGOTIATIONS

Bargaining is inherent to people of many nations. Culturally, nothing comes less natural to Americans. The United States is a nation that operates on a fixed-price system. Most buyers have grown up with the notion that you either purchase off the shelf at the price offered or you don't buy at all. Of course, comparative shopping is native to everyone's buying psychic. So when the international stakes and competition increase, company representatives who are born cultural negotiators might begin to force your hand. In these cases, you will need to rely on your instincts. Before you find yourself in such a position, it is best to be prepared.

Preparations

Unfortunately, all too many people wander into international bargaining situations with no plan and no idea how to proceed. For them, its an ad-lib and ad-hoc operation. For some, lack of preparation is the result of a sense of superiority, but for most it's pure ignorance of the number and competence of the ferocious competitors scouring the world for scraps of business.

The first step in preparing for international negotiations is to develop a complete assessment of your firm's capabilities. Analyze your strengths and weaknesses, particularly in terms of managerial skills, product delivery, technical abilities, and global resources.

Next, analyze your target—the company or country to which you intend to sell your product. Keep in mind that the human and behavioral aspects of your negotiations will be vital.

Understand the place in the world you will be traveling. Know the culture, history, and political process. Pay particular attention to the importance of saving face to the people of the country where you will be negotiating. Find out about the host government's role in country negotiations. Learn about the importance of personal relations. Decide how much time you should allow for negotiations.

Be sure the final agreement specifies terms for the cost, quality, and delivery of the product. Quality can only be assured by someone seeing the product, but cost and delivery terms are the result of a quote agreed to by the seller.

In Japan, young executives role-play negotiations before they make an initial quote. They form teams, sit around a table with a chalkboard nearby, and pretend to negotiate the deal. Each team has a set of negotiating alternatives related to the country they are pretending to represent. Sometimes they cut their offer price by 10%; if that doesn't work, they cut it another 5% or 10%. Other ploys are: (a) offer lower interest rate loans than their competitors; (b) offer better after-sales service warranties; or (c) provide warehouses for parts. Sometimes, even the cost of advertising can make the difference in the sale.

Agreeing to a Contract

After obtaining the initial quotations, as explained in Chapter 2, the next step in any international business arrangement is to reach an agreement or a sales contract with your overseas partner.

Negotiating is integral to international trade and an importer/exporter should be ready to offer or ask for alternatives using simple letters or a fax. In the highly competitive international business world, a trader's ability to offer reasonable terms to customers could mean the difference between winning and losing a sale.

Exporters are finding it increasingly necessary to offer terms ranging from cash against shipping documents to time drafts, open accounts, and even installment payments spread over several years. More sophisticated ideas such as countertrade, counterpurchase, and after-sales service are also negotiable.

Countertrade. International trade means the seller accepts goods or other instruments of trade in partial or whole payment for its products.

Counterpurchase. One of the most common forms of countertrade is one in which the seller receives cash but contractually agrees to buy local products or services as a percentage of cash received and over an agreed period of time.

As a trader, you must have a list of alternatives ready. Keep negotiations open and don't firm them up on paper until a general agreement has been reached. Consider alternatives and conditions that you could use as part of your negotiations, including quantity price breaks, discounts for cash deals or even down payments, countertrade to those countries short on foreign exchange, guaranteed loans, low-interest loans, time payments, and/or home factory trips for training.

Let your banker, freight forwarder, or customhouse broker review the final offer or quotation. A second pair of experienced eyes can save you money. (See Chapters 6 and 7 respectively for an explanation of the freight forwarder and customhouse broker.)

Foreign Corrupt Practices Act

During your negotiations, make sure you stay on the right side of the Foreign Corrupt Practices Act (FCPA) of 1977. In essence, this act makes it illegal for companies to bribe foreign officials, candidates, or political parties. Make certain that everything is in the contract and has a price. Don't get caught making illegal payments or gifts to win a contract or sale. The penalties are severe: a five-year jail sentence and a fine of up to $10,000.

The law does not address itself to *facilitating payments*, those small amounts used to expedite business activities euphemistically called in various countries: *mordida*, *grease*, *bakshish* (small amount of money), *rashoa* (big amount of money), *cumsha*, or *squeeze*. Nevertheless, great care should be exercised in this regard as well.

TIPS AND TRAPS OF CULTURE

The very thought of doing business in a foreign culture can be a major barrier to negotiations, but it shouldn't be. After all, traders are known for their spirit of curiousness, inquisitiveness, and risk-taking.

Can one culture be superior to another? Political systems, armies, navies, and even economic systems might be superior, but cultures are not. The best way to appreciate another culture is to "walk in the other fellow's shoes." That is, visit or live in the country and get a feel for the similarities and differences. Short of that, this section of the chapter is the next best thing because its purpose is to help you break through cultural barriers. Foremost, is that you take heed to be careful. To be effective in your business dealings, it is essential that you be prepared. Do your homework before you interact in a new country, and then get on with business.

Does understanding foreign cultural values really make a difference? You bet it does! One person who had traveled overseas regularly and had made friends in many countries said, "They're more like us than they're different." What he meant was that individuals in other countries like kids, want them to be educated, understand business, and work hard. What he didn't say was the differences are what affect attitudes. Attitude differences can be such that some managers won't even consider entering the market to do business with "them."

Practical Applications

Now that you have an appreciation of culture, lets take a look at the practical side. Most business trips are usually short-term. Nevertheless, it's important to understand as much about the culture of a country as possible, even when just visiting. To begin, let's look at some generalities—some ideas that will help you make a good impression no matter where you're doing business.

Saving face is not just an Asian concept, although it is particularly important in these countries. Avoiding embarrassment to others, particularly ranking persons, is essential wherever you are in the world.

People of any country like to talk about their own land and people. If you ask questions that show genuine interest, it will cultivate their respect for you. But no one likes critical questions such as: Why don't you do it this way? Or, how come you do it that way? Above all, they don't want to hear how much better it is where you come from.

First impressions do count, and the wrong first impression can stop your business deal in its tracks. Bad first impressions are all but impossible to overcome. So smile! It's the universal business language and saves many problems. But smile right. The smile in which the lips are parted in a sort of an ellipse around the teeth comes across as phony and dishonest. Smile easy—the kind where your full teeth are exposed and the corners of your mouth are pulled up. This kind of smile says, "Hi, I'm sure pleased to meet you!"

Another important consideration is grooming. Grooming is important all over the world. Studies indicate that most people are more attracted to others who are neat, well groomed, and dress crisply.

Flash your eyebrows. In most cultures, raising the eyebrows almost instinctively in a rapid movement and keeping them raised for about a half-second is an unspoken signal of friendliness and approval.

Lean forward. Liking is produced by leaning forward.

Look for similarities. People tend to like others who are like them, so common experiences and interests are often a starting point for producing liking.

Nod your head. People like other people who agree with them and are attentive to what they are saying.

Open up. A position in which your arms are crossed in front of your chest might project the impression that you're resisting the other person's ideas. Open, frequently outstretched arms and open palms project the opposite.

Tips for Women. Never give a man a gift, no matter how close the business relationship. A small gift for his family might do. Give gifts from the company, never from you. If you are married, use Mrs. when overseas, even if you don't at home. Avoid eating or drinking alone in public. Use room service or invite a woman from the office where you are doing business to join you at a restaurant.

If the question of dinner arises and is useful to cement the deal, avoid any doubts by inviting your counterpart's family. Make a point to mention your husband and ask about your male counterpart's family. Some businesswomen who are not married invent a fiancé or steady back home. Try not to be coy about flirtations; turn them off immediately with a straightforward, "no."

Be aware of the culture, and dress to fit as closely as your wardrobe will permit. Conservatism works.

Jokes. People of every country enjoy humor and they all have their funny stories, but explaining complicated jokes to businesspersons who don't share your culture can be very tricky. Remember that each culture reacts differently to jokes. Don't tell foreigners a joke that depends on word play or punning. Do be careful of the subject of your joke. It could be taken seriously in a culture different than your own. Be informed about the sensitive issues in the country where you are visiting. Ask to hear a few local jokes. They will give you a sense of what's considered funny. Do tell jokes, everyone enjoys a good laugh.

SUCCESS STORY: Creative Tour Consultants, founded by two women, took advantage of their knowledge of Northern Europe and combined it with a background in the travel industry. Their market plan offered an introductory tour package called "Viking Tour" to a micro segment interested in touring Sweden. Soon they were booking all over Scandinavia.

INTELLECTUAL PROPERTY RIGHTS

"The Japanese stole my stuff! They just drove down the road, passed our factory, and copied our trademark. It took us two and a half years and $5000 to get it back," said one executive. On the other hand, because this company had the trademark registered, no one else in the United States could use it, and the litigation against the guilty Japanese firm was considerably easier than it would have been had the trademark not been properly registered.

Intellectual property is a general term that describes inventions or other discoveries that have been registered with government authorities for the sale or use by their owner. Such terms as patent, trademark, copyright, or unfair competition fall into the category of intellectual property.

Patent Registration. You can obtain information about patents and trademarks from the U.S. Patent Office by calling (703) 308-HELP or by writing to the Patent and Trade Mark Office, Division of Patents and Trade Marks, Washington, DC 20231. The booklet, *General Information on Patents*, can be ordered from the U.S. Government Printing Office (see Appendix F). Table 3-1 summarizes the basic elements of intellectual rights in the United States.

Recognize that registration in the United States does not protect your product in a foreign country. In general, protection in one country does not constitute protection in another. The rule of thumb is to apply for and register all intellectual property rights in each country where you intend to do business. Registration can be expensive; therefore, several multilateral organizations have been formed that make it possible to make a patent application covering all member countries:

- The European Patent Convention (16 European-area countries)
- The Community Patent Convention (9 countries)
- The Patent Cooperation Treaty, which gives, by far, the greatest international coverage (more than 35 signature countries, including several from the former Soviet Union)

Trademark Registration. Trademark registration is less costly and time-consuming than patents. The following are two organizations that can help:

- The International Convention for the Protection of Industrial Property, better known as the Paris Union. This organization is 90 years old and covers patents as well as trademarks. Under this convention, 6-month protection is provided the firm, during which time the trademark can be registered in the other member countries.
- The Madrid Arrangement for International Registration of Trademarks has 22 members, but it offers the advantage that registration in one country qualifies as registration in all other member countries.

Table 3-1. Intellectual Property Rights.

	Patents	Copyright	Trade and service marks	Trade name	Trade dress	Trade secrets
Duration (yrs)	14–17 years	Life + 50 years	As long as in use	As long as in use	As long as in use	Until public disclosure
How	Apply to Patent Office	By original creation in permanent form	By use	By use	By use	By security measures
Req'ts	Useful/ novel	Nonfunctional original creation	Fanciful and distinguishing-	Non-confusion with others	Fanciful nonfunctional	Not known
Prevents	Manufr. use or sale	Copying or adapting	Confusing or misleading use	Confusing or misleading use	Confusing or misleading use	Disclosure
Protects	Utility and design attributes	Author-ship	Reputation and goodwill	Goodwill	Reputation	Info for competitive advantage
Examples	Product/ mechanism/ process/style	Label design/ operating manual	Coca Cola	Computer-land, Inc.	Container shape	Formula
Legal costs	$1500–$3000	$10–100 $400	$100–			

COMMUNICATIONS

Although nothing substitutes for personal contact when developing an international marketing structure, it is not always possible. Therefore, the tone of initial written communications is crucial. It often makes the difference between a profitable long-term arrangement and a lost opportunity.

The Introductory Letter or Facsimile

Your introductory letter or fax most often can be written in English. With the exception of Latin American countries, English has become the language of international business. Use simple words. If the letter or fax is to be translated and transmitted into a foreign language, make sure you have it translated back to English by a third party before you send it. However proficient a person is in another language, funny things can happen in translation.

From the beginning, establish your company's favorable reputation, and explain the relationship that you seek. Describe the product you want to market (export) or to purchase (import). Propose a personal meeting and offer the buyer a visit to your firm during the person's next visit to your country. Ask for a response to your letter. Figure 3-1 shows a sample letter of introduction.

Follow-Up Communications

As technology improves, more alternative forms of communications become available and choosing the best alternative might result in the competitive difference. Successful importing/exporting depends on reliable two-way communication; it is critical in establishing and running an import/export marketing network.

Telephone

Speech is the fastest way to convey ideas and receive answers. Voice communications allow for immediate feedback—quick response to fast-breaking problems or opportunities. Most countries can be dialed directly and the rates for international telephone service range from about $1 to $2 for the first minute (depending on the time of day), and about $1 a minute for each additional minute. While international telephone calls can be expeditious, it can be very expensive if you have a lot to say.

Our Company, Inc.
Hometown, U.S.A.

Ref:
Date:

Your Company, Ltd.
2A1 Moon River
Yokohama, Japan

Gentlemen:

Our Company, Inc. markets a line of highway spots. When secured to the centerline of highways these spots provide for increased safety for motorists. We believe that these spots might interest foreign markets, especially the Japanese market. Our major customers include highway contractors and highway departments of the states of ABC and DEF.

Our Company, founded in 1983, has sales of $1.5 million. Further details are given in the attached brochure. The attached catalogs and specification sheets give detailed information about our products.

We are writing to learn whether: (1) Your Company has a requirement to purchase similar products for use in Japan; and (2) Your Company would be interested in representing Our Company in Japan.

Don't hesitate to telephone if you need further details. We look forward to meeting with representatives of Your Company about our highway spots.

Sincerely,

W.T. Door
President

Fig. 3-1. Sample letter of introduction

Facsimile

A fax, or telecopier service, is one of the fastest growing means of business communication. The advantage of the fax is that any image up to 8½ × 14 inches can be transmitted directly to the receiving unit. Letters, pictures, contracts, forms, catalog sheets, drawings, and illustrations—anything that would reproduce in a copy machine can be sent.

HISTORY NOTE: The fax is not new. It was invented more than a century ago in 1842 by Alexander Bain, a Scottish clockmaker. His devise used a pendulum that swept a metal point over a set of raised metal letters. When the point touched a letter, it created an electrical charge that traveled down a telegraph wire to reproduce on paper the series of letters the pendulum had touched. Wire service photos were transmitted by fax as early as 1930. The U.S. Navy used them aboard ships to transmit weather data during World War II.

The earliest fax machines were clunkers and very expensive, taking more than 10 minutes to send a single page and costing more than $18,000. Today, there are more than 2 million faxes in use, and dedicated fax terminals now cost as little as $200. Their speed equates favorably to the telex.

A fax transmits over the ordinary voice-phone network. Several private bureaus manage the worldwide fax service, but there is no effective proof of delivery of a faxed document.

Internet

It wasn't that long ago that *Internet* was just a public, amorphous collection of computer networks—a techno-fad made up of a few personal computers and citizen's band radio enthusiasts.

Today, Internet is the fastest growing and most exciting place to do business. New cross-indexing software and imaginative services are connecting the home computer masses to electronic commerce through web servers and high-speed circuits into what is called the World Wide Web.

As the concept matures, the linking of buyers and sellers and the elimination of paperwork will drive down the cost of transactions. Internet is becoming the low-cost alternative to fax, express mail, and other communications channels such as toll-free telephone sales.

In the United States, the major operators of online services are AmericaOnline, CompuServe, Delphi, and Prodigy. Internet's user population has grown from 1 million in 1988 to more than 20 million in 1995, with hundreds of thousands joining each month.

Internet knows no international boundaries. Internauts are logging on from Bangkok to New York's Broadway on computers that are expected to swell to more than 100 million by the turn of the century. Already the network extends to 140 countries. The most interesting part of it is nobody owns the Internet. It is not guided by a single company or institution. The Internet Protocol (IP) allows any number of computer networks to link up and act as one. Users pay a flat fee, based on the length of time they're connected to a local subnetwork and the potential capacity, or bandwith, of that connection.

How would you use it for your import/export business? One way would be to advertise through an internet advertising agency. When a browser decides to buy your product(s) they just click a "buy" button. The sale is consummated when they fill out an online order form with shipping and credit card information.

HISTORY NOTE: Internet also is not new. It got its beginning in the late 1960s when the Pentagon asked computer scientists to find the best way for an unlimited number of computers to communicate without relying on any single computer to be traffic cop so that the system would not be vulnerable to nuclear attack. The outcome was the decision to fund experimental packet-switching communications using a Transmission and Control Protocol/Internet Protocol (TCP/IP) technology called ARPAnet, which quickly expanded to dozens of universities and corporations. Programs were written to help people exchange electronic mail (E-mail) and tap into remote databases. In 1983, ARPAnet was split into two networks: ARPAnet and Milnet and the Pentagon mandated TCP/IP as the standard protocol. These two networks evolved into Internet.

Telex

Telex terminals in government and business offices worldwide can receive information automatically, even when unattended. Telex charges are based on transmission time—the time the circuit is actually used. It is possible to transmit up to 1800 characters (about 180 words or more) per minute for the price of a telephone call. The carrier charge varies from $1 to $3 per minute, with service charge costs of about $3 per minute.

By custom, telex messages are brief. Standard abbreviations and terminology are widely understood. When you compare:

```
KS UR TX N TEL CALL RCNTLY. SEE U AT ARPRT TUES 3.9.88
```

with:

```
THANKS FOR YOUR TELEX MESSAGE AND TELEPHONE CALL RECENTLY.
I WILL SEE YOU AT THE AIRPORT ON TUESDAY, THE THIRD OF SEPTEMBER
1988.
```

You can easily see the need for abbreviations. Table 3-2 lists many of the common abbreviations. Figure 3-2 shows a sample telex message.

Table 3-2. Commonly Used Telex Abbreviations.

ADS	address	NBR	number
ANS	answer	NL	night letter telegram
CFM	confirm	NR	no record
CHGS	charges	OFC	office
CK	check	OGNL	original
CST	cost	OK	agreed
DLD	delivered	PLS	please
DLR	deliver	R	received
DLY	delivery	R	are
DSTN	destination	RE	reference
DUP	duplicate	RGDS	regards
FM	from	RPT	repeat
GOVT	government	SGD	signed
HW	herewith	SPL	special
ICW	in connection with	SVC	service
	(concerning)		
INTL	international	TKS	thanks
LT	letter telegram	TLX	telex
MGR	manager	U	you
MK	make	WD	word
MGS	message	YR	your
N	and		

When you draft messages that include tables or other columnar information, consider that each "space" is a chargeable character up to the carriage return. The general rule is that horizontal

```
TRT

188912 ATSD UT

1243 9/16

GA

20801 MYMCO TH

188912 ATSD UT

ATTN: MR. CHIEHAT PONG

PLS SEND SAMPLES N CST INFO FOR RINGS GOLD AND
SILVER
RGDS

W.T. DOOR

OUR COMPANY

U.S.A.

TEL: (AREA CODE) XXX-XXXX

FAX: (AREA CODE) XXX-XXXX

188912 ATSD UT
```

Fig. 3-2. Sample telex message

space is expensive, but vertical space is not. It takes but two characters, a carriage return, and a line feed, to skip a line. Use line skipping generously to separate logical units and to give length to the received message to make it easier to handle. For example, compare:

```
DESCRIPTION              QTY      PRICE
LEFT-HANDED WRENCH        1       11.78
BOX                       2        7.52
```

with:

```
QTY        PRICE        DESCRIPTION
1          11.78        LEFT-HANDED WRENCH
2           7.52        BOX
```

HOT TIP: Though print lacks speed (compared to voice), it provides written documentation that can be read and reread at the reader's pace and schedule.

Cables

International mailgrams, telegrams, or cables can be sent anywhere mail goes. Cables require a complete mailing address, including any postal codes.

Cables are sent electronically to the major city nearest the recipient. There, the message might be telephoned and mailed, mailed only, or (in a few locations) delivered by messenger. Cables don't offer proof of delivery that a telex message does, and because of the extra handling, cables are significantly more expensive than telex messages. But a cable can be sent to anyone, anywhere.

Communications Equipment

Electronic data transmission will grow rapidly throughout the 1990s and into the new century. As an international marketing network develops, data will flow back and forth among the importer/exporter and agencies, distributors, and customers. You must decide whether you'll be wiser to purchase your own equipment or to use a service bureau. The volume of messages will dictate the break-even point for your growing international import/export organization. If you send less than one message per day, a service company is your best bet.

When your message volume grows to more than one message per day, consider purchasing equipment and transmitting your own messages. E-mail is now commonly delivered over international phone lines. Practically any computer can be interfaced with a modem via a cable, ordinary telephone, satellite, or microwave to any other computer or word processor anywhere in the world so long as the receiving country does not restrict or prohibit transborder data flows. If you have a personal computer and a modem, you might want to consider this, because a data communications software package costs less than $300.

HOT COMMUNICATIONS TIPS: Write out your message and check it by reading it aloud. Some situations in international business can be frustrating, so take care not to lose your temper and send a "zinger" that you'll regret later. Develop a cordial and professional style, and stick to it at all times. Try to draft replies in the morning when you are fresh. Whenever possible, let a second party read each message. Send messages early in the day and early in the week to avoid the heavy calling periods and possible delay of your message.

Keep your messages brief, but avoid any abbreviation that might not be understood. Remember that telex is UPPERCASE ONLY and does not provide for the dollar ($) or percent (%) symbol, among others. For $, use USDOL, and for %, use PCT. Cables are generally more expensive than telex messages. They are charged by the word. Words have a maximum of 10 characters, 11 characters count as 2 words. Try to reply to every fax/telex/Internet message the day it is received, even if only to give a date when a more complete reply will be sent.

Use "ATTN: Name" rather than "DEAR Name" and almost all fax/telex/Internet messages, by custom, end with "REGARDS," "BEST REGARDS," or occasionally "CORDIALLY."

TRAVEL

Mistrust across international borders can be a barrier to a successful import/export business. Therefore, visiting the country and the people who offer goods for your importation or the agents or distributors who market your export products is essential. These personal contacts remind us that we have more in common with people from other nations than differences. Travel to exotic places is not only fun, it is a tax deductible expense of international trade.

HOT TIP: The Internal Revenue Service looks closely at travel expenses to make sure you are actually doing business and not indulging your travel hobby. For this purpose, keep good records during your travels and make sure you profit from your trips.

Planning a Trip

You alone know your itinerary, how long you can stay in each place, and what you expect to accomplish. So lay out your own trip before turning it over to the travel agent. Make certain your local arrival time allows for time changes and scheduled business meetings. Allow time for rest prior to negotiating.

After you have laid out your trip, take it to the travel agent for booking. Allow three to five days and expect some changes. Occasionally you need to go through country B in order to get to country C.

Foreign Travel Information. To stay alert to any possible danger areas in the world, contact the Citizens Emergency Center at the U.S. Department of State, Washington, DC by calling (202) 647-5225.

Packing for a Trip. Travel light. The usual arrival sequence is immigration followed by customs. Be ready to open your luggage and sometimes declare each item.

Transportation. Request business class to most countries; it's more comfortable than coach and less expensive than first class. However, one traveler remembered the time the Pakistani lady sat next to him with five boxes, two kids, and a cage full of chickens. In some Middle European and Eastern countries, it's better to pay the difference and go first class.

Hotels. Unless you are familiar with the better hotels in a country, you are usually better off to stay at one that is internationally recognized. Most major travel companies, agents, or your local library can give you the names of the best hotels.

Food and Drink. Are you a bit overweight? Now is the time to drop a few pounds. The food may be the best in the world, but eat light and drink only sterilized water.

Time Changes. Plan for changing time zones. Think ahead and figure the local time of arrival for the plane you have booked. Remember, time is reckoned from Greenwich, England, and watches are normally set to some form of zone time. Time is changed near the time of crossing of the boundary between zones, usually at a whole hour. If you know the time zone, you can calculate the local time. Figure 3-3 contains international time zones as they appear at noon Eastern Standard Time (EST).

Passport. This travel document identifies the holder as a citizen of the country from which it is issued. In the United States,

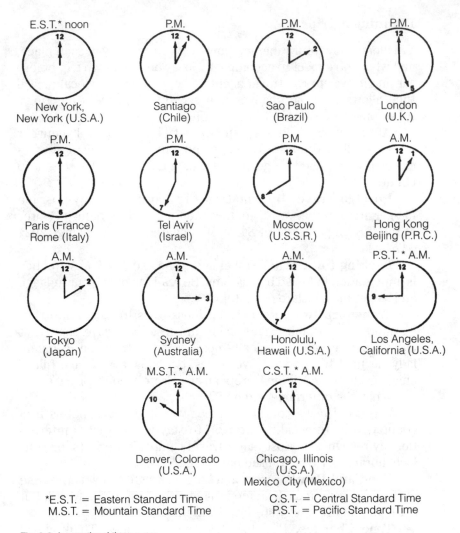

Fig. 3-3. International time zones

the Department of State issues passports. You can apply for one at your local post office. The cost is about $50 to $60. Allow about two to three weeks for processing.

Visa. A *visa* is an official endorsement from a country a person wishes to visit. You must receive it before entry into that country is permitted. Some nations don't require a visa. Check with your travel agent or local consul/embassy. You might prefer to have "visa service"—you provide your passport and three photos and let them make the rounds of embassies. Count on waiting a week for the completion of this service.

Arrival/Departure. When you arrive at a country you have never visited before, ask the airline crew or counter personnel for such tips as normal taxi fare from the airport to the hotel, sights to see, and local travel problems. Exchange your currency at the best rate. On departure, use any excess local currency to pay your hotel bill, but be sure to save enough local currency for taxi fare and airport departure tax.

Smile and be cheerful as you pass through immigration and customs. A smile can head off many problems.

Carnet. Use an ATA Carnet to get your business samples and other equipment through customs. The initials "ATA" are a combination of both French and English words meaning "Admission Temporaire/Temporary Admission." To obtain ATA Carnet, make application to the Council for International Business, which has offices in major cities such as London, Paris, San Francisco, Los Angeles, and New York.

The Carnet is a special customs document to simplify and streamline customs procedures for business and professional travelers. It guarantees payment in case of failure to re-export. Commercial samples, advertising material, medica, or other professional equipment, whether accompanied by a person or not, can be taken into participating countries for up to one year under this system. The applicant must furnish security in the amount of 40% of the total value of all items listed on the application form. The fee schedule ranges from a minimum of $50 to as much as $200 depending on the value of the merchandise. If you don't get a Carnet, check your samples at the airport with customs and allow plenty of time to get them before the next flight.

The next chapter further expands the concepts related to both import and export, developing the fundamentals needed to "complete the transaction," i.e., financing, avoiding risk, shipping, and documentation.

4

Completing a
Successful Transaction

YOU ARE NOW READY TO TAKE THE STEPS NEEDED TO COMPLETE AN import or export transaction. In Chapter 2, you learned the basics of start-up. Chapter 3 led you through the concepts of planning and negotiating a transaction. This chapter covers the four remaining commonalities associated with paying for and physically moving goods: financing, avoiding risk, physical distribution (packing and shipping), and documentation.

FINANCING

Why do you need financing for your import/export business? To start, expand, or take advantage of opportunities; all businesses need new money sooner or later. By "new money," I mean money that has not yet been earned. This money can become the engine for growth.

As an importer, financing offers you the ability to pay for the overseas manufacture and shipment of foreign goods destined for the domestic market. As an exporter, financing could mean working capital to pay for international travel and marketing efforts. New money might also be used as loans to foreign buyers so they can purchase an exporter's goods.

If you have done your homework and have purchase orders for the product(s) in hand, there is plenty of currency available—banks or factors are waiting to assist.

Banks

Financing for importing/exporting businesses comes primarily from commercial banks and is an essential part of the team you will require for international trade success. When you are selecting a banking partner, look for the following:

- A strong international department
- Speed in handling transactions (Do they want to make money on your money—called the float?)
- The bank's relationship with overseas banks (That is, do they have corresponding relationships with banks in the countries in which you wish to do business?)
- The bank's credit policy (Do they have an aggressive policy toward trade finance, particularly working capital loans and letters of credit?)

HOT TIP: In the import/export industry there is a saying: "Walk on two legs." This means choose carefully then work closely with a good international bank and a customs broker/freight forwarder.

Forms of Bank Financing

Loans for international trade fall into two categories: secured and unsecured. Banks are not high risk-takers. To reduce their exposure to loss, they often ask for collateral.

Financing against collateral is called secured financing and is the most common method of raising new money. Banks will advance funds against payment obligations, shipment documents, or storage documents.

Most commonly, advancement of funds is made against payment obligations or documentary title. The trader pledges the goods for export or import as collateral for a loan to finance them. The bank maintains a secure position by accepting as collateral documents that convey title to these goods, such as negotiable bills of lading, warehouse receipts, or trust receipts.

Another popular method of obtaining secured financing is the *Banker's Acceptance* (B/A). A B/A is a time draft presented to a bank by an exporter. This differs from what is known as *trade acceptance* between buyer and seller in which a bank is not involved. The bank stamps and signs the draft "accepted" on behalf of its client, the importer. By accepting the draft, the bank undertakes and recognizes the obligation to pay the draft at maturity and has placed its creditworthiness between the exporter (*drawer*) and the importer (*drawee*).

B/As are negotiable instruments that can be sold in the money market. The B/A rate is a discount rate generally 2 to 3 points below the prime rate. With the full creditworthiness of the bank behind the draft, eligible B/As attract the very best market interest rates. The criteria for eligibility are:

- The B/A must be created within 30 days of the shipment of the goods.
- The maximum tenor is 180 days after shipment.
- The B/A must be self-liquidating.
- The B/A cannot be used for working capital.
- The credit recipient must attest to no duplication.

> Shipping documents are commercial invoices, bills of lading, insurance certificates, consular invoices, and related documents.

A draft or bill of exchange is a written order for a certain sum of money to be transferred on a certain date from the person who owes the money or agrees to make the payment (the drawee) to the creditor to whom the money is owed (the drawer of the draft). See the glossary for complete definitions of *date draft, documentary draft, sight draft,* and *time draft.*

Unsecured financing is only for those who have a sound credit standing with their bank or have had long-term trading experience. It usually amounts to expanding already existing lines of working credit. For the small importer/exporter, unsecured financing will probably be limited to a personal line of credit.

Factors

A *factor* is an agent who will buy your receivables at a discount (usually 5% to 8% of the gross). Banks do 95% of the factoring; the remainder is done by private specialists. The factor makes a profit on the collection and provides a source of cash flow for the seller, albeit less than if the business had held out to make the collection itself.

For example, suppose you had a receivable of $1000. A factor might offer you a $750 advance on the invoice and charge you 5% on the gross of $1000 per month until collection. If the collection is made within the first month, the factor would only keep $50 and return $200. If it takes two months, the factor would keep $100 and return only $150, etc.

The importer benefits from having the cash to reorder products from overseas. For a manufacturer, the benefit might be available cash flow for increased or new production.

Private Sources of Financing

The United States has several major private trade financing institutions, all in competition to support your export programs.

PEFCO. The *Private Export Funding Corporation* (PEFCO) was established in 1970 and is owned by about 60 banks, 7 industrial corporations, and an investment banking firm. PEFCO operates with its own capital stock, an extensive line of credit from the U.S. government's Export-Import Bank, and the proceeds of its secured and unsecured debt obligations. It provides medium- and long-term loans, subject to Export-Import Bank approval, to foreign buyers of U.S. goods and services. PEFCO generally deals in sales of capital goods with a minimum commitment of about $1 million—there is no maximum. PEFCO can be contacted at 747 Third Avenue, New York, NY 10017 or you can call (212) 826-7010.

OPIC. The *Overseas Private Investment Corporation* (OPIC) is a private, self-sustaining institution whose purpose is to promote economic growth in developing countries. OPIC's programs include: insurance; finance; missions; contractors and exporters insurance program; small contractors guarantee program; and investor information services. For more information, write OPIC at 1615 M Street, N.W., Washington, DC 20527 or call them at (202)336-8400.

Government Sources. Many nations are short on foreign exchange, and what they have, is earmarked for priority national imports and to service large international credit commitments.

Nevertheless, there are probably more sources of competitive financing available today to support exporting than at any other time in history. The major complaint is that not enough firms are taking advantage of the programs.

Small Business Administration (SBA). All nations support the growth of small business. For example, the United States has a Small Business Administration (SBA) that guarantees small companies, which can show a reasonable ability to pay, eight-year working capital loans for about 2.25% over prime. The maximum maturity period can be up to 25 years depending on the use of the loan proceeds. The SBA's export revolving line of credit guarantee program provides preexport financing for the manufacture or purchase of goods for sale to foreign markets and to help a small business penetrate or develop a foreign market. The maximum maturity for this financing is 18 months. The SBA, in cooperation with the Export-Import Bank, participates in loans between $200,000 and $1 million.

Export-Import Bank. For those exporters who have found a sale but the buyer can't find the financing in her or his own country, the Export-Import Bank (Eximbank) has funds available to provide credit support in the form of loans, guarantees, and insurance for small businesses. The Export-Import Bank of the United States is a federal agency charged with helping to finance the export of U.S. goods and services. Rates vary but are available for a 5- to 10-year maturity period.

Programs include medium- and long-term loans and guarantees that cover up to 85% of a transaction's export value, with repayment terms of 1 year or longer. Long-term loans and guarantees are provided for more than 7 years, but not usually more than 10 years. The Medium-Term Credit Program has more than $300 million available for small businesses facing subsidized foreign competition. The Small Business Credit Program also has funds available with direct credit for exporting medium-term goods; competition is not necessary. The EXIM Working Capital Program guarantees the lender's repayment on capital loans for exports.

The Agency for International Development (AID). This organization, a subordinate division of the U.S. State Department, provides loans and grants to Third World nations for both developmental and foreign policy reasons. Under the AID Development Assistance Program, funds are available at rates of 2% and 3% over 40 years. The AID Economic Development Fund also has funds at similar interest rates. Generally, these funds are available through invitations to bid through the *Commerce Business Daily*, a publication available from the U.S. Government Printing Office, Washington, DC 20402.

The International Development Cooperation Agency (IDCA). This organization sponsors a Trade and Development Program (TDP) that loans funds on an annual basis for friendly countries to procure foreign goods and services for major development projects. Often, these funds support smaller firms in subcontract positions.

SUCCESS STORY: One in every 1.5 Japanese own a bicycle. When Ken Orito also learned that 36,630 all-terrain bicycles (ATB) were bought in 1989 and that the number increased to about 500,000 by 1991, he decided to export high-grade bikes from the United States. He borrowed $160,000 from his family, established the International Express Bicycle company, and began by sending 10 bikes a month, 5 to a retail shop in Tokyo and 5 to one in Osaka. By the summer of 1994, he had increased his sales of $1000 and $1500 bikes to 20 a month. His net profit for the first year was only $2440 on $150,000 sales but the future looks very bright.

AVOIDING RISK

Doing business always involves some risk, so you should expect across-border business to be no different. Uncertainty is always present in doing business across international borders, but much of it can be hedged, managed, and controlled. All major exporting countries have arrangements to protect exporters and the bankers who provide their funding support. Avoiding and/or controlling risks in global trade is an everyday occurrence for importers/exporters. Understanding the instruments available for avoiding risk is not difficult, but it is vital. Essentially, there are four types of risks:

- Commercial (not being paid; nondelivery of goods; insolvency or protracted default by the buyer; competition; and disputes over product, warranty, etc.)
- Foreign exchange (foreign exchange fluctuations)
- Political (war, coup d'etat, revolution, expropriation, expulsion, foreign exchange controls, or cancellation of import or export licenses)
- Shipping (risk of damage and/or loss at sea or via other transportation method)

Most risks allow for a method of avoidance. Of course, there is no insurance for such problems as disputes over quality or loss of markets due to competition, but there are management instruments for three aspects of risk: not being paid, loss or damage, and foreign exchange exposure.

Avoiding Commercial Risk

The *seller* would like to be certain that the buyer will pay on time once the goods have been shipped. He or she wants to at least minimize the risk of nonpayment. On the other hand, the *buyer* wants to be certain the seller will deliver on time and that the goods are exactly what the buyer ordered.

These concerns are often heard from anyone beginning an import/export business. Mistrust across international borders is natural; after all, there is a certain amount of mistrust even in our own culture. One key to risk avoidance is a well written sales contract. In Chapter 3, you learned that an early step in the process of international trade is to gain contract agreement between yourself and your overseas business associate. The contract agreement should include method of payment.

Getting Paid

Ensuring prompt payment often worries exporters more than any other factor. The truth is that the likelihood of a bad debt from an international customer is very low. In the experience of most international businesspeople, overseas bad debts seldom exceed 0.5% of sales. The reason is that in overseas markets, credit is still something to be earned as a result of having a record of prompt payment. Use common sense when you extend credit to overseas customers, but don't use tougher rules than you use for your domestic clients.

Methods of payment, in order of their risk to the seller, are: open account, consignment, time draft, sight draft, authority to purchase, letter of credit, and cash in advance. Table 4-1 summarizes and compares the various methods of payment in order of decreasing risk to the exporter and increasing risk to the importer.

Open Account. The *open account* is a trade arrangement in which goods are shipped to a foreign buyer without guarantee of payment. Though the riskiest trade arrangement, many firms that have a long-standing business relationship with the same overseas

Table 4-1. Comparison of Various Methods of Payment.

(In order of decreasing risk to exporter and increasing risk to importer)

Method	Goods available to buyers	Usual time of payment	Exporter risk	Importer risk
Open account	Before payment	As agreed	Most Relies on importer to pay account	Least
Consign-ment	Before payment	After sold	Maximum Exporter retains title	Minor inventory cost
Time draft	Before payment	On maturity of draft	High Relies on importer to pay draft	Minimal check of quantity/ quality
Sight draft	After payment	On presenting draft to importer	If unpaid goods are returned/ disposed	Little if inspection report rq'd
Authority to Purchase	After payment	On presenting draft	Be careful of recourse	Little if inspection report rq'd
Letter of Credit	After payment	When documents are available after shipment	None	None if inspection report rq'd
Cash	After payment	Before shipment	Least	Most

firm use this method. Needless to say, the key is to know your buyer and your buyer's country. You should use an open account when the buyer has a continuing need for the seller's product or service.

Some experienced exporters say that they only deal in open accounts, but they always preface that statement by saying that they have close relationships and have been doing business with their overseas clients for many years.

Open accounts can be risky unless the buyer is of unquestioned integrity and has withstood a thorough credit investigation. The advantage of this method is its ease and convenience, but with open-account sales, you bear the burden of financing the shipment. Standard practice in many countries is to defer payment until the merchandise is sold, sometimes even longer. Therefore, among the forms of payment, open-account sales require the greatest amount of working capital. In addition, you bear the exchange risk if the sales are quoted in foreign currency. Nevertheless, competitive pressures could force you to use this method.

HOT TIP: Relationships between buyer and seller make the difference by reducing mistrust. Make an effort to meet and get to know your trading partner.

Consignment. The seller (*consignor*) retains title to the goods during shipment and storage of the product in the warehouse or retail store. The consignee acts as a selling agent selling the goods and remitting the net proceeds to the consignor. Like open account sales, consignment sales also can be risky and lend themselves only to certain kinds of merchandise. Great care should be taken in working out this contractual arrangement. Be sure it is covered with adequate risk insurance.

Bank Drafts. Payment for many sales are arranged using one of many time-tested banking methods. *Bank drafts* (bills of exchange), *sight drafts*, and *time drafts* are each useful payment arrangements under certain circumstances.

Bank drafts are simply written orders that activate payment either at sight or at "tenor," a future time or date. A bank draft is a check, drawn by one bank on another bank. Drafts are used primarily when it is necessary for the customer to provide funds payable at a bank in some distant location. The exporter who undertakes this payment method can offer a range of payment options to the overseas customer.

SUCCESS STORY: Elizabeth Ortola opened Las Brisas Exports on an initial capitalization of $10,000, half from her Spanish business partner and half from her own Master Card line of credit. In her first year she sold 180 units of top-of-the-line ceiling fans and had profits of $24,000 on sales of $144,000. She sold 480 units in her second year with $69,256 in net earnings on $395,520. Conservative fifth-year projections show sales of more than 600 units and net profits of $262,000 on sales of greater than a half million dollars.

A *time (date) draft* is an acceptance order drawn by the exporter on the importer (customer) that is payable a certain number of days after sight (presentation) to the holder. Think of it as nothing more than an IOU, or promise to pay in the future.

Documents such as negotiable bills of lading, insurance certificates, and commercial invoices accompany the draft and are submitted through the exporter's bank for collection. When presented to the importer at his bank, the importer acknowledges that the documents are acceptable and commits to pay by writing "Accepted" on the draft and signing it. The importer normally has 30 to 180 days depending on the draft's term to make payment to his or her bank for transmittal.

A *sight draft* is similar to a time draft except that the importer's bank holds the documents until the importer releases the funds. Sight drafts are the most common payment method employed by exporters throughout the world. It is nothing more than a written order on a standardized bank format requesting money from the overseas buyer. While this method costs less than a letter of credit, it is riskier because the importer can refuse to honor the draft.

A *bill of lading* is a document that provides the terms of the contract between the shipper and the transportation company to move freight between stated points at a specified charge.

A *commercial* or *customs invoice* is a bill for the goods from the seller to the buyer. It is one method used by governments to determine the value of the goods for customs valuation purposes.

At sight indicates that a negotiable instrument is to be paid upon presentation or demand.

Authority to Purchase. The *authority to purchase* method of payment is occasionally used in the Far East. It specifies a bank where the exporter can draw a documentary draft on the importer's bank. The problem with this method is that if the importer fails to pay the draft, the bank has *recourse* to the exporter for settlement. If an exporter consents to this method, it is suggested that the authority to purchase specify *without recourse* and state so on drafts.

The major risk with the time, sight, and authority to purchase payment methods is the buyer can refuse to pay or to pick up the goods. The best way to avoid this is to require cash against documents. Unfortunately, this method is slow because banks are slow in transferring funds because they want to use the time float (short-term investment of bank money) to make interest. A wire transfer can get around this.

Letters of credit. Ideally, an exporter will deal only in cash, but in reality, few business persons are initially able or willing to do business under these terms. Because of the risk of nonpayment due to insolvency, bankruptcy, or other severe deterioration, procedures and documents have been developed that help to ensure that foreign buyers honor their agreements.

The most common form of collection is payment against a letter of credit (L/C), a time-tested method whereby an importer's bank guarantees that if all documents are presented in exact conformity with the terms of the L/C, they will pay the exporter. The procedure is not difficult to understand, and most cities have banks with persons familiar with the mechanics of an L/C. Internationally, the term documentary credits is synonymous with L/C.

L/Cs are well understood by traders around the world, they are simple, and they are as good as your bank. L/Cs involve thousands of transactions and billions of dollars every day in every part of the world. They are almost always operated in accordance with the Uniform Customs and Practice for Documentary Credits of the International Chamber of Commerce, a code of practice that is recognized by banking communities in 156 countries.

A *Guide to Documentary Operations*, which includes all of the standard forms, is available by writing either:

ICC Publishing Corporation, Inc.
156 Fifth Ave., Suite 302
New York, NY 10010
(212) 206-1150
fax: (212) 633-6025

ICC Services S.A.R.L.
38 Cours Albert ler
75008 PARIS
Telephone: 49-53-28-28
fax: 33-01-49-53-29-24 or telex: 650770

An L/C is a document issued by a bank at the importer's or buyer's request in favor of the seller. It promises to pay a specified amount of money upon receipt by the bank of certain documents within a specified time or at intervals corresponding with the shipment of goods. It is a universally used method of achieving a commercially acceptable compromise. Think of an L/C as a loan against collateral wherein the funds are placed in an escrow account. The amount in the account depends on the relationship of the buyer and the buyer's bank.

If you don't already have an account, the bank typically will require 100% collateral. With an account, the bank will establish a line of credit against your account. For instance, if you have $5000 in your account and the transaction is expected to cost $1000, your account will be reduced to $4000 and the line of credit established as $1000.

Typical commercial letters of credit charges for domestic, import, and export are shown in Table 4-2.

Standby L/Cs. Sometimes when dealing in an open account, the exporter requires a *standby letter of credit*. This means just what the name implies, the L/C is not to be executed unless payment is not made within the specified period, usually 30 to 60 days. Bank handling charges for standby L/Cs are usually higher than for commercial (import) L/Cs.

Issuing, Confirming, and Advising Banks. L/Cs are payable either at *sight* or on a *time* draft basis. Under a sight L/C, the *issuing* (buyer's) bank pays, with or without a draft, when satisfied that the presented documents conform with the required forms. An *advising* bank (most often the *confirming* or seller's bank) informs the seller or beneficiary that an L/C has been issued. With a time (acceptance) L/C, once the associated draft is presented and found to be in exact conformity, the draft is stamped "accepted" and can then be negotiated as a *bankers acceptance* by the exporter, at a discount to reflect the cost of money advanced against the draft.

Once the buyer and the seller agree that they will use an L/C for payment, and they have worked out the condition(s), the buyer or

Table 4-2. Typical L/C Charges.

Import and domestic charges

Transactions	⅛ of 1% of transaction with a minimum of $75–$100
Amendments	⅛ of 1% flat with min. of $70
Payment fee	¼ of 1% flat with min. of $90 per draft
Acceptance fee	Per annum fee (360) day basis, min. $75 per each draft accepted
Discrepancy fee	$40

Export

Advising	$60
Confirmation	Subject to country risk conditions, min. $75
Amendments	$55
Assignment of proceeds/transfers	⅛ of 1% of the transaction with a minimum of $75
Discrepancy fee	$45
Payment/negotiation	⅒ of 1%, min. $85–$95

Standby letters

Issuance fee	An annual percentage (360-day basis) based on credit risk considerations, min. $250
Amendment fee	Risk-related fee is charged, min. $250
Payment fee	¼ of 1% flat, min. $90 per draft

Collections—Documentary

Incoming	sight $75/time $95
Outgoing	sight $75/time $95

importer applies for the L/C to his or her international bank. Figure 4-1 is an example of an L/C application.

Types of L/Cs. There are two types of L/Cs: revocable and irrevocable. *Revocable credit* means the document can be amended or canceled at any time without prior warning or notification of the seller. *Irrevocable* simply means that the terms of the document can be amended or canceled only with the agreement of all parties thereto.

Confirmation means the U.S. bank guarantees payment by the foreign bank. Using the application as its guide, the bank issues

To: Importer's international bank

> Request to open documentary credit (commercial letter of credit and security agreement)

> Date _____

Please open for my/our account a documentary credit (letter of credit) in accordance with the undermentioned particulars.

We agree that, except so far as otherwise expressly stated, this credit will be subject to the Uniform Customs and Practice for Documentary Credits, ICC Publication #290.

We undertake to execute the Bank's usual form of indemnity.

Type of Credit: Irrevocable, i.e., cannot be cancelled without beneficiary's agreement.
Revocable, i.e., subject to cancellation.
Method of Advice: [ ]   Airmail   [ ]   Cable, short details   [ ]   Cable, full details.
Beneficiary's bank: _____

In favor of Beneficiary: Company name and address.

Amount or sum of:

Availability: Valid until_____in_____for negotiation/date place acceptance/ payment.

This credit is available by drafts drawn at _____ sight/ accompanied by the required documents.

Documents required: Invoice in three copies
Full set clean "on board" bills of lading to order of shipper, blank endorsed. In case movement of goods involves more than one mode, a "Combined Transport Document" should be called for.

Fig. 4-1. Request to open a letter of credit (L/C)

Negotiable Marine and War risk insurance for %
(usually 110%) of invoice value covering all
risks.

Certificate of Inspection

Other
Documents: Certificate of origin issued by Chamber of
Commerce in three copies.

Packing List

Quantity &
Description
of Goods

Price per unit:

Terms &
relative port
or place: C.I.F./C.&F./F.O.B./F.A.S./_____
Place _____

Dispatch/
Shipment   From _____ to _____

Special
Instructions
(if any):

a document of credit incorporating the terms agreed to by the parties. Figure 4-2 exemplifies an L/C.

Figure 4-3 shows the three phases of documentary credit in their simplest form. In Phase I, your (*issuing*) bank notifies the seller through an *advising* bank or the seller's (*confirming*) bank that a credit has been issued. In Phase II, the seller then ships the goods and presents the documents to the bank, at which time the seller is paid. Phase III is the *settlement* phase, wherein the documents are then transferred to the buyer's bank. Upon transfer, the buyer pays the bank any remaining moneys in exchange for the

Name of Issuing Bank	Documentary Credit No._____
Place and date of issue	Place and date of expiration
Applicant	Amount
	Credit available with [ ] Payment [ ] Acceptance [ ] Negotiation
Shipment from _____ Shipment to _____	Against presentation of documents detailed herein
.	[ ] Drawn on _____ Bank

Invoice in three copies

Full set clean "on board" bills of lading to order of shipper, blank endorsed. In case movement of goods involves more than one made, a "Combined Transport Document" should be called for.

Negotiable Marine and War risk insurance for _____% (usually 110%) of invoice value covering all risks.

Certificate of Inspection

Certificate of origin issued by Chamber of Commerce in three copies.

Packing List

Documents to be presented within _____ days after date of issuance of the shipping document(s) but within the validity of the credit.

We hereby issue this Documentary Credit in your favor.

                    Issuing Bank

Fig. 4-2. Sample letter of credit (L/C)

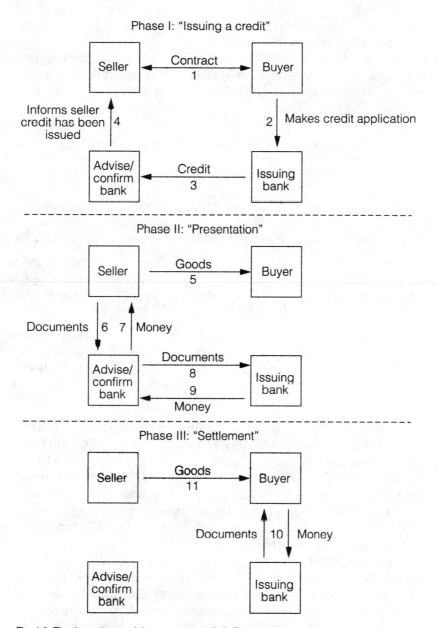

Fig. 4-3. The three phases of documentary credit (L/C)

documents. Thus, when the goods arrive, the buyer or importer has the proper documents for entry.

Special Uses of the L/C. Import/export middlemen have three special uses for commercial L/Cs: transferable, assignment of proceeds, and back-to-back L/Cs. Table 4-3 compares the risks involved with each method.

Table 4-3. Risk Comparison for Various L/Cs.

	Assignment of Proceeds	*Transferable Letter of Credit*	*Back to Back*
Risk to Middleman	Supplier relies on middleman to comply with L/C	Middleman relies on supplier to comply with L/C	Supplier's performance must satisfy both L/C's
Risk to Middleman's Bank	None	Minimal	Supplier's do not comply with master L/C
Disclosure	Buyer and seller are not disclosed	Buyer and seller are disclosed	Buyer and seller are not disclosed (with third-party documents)

Figure 4-4 shows how the transferable L/C works. The buyer opens the L/C, which states clearly that it is transferable, on behalf of the middleman as the original beneficiary. The middleman then transfers all or part of the L/C to the supplier(s). The transfer must be made under the same terms and conditions as the original L/C with the following exceptions: amount, unit price, expiration date, and shipping date. In this instance, the buyer and supplier are usually disclosed to each other.

The assignment of proceeds method is a typical letter of assignment (see Figs. 4-5 and 4-6). Note that the proceeds of all L/Cs can be assigned. In this instance, the buyer opens the L/C as the beneficiary and relies on the middleman to comply so that he or she can be paid. Any discrepancy in middleman documents will prevent payment under the L/C. The middleman instructs the advising bank to effect payment to the supplier when the documents are negotiated. In this way, buyers and sellers are not disclosed to each other.

When using the back-to-back method shown in Fig. 4-7, the middleman must have an L/C because the middleman is responsi-

Transferable Letter of Credit

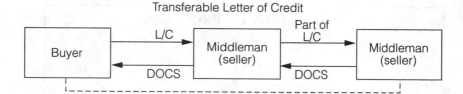

- L/C must state that it is transferable
- Original beneficiary transfers all or part of L/C to supplier(s)
- Transfer must be made under the same terms and conditions with the following exceptions:
  Amount
  Unit price
  Expiration date
  Shipping date
- Buyer and supplier usually disclosed to each other

Fig. 4-4. Transferable letter of credit

ble for paying the second (backing) L/C regardless of receipt of payment under the first (master) L/C. Great care should be exercised when using this method because discrepancies on the first L/C will result in nonpayment. The middleman's ability to pay could be a substantial credit risk. Back-to-back L/Cs should be issued on nearly identical terms and must allow for third-party documents.

Cash in Advance. The cash-in-advance method of getting paid is the most desirable, but the foreign buyer usually objects to tying up his or her capital. On the grounds that seeing the merchandise is the best insurance, most foreign businesspeople try not

Assignment of Proceeds

| Buyer | L/C → | Middleman (seller) | A/P → | Supplier |
| | ← DOCS | | | |

- Supplier relies on middleman to comply with L/C so that he or she can be paid. Discrepancy in middleman's documents will prevent payment under L/C
- Middleman instructs advising bank to effect payment to supplier when documents are negotiated
- Buyer and seller are not disclosed to each other
- Proceeds of all letters of credit can be assigned

Fig. 4-5. Assignment of proceeds

ASSIGNMENT OF PROCEEDS

Gentlemen:

Here is Letter of Credit No. _____
issued by _____ in favor of _____
_____ for an amount in excess of $ _____
expiring _____.

Our drafts and documents in terms of this credit will be presented by us to your office, and they are negotiated/paid, we authorize and direct you to pay to _____
the sum of $ _____ from the proceeds of these drafts, in consideration of value received.

These instructions are irrevocable and shall continue under any extension of this Letter of Credit. Please acknowledge receipt of these instructions directly to _____ by forwarding them a copy of this letter.

Sincerely yours,

_____

Signature verified:

_____
    Name of Bank

_____
    Authorized Signature

The above assignment has been duly noted on our records.

_____
    The Bank of San Diego International Banking Department
    Authorized Signature

Fig. 4-6. Assignment of proceeds letter

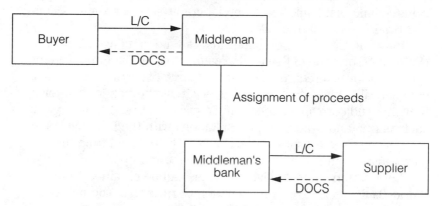

Fig. 4-7. Back-to-back letter of credit

* Requires credit line for middleman
* Middleman is responsible for paying the second (backing) L/C regardless of receipt of payment under first (master) L/C
* Substantial credit risk in that discrepancies on the first L/C will result in non-payment
* L/Cs are issued on nearly identical terms
* Middleman's ability to pay is a key consideration
* L/C must allow third-party documents

to pay until they actually receive the goods. Furthermore, the buyer might resent the implication that he or she is not creditworthy.

Avoiding Bad Credit

Pick your customer carefully. Bad debts are more easily avoided than rectified. If there are payment problems, keep communicating and working with the firm until the matter is settled. Even the most valued customers have financial problems from time to time. If nothing else works, request your department of industry or commerce or the International Chamber of Commerce (ICOC) to begin negotiations on your behalf.

Information that is current and accurate is the basis of good financing decisions. Basically two types of international credit information exists: (1) the ability and willingness of importing firms to make payment, and (2) the ability and willingness of foreign countries to allow payment in a convertible currency.

You can obtain credit information about domestic companies from commercial banks, commercial credit services such as Dun and Bradstreet, and trade associations.

Information about foreign firms can be obtained from the National Association of Credit Management (NACM), foreign credit specialists in the credit departments of large exporting companies, commercial banks, which check buyer credit through their foreign branches and correspondents, commercial credit reporting services such as Dun and Bradstreet, consultations with the Eximbank and the Foreign Credit Insurance Association (FCIA), and from the Department of Commerce's World Trade Directory Reports.

Information about foreign countries can be obtained from the World Bank, Chase World Information Corporation, the magazine *Institutional Investor*, and NACM.

Avoiding Foreign Exchange Risk

When the dollar is strong—as strong as it was in the early 1980s—traders prefer to deal in the dollar. When the opposite is true, traders begin to deal in other currencies. Of course, the dollar is as good as gold because it is a politically stable currency that is traded internationally. Because of its stability, the dollar has become the vehicle currency for most international transactions.

As long as exporters deal only in their currency, there is no foreign exchange risk. However, the strength and popularity of currencies is cyclical and the dollar is not always the leader. Often, an exporter is faced with the prospect of pricing products or services in currencies other than dollars. Importers must buy foreign currency to pay for products and services from risk-avoiding foreign suppliers demanding payment in their own currency. In the current era of floating exchange rates, risks due to exposure are real whenever cash flows are denominated in foreign currencies.

Exposure is the effect on a firm or an individual if there is a change on exchange rates.

Hedging or *covering* is the use of the forward foreign exchange market to avoid foreign currency risk.

The *forward* or *future exchange rate* is the rate that is contracted today for the delivery of a currency at a specified date in the future at a price agreed upon today.

Successfully managing currency risk is imperative. No longer can an importer/exporter speculate by doing nothing, then passing his foreign exchange losses on to customers in the form of higher prices.

The best business decision for an importer/exporter is to hedge or cover in the forward market when there is risk of exposure. To do otherwise is to be a speculator, not a businessperson. Use the forward rate for the date on which payment is required. This avoids all foreign exchange risk, is simple, and reasonably inexpensive. The cost of a forward contract is small—the difference between the cost of the spot market (today's cost of money) and the cost of the forward market.

Major international banks and brokerage houses can help you arrange a foreign-exchange forward contract. Spot and forward markets are quoted daily in the *Journal of Commerce* and the *Wall Street Journal*.

Avoiding Political Risk

No two national export credit systems are identical. However, there are similarities, the greatest of which is the universal involvement of government through the export credit agency concerned and of the commercial banking sector in the workings of the system.

Most countries have export-import banks. In the United States, the Eximbank provides credit support in the form of loans, guarantees, and insurance. All Eximbanks cooperate with commercial banks in providing a number of arrangements to help exporters offer credit guarantees to commercial banks that finance export sales. OPIC and FCIA also provide insurance to exporters, enabling them to extend credit terms to their overseas buyers. Private insurers cover the normal commercial credit risks; Eximbank assumes all liability for political risk.

To contact FCIA, write FCIA, Marketing Department 11th Floor, 40 Rector, New York, NY 10006 or call (212) 306-5000.

The programs available through OPIC and FCIA are well advertised and easily available. Commercial banks are essentially intermediaries to the Eximbank for export guarantees on loans (beginning with loans of up to 1 year and ending at loans from 10 to 15 years).

FCIA offers insurance in two basic maturities: (1) a short-term policy of up to 180 days, (2) a medium-term policy from 181 days to 5 years; or you can obtain (3) a combination policy of those maturities. FCIA also has a master policy providing blanket protection (one policy designed to provide, under one policy, coverage for all the exporter's sales to overseas buyers).

Avoiding Shipping Risk

Marine cargo insurance is an essential business tool for import/export. Generally, coverage is sold on a warehouse-to-warehouse basis (i.e., from the sender's factory to the receiver's platform). Coverage usually ceases a specific number of days after the ship or plane is unloaded. You purchase policies on a per shipment or *blanket* basis. Freight forwarders usually have a blanket policy to cover clients who do not have their own policy. Most insurance companies base cargo insurance on the value of all charges of the shipment, including freight handling, etc., plus 10% to cover unforeseen contingencies. Rates vary according to product, client's track record, destination, and shipping method. Ocean cargo insurance costs about $.50 to $1.50 per $100 of invoice value; air cargo is usually about 25% to 30% less.

Agency/Distributor Agreements

Chapter 3 covered your relationship with overseas distributors. A manufacturer or importer/exporter seldom agrees to meet all of a distributor's conditions. Most conditions are negotiable, and a firm that is not internationally known might have to fulfill more demands than others in a more favorable position. The following five tips can help you avoid unnecessary risk when doing business with distributors:

1. *Put the agency agreement in writing.* The rights and obligations resulting from a written agreement require no extraneous proof and are all that is necessary to record or prove the terms of a contract in most countries.

2. *Set forth the benefit(s) to both parties in the agreement.* Well-balanced agreements should not place an excess of profitless burden on one of the parties. Performance of the agreement could be impossible to enforce with a party who receives no apparent benefit from it.

3. *Provide clear definitions for all contract terms.* Many English terms that are spelled similarly in a foreign lan-

guage have entirely different meanings. Require that the English version prevail when there is doubt. To avoid conflict use INCOTERMS.

4. *Expressly state the rights and obligations of the parties.* The agency contract should contain a description of the rights and duties of each party, the nature and duration of the relationship, and the reasons for which the agreement may be terminated.

5. *Specify a jurisdictional clause.* If local laws will allow, specify in the contract the jurisdiction that is to handle any legal disputes that might arise. When possible, use arbitration. Basic arbitration rules and principles are generally the same everywhere. Clauses in the contract should contain identification of the arbitration body or forum. Model arbitration clauses can be obtained from the following organizations:

American Arbitration Association
140 West 51st Street
New York, NY 10020
(212) 484-4000
fax: (212) 765-4874

The International Chamber of Commerce
1212 Avenue of the Americas
New York, NY 10036
(212) 354-4480
fax: (212) 575-0327

PHYSICAL DISTRIBUTION (SHIPPING AND PACKING)

Physical distribution, often referred to as logistics, is the means by which goods are moved from the manufacturer in one country to the customer in another. This section discusses two vital aspects the importer/exporter should have an appreciation for: shipping and packing.

Shipping

The importer/exporter can arrange directly land, ocean, and air shipping of international cargo. You handle inland transportation much the same as a domestic transaction, except that certain export marks must be added to the standard information shown on a domestic bill of lading. Also include instructions to the inland carrier to notify the ocean or air carrier.

Water Transportation

There are three types of ocean service: conference lines, independent lines, and tramp vessels. An *ocean conference* is an association of ocean carriers that have joined together to establish common rates and shipping conditions. Conferences have two rates: the regular tariff and a lower, contract rate. You can obtain the contract rate if you sign a contract to use conference vessels exclusively during the contract period.

Independent lines accept bookings from all shippers contingent on the availability of space and are often less expensive than conference rates. An independent usually quotes rates about 10% lower than a conference carrier in situations where the two are in competition.

Tramp vessels usually carry only bulk cargoes and do not follow an established schedule; rather they operate on charters.

Regardless of the type of carrier you use, the carrier will issue a booking contract, which reserves space on a specific ship. Unless you cancel in advance, you might be required to pay even if your cargo doesn't make the sailing.

You must be insured with ocean marine insurance. An insurance broker or your freight forwarder can make the arrangements for you. *Marine insurance* compensates the owner of goods transported on the seas in the event of a loss that would not be legally recovered from the carrier. It also covers air shipments.

Air Transportation

Air freight continues to grow as a popular and competitive method for international cargoes. The growth has been facilitated by innovation in the cargo industry. Air carriers have excellent capacity, use very efficient loading and unloading equipment, and handle standardized containers. The advantages are (a) the speed of delivery, which gets perishable cargoes to the place of destination in prime condition, (b) the ability to respond to unpredictable product demands, and (c) the rapid movement of repair parts.

Air freight moves under a general cargo rate or a commodity rate. A special unit load rate is available when using approved air shipping containers.

Land Transportation

Transportation over land has become less regulated and, therefore, more competitive and efficient. The largest import/export market—the North American Free Trade Area (NAFTA)—can be served directly by road and rail. Importers and exporters look primarily to land transportation to move their goods to the nearest port of departure or as one leg of a sea, land, or air combination, often referred to as *intermodalism*.

Intermodalism

The movement of international shipments via container using sequential transportation methods is the system of the future. The concept makes use of the most efficient and cost-effective methods to move goods.

Load Centering. This concept stimulated the sophistication of today's intermodal world. As ships grew to hold more containers, they became more expensive to operate. One way to reduce costs was to hold down the number of port calls. In order to fill the ships at fewer ports, the cargo has to be funneled into these load centers. The simplification and organization of movements of cargo has become the "fair haired" child of transportation specialists. An entirely new set of terms have developed around the concept.

Land Bridges. A *micro-bridge* is the routing of a container to or from anywhere in the United States to or from any port. A *mini-bridge* moves a container that originates or terminates in a U.S. port other than the one where it enters or leaves the country. A *land-bridge* off-loads a container at any U.S. port, ships it cross-country by rail, then reloads it aboard a vessel for final movement to a foreign destination. *RO/RO* refers to the roll on/roll off capability of containerized cargo, which is the foundation of intermodalism.

An example of intermodalism might be a container of goods originating in Europe but destined for Japan. It could be rolled off a ship by truck then onto a train in Newport News, Virginia (RO/RO), where it would be joined by another container trucked in from Florida, (mini-bridge) also destined for Japan. The containers would then be moved across the United States (land-bridge) and then rolled off the train and onto a ship in Long Beach, California that would complete the movement to Tokyo. Figure 4-8 illustrates the intermodal concept.

HOT TIP: If the details of transportation and all the "new fangled" ideas are not for you, then see your nearest freight forwarder (see Chapter 6).

Fig. 4-8. The intermodal concept

Packaging and Marking for Overseas Shipment

Whether importing or exporting, your product(s) must travel thousands of miles in an undamaged condition. Your package must protect against breakage, dampness, careless storage, rough handling, thieves, and weather. Insurance might cover the loss, but lost time and the ill will of your overseas trading partner is a high price to pay. It has been estimated that as much as 70% of all cargo loss could be prevented by proper packaging and marking.

An excellent source on all aspects of packing and packaging is the *Modern Packaging Encyclopedia* (Annual), McGraw-Hill, New York.

Breakage. Ocean shipments are often roughly loaded aboard by stevedores using forklifts, slings, nets, and conveyors. During the voyage, rough water and storms can cause loads to shift and sometimes crash into other containers. Even small packages sent through the mail can be squeezed, thrown, or crushed.

Assume the Worst. Use stronger and heavier materials when packaging for overseas delivery than you would use for domestic shipments. On the other hand, don't overpack—you pay by weight and volume. For large ocean shipments, consider standardized containers that can be transferred from truck or railcar without opening.

Pilferage (Theft). Use strapping and seals and avoid trademarks or content descriptions to avoid pilferage.

Moisture and Weather. The heat and humidity of the tropics as well as rainstorms and rough weather at sea can cause moisture to seep into the holds of a ship. From that moisture comes fungal growth, sweat, and rust. Waterproofing your shipment is essential for most ocean shipments. Consider plastic shrink-wrap or waterproof inner liners, and coat any exposed metal parts with grease or other rust inhibitors.

Marking (Labeling). Foreign customers have their needs, shippers have theirs, and terminal operators have theirs. Each will specify certain marks (port, customer identification code, package numbers, and number of packages) to appear on shipments. Other markings such as weight, dimensions, and regulations that facilitate clearing through customs can be specified.

When you mark your containers, write your customer's name and address or shipping code on the package. Use black, waterproof ink for the stencils. Include port of exit and port of entry on your label. Don't forget package and case number.

Include dimensions (inches and metric). Mark exports: "Made in U.S.A.," etc., to get through customs in most foreign countries. Express gross and net weight in pounds and/or kilograms. Don't forget cautionary markings such as "This side up" or "Handle with care" in *both* languages. Don't use brand names or advertising slogans on packages. Any shipments that carry explosives or volatile liquids must conform to local laws and international agreements. Figure 4-9 is a sample of such markings.

DOCUMENTATION

"Attention to detail" is the byword when preparing documentation. The naive pass it off as a byproduct of the transaction, but the experienced trader knows that shipments can be detained on the pier for weeks because of inattention. As ex-Yankee baseball player,

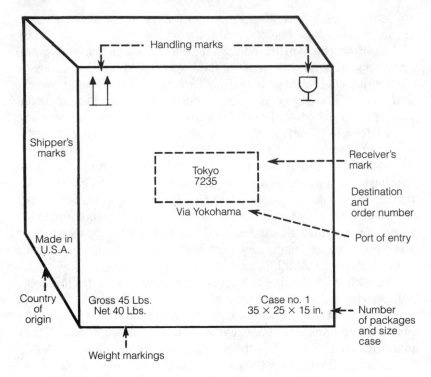

Fig. 4-9. Example of markings

Yogi Berra once said, "It ain't over 'til it's over," and that's the way it is in international trade. The exporter doesn't get his or her money and the importer doesn't get his or her goods unless the paperwork is complete and accurate. Therefore, be attentive to detail!

Basically, documentation falls into two categories; *shipping* and *collecting. Shipping documents* permit an export cargo to be moved through customs, loaded aboard a carrier, and shipped to its foreign destination. Shipping documents include export licenses, packing lists, bills of lading, and export declarations.

Collection documents are documents that are submitted to the importer (in the case of a draft) or to the importer's bank (in the case of an L/C) in order to receive payment. Collection documents include commercial invoices, consular invoices, certificates of origin, inspection certificates, and bills of lading.

When endorsed by the shipper, you can use the bill of lading for sight draft or for L/C shipments. Other documents sometimes required for collection are manufacturing and insurance certificates and dock or warehouse receipts. Keep in mind that customhouse brokers and freight forwarders are specialists in documentation as well as physical distribution. The following section describes the various documents in detail and provides samples of each.

Collection is the procedure whereby a bank collects money for a seller against a draft drawn on a buyer abroad, usually through a correspondent bank.

Certificate of Origin. The *certificate of origin* is a document that certifies to the buyer the country in which the goods were produced. A recognized chamber of commerce (COC) usually performs the certificate of the origin of merchandise. Some countries require a separate certificate, sometimes countersigned by a COC and possibly even visaed by their resident consul at the port of export. These statements are required to indicate preferential rates of import duties such as *most favored nation*. Often as little as 35% of a nation's materials and/or labor can qualify it for favorable duties. Some nations require special forms, while others accept a certification on the shipper's letterhead. (See Fig. 4-10 for an example of a certificate of origin.)

When preparing the certificate of origin, make sure that the letter or form originates from the address of the product manufacturer and that a responsible and knowledgeable person within the manufacturing company (an *officer* of the corporation) signs the letter. The letter or form will not be accepted if it is from an outside sales office or distributor. It cannot be signed by a salesperson. The letter also should clearly state where the product in question was manufactured.

Commercial Invoice. The *commercial invoice* is a bill that conforms in all respects to the agreement between importer and exporter. It could have the exact terms of the pro forma invoice first offered in response to a quotation or it could differ in those terms that were the result of final negotiations. In any case, there should be no surprises for the importer. The commercial invoice should: (a) itemize the merchandise by price per unit and any charges paid by the buyer, and (b) specify the terms of payment and any marks or numbers on the packages. See Fig. 4-11.

Our Company, Inc.

Hometown, Wherever

Date _____

Your Company

Hometown, Wherever

Point of Origin Declaration

For the purpose of positively identifying certain components

as being manufactured in _____ and therefore qualifying for
(Country)

entry under _____.
(Tariff code identification)

Component(s) description: _____

_____

Part number: _____

_____

The manufacturer _____ warrants and

represents that the articles supplied to _____

_____
(Company)

and described above are articles of _____.
(Country)

The articles were manufactured at _____
(Address of location of plant)

_____.

Authorized signature and date

_____

Title

Fig. 4-10. Certificate of origin

XYZ Foreign Co.
2A1 Moon River
Yokohama, Japan

Purchase Order:
Invoice Number: 00012
Invoice Date:

Sold To: Our Company, Inc.　　　Ship To: Our Company, Inc.
　　　Hometown, U.S.A.　　　　　　　Hometown, U.S.A.

Forwarding Agent:

Via:　　　　　　　　　　　Country of Origin: Japan

QUANTITY	PART NO.	DESCRIPTION	PRICE EACH	TOTAL PRICE
10	A2Z	Machines	$100.00	$1,000.00

Inland freight, export packing & forwarding fees　　$ 100.00

Free alongside (F.A.S.) Yokohama　　　　　　　$1,100.00
Estimated ocean freight　　　　　　　　　　　$ 100.00
Estimated marine insurance　　　　　　　　　$ 50.00

Packed in 10 crates, 100 cubic feet
Gross weight 1000 lbs.
Net weight　　900 lbs.
Payment terms: Confirmed irrevocable letter of credit confirmed by a
U.S. bank. Shipment to be made two (2) weeks after receipt of firm order.
Additional conditions of sale: XYZ, Foreign Co. to provide:
Certificate of Origin
Consular Invoice
Certificate of Manufacture
Insurance Certificate
Inspection Certificate

Fig. 4-11. Commercial invoice

Consular Invoice. This invoice is not required by all countries. It is obtained from the commercial attache or through the
consular office of that country in the port of export. When required, it is in addition to a commercial invoice and must conform

in every respect to that document, as well as the bill of lading and any insurance documents. Its purpose is to allow clearance of your shipment into the country that requires it. (See Fig. 4-12.)

> The *commercial attache* is the commercial expert on the diplomatic staff of his country's embassy or large consulate in a foreign country.

Certificate of Manufacture. This document certifies that the goods ordered by the importer have been produced and are ready for shipment. For example, the certificate might be used in those cases when the manufacturer has moved ahead in production with only a down payment, thus allowing the importer to avoid allocation of the full amount too far in advance. Generally, invoices and packing lists are forwarded to the importer with the certificate of manufacture. (See Fig. 4-13.)

Export Licenses. Export licensing procedures are described in detail in Chapter 6 as one of the six topics unique to exporting. These licenses are of two basic varieties: general and validated. *Validated licenses* require careful attention because they apply to products that the government wants to control closely for either strategic or economic reasons. The Commodity Control List (CCL) sets forth items such as certain weapons, technologies, and high-tech products. Export administration regulations set forth all licensing requirements for commodities under the jurisdiction of the Office of Export Administration (OEA), International Trade Administration. Once it has been determined that a license is needed, the form *Application for Export License* must be prepared and submitted to the OEA. (See Fig. 6-1 in Chapter 6.)

Insurance Certificates. *Insurance certificates* provide evidence of coverage and can be a stipulation of a contract, purchase order, or commercial invoice in order to receive payment. These documents indicate the type and amount of coverage and identify the merchandise in terms of packages and identifying marks. Make certain that the information on this certificate agrees exactly with invoices and bills of lading. (See Fig. 4-14.)

Inspection Certificates. This document protects the importer against fraud, error, or quality performance. It is most often conducted by an independent firm, but it is sometimes accomplished by the shipper. An affidavit that certifies the inspection is of-

FACTURA COMERCIAL

No. de la Factura............
(Commercial Invoice #)

Lugar (Ciudad)............
Place (City)

Fecha: Día. ....   Mes.........   Año..........
Date: Day   Mo.   Year

INTERVIENEN	Nombre de la Cía. o del Agente autorizado	DOMICILIO (Address)		
		Número (No.)	Calle (Street)	Ciudad (City)	Tel. (Phone)
Vendedor o remitente (Seller or shipper)					
Comprador (Buyer)					
Consig. a Destinatario (Consigned to)					
Agente o Gestor Agent-Broker					

Lugar y Puerto de Embarque Port of Loading	Lugar y Puerto de Destino Port of Unloading	Fecha de Embarque Date of Shipment	Nombre del Buque o Cía. Aérea Transp. Vessel/Airline Name

CONDICIONES DE VENTA: FOB - CIF   SEGURO (Insurance): ....

Cantidad y Número de Bultos	PESO		Detalle descriptivo de la mercadería, indicando marca, lugar de fabricación, clase o tipo del producto, series, números, etc. y cualquier otra información adicional relacionada. (Denomination and details of each article: quantity, quality, measure, merch. origin, etc.)	Precio de la Mercadería (Merchandise Price)
	Kilogramos	Libras		

Fig. 4-12. Consular invoice

El agente autorizado que firma la presente, declara bajo juramento que todos los datos declarados en la presente factura, son exactos y verdaderos y que los precios pagados o por pagarse, son los reales y convenidos, que no existe convenio o arreglo alguno que permita la alteración o modificación de éstos, ni tampoco de su cantidad o calidad.

Firma del Agente, Vendedor o
Despachante autorizado. Fecha: ......

Importe mercad. ....U$S
Merch. Price

Transporte .... U$S

Otros (other) ......U$S

SUB-TOTAL ......U$S

Tasa Consular, Fee U$S

IMPORTE TOTAL U$S

FACTURA COMERCIAL No.

Certifico que la firma que aparece en este

documento y dice ......

es auténtica y pertenece al funcionario descripto.

Los Angeles, Calif......

Número de orden ......

No. del arancel ......

Der. percib. U$S. ......

Depositado en el Banco

The ......
A recognized Chamber of Commerce under the laws or the State of California has examined the manufacturer's invoice or shipper affidavit concerning the origin of the merchandise and according to the best of its knowledge and belief, finds that the products named originated in the United States of North America.

Authorized Officer...... Date......

Espacio para Certificacion Consular

REPUBLICA ARGENTINA
CONSULADO DE LA

Fig. 4-12. Continued

DATE:

REFERENCE: ACCOUNT NAME & ADDRESS
              PURCHASE ORDER NO. AND/OR
              CONTRACT NO.

BANK NAME AND LETTER OR CREDIT NO:

MERCHANDISE DESCRIPTION:

CERTIFICATE OF RECENT MANUFACTURE

WE HEREBY CERTIFY THAT THE HEREIN DESCRIBED
MERCHANDISE IS OF RECENT MANUFACTURE IN THIS
CASE NOT OLDER THAN _____ YEAR(S) FROM THIS DATE.

NAME AND ADDRESS OF MANUFACTURER:

BY: _____
              (Original signature)

Fig. 4-13. Certificate of manufacture

ten required under the terms of an L/C. For example, a Taiwanese firm wanted to import used diesel generators from the United States. That company insisted that an independent engineer certify satisfactory operation of each generator, at specifications, prior to shipment. (See Fig. 4-15.)

Packing Lists. A packing list accompanies the shipment and describes the cargo in detail. It includes the shipper, the consignee, measurements, serial numbers, weights, and any other data peculiar to the shipment. When correctly completed it is placed in a waterproof bag or envelop and attached with the words: "Packing List Enclosed." (See Fig. 4-16.)

Shippers Export Declaration. The *shippers export declaration* (SED) is prepared by the exporter or freight forwarder for the U.S. government. It is a data collection document required on all exports in excess of $2500. It is prepared for purposes of

No. 573951

CERTIFICATE OF MARINE INSURANCE

International Cargo & Surety Insurance Company

* $ _____
(sum insured)

This is to Certify, That on the _____ day of _____ 19___ , this Company

insured under Policy No. _____ made for _____

for the sum of _____ Dollars,

on _____

*(Amounts in excess of $1,000,000.00 cannot be insured under this Certificate)

Valued at sum insured. Shipped on board the S/S or M/S _____ and/or following
steamer or steamers

at and from _____ , via _____
(Initial Point of Shipment)   (Port of Shipment)

to _____ and it is understood and agreed, that in case of loss, the same
(Port of Places of Destination)

is payable to the order of _____
conveys the right of collecting any such loss as fully as if the property were covered by a special policy direct to the holder hereof, and free from any liability for unpaid premiums. This certificate is issued subject to the standard International Cargo & Surety Insurance Company open cargo policy, which is incorporated herein by reference. To the extent that any terms or conditions in this certificate are inconsistent with the standard policy, the standard policy shall govern the rights and duties of all parties subject to the contract of insurance. Copies of the standard policy are available, upon request, from International Cargo & Surety Insurance Company, 1501 Woodfield Road, Schaumburg, Illinois 60173.

SPECIAL CONDITIONS

Merchandise shipped with an UNDER DECK bill of lading insured –
Against all risks of physical loss or damage from any external cause, irrespective of percentage, excepting those excluded by the F.C.& S. and S.R.& C.C. Warranties, arising during transportation between the points of shipment and of destination named herein

ON DECK SHIPMENTS (with an ON DECK bill of lading) and/or shipments of used merchandise insured:
Warranted free of particular average unless caused by the vessel being stranded, sunk, burnt, on fire or in collision, but including risk of jettison and/or washing overboard, irrespective of percentage.

MARKS & NUMBERS

SCHEDULE B CODE (commodity)	SCHEDULE C-E CODE (country)

TERMS AND CONDITIONS—SEE ALSO BACK HEREOF

WAREHOUSE TO WAREHOUSE This insurance attaches from the time the goods leave the Warehouse and/or Store at the place named in the Policy for the commencement of the transit and continues during the ordinary course of transit, including customary transhipment if any, until the goods are discharged overside from the overseas vessel at the final port. Thereafter the insurance continues whilst the goods are in transit and/or awaiting transit until delivered to final warehouse at the destination named in the Policy or until the expiry of 15 days (or 30 days if the destination to which the goods are insured is outside the limits of the port) whichever shall first occur. The time limits referred to above to be reckoned from midnight of the day on which the discharge overside of the goods hereby insured from the overseas vessel is completed. Held covered at a premium to be arranged in the event of transhipment, if any, other than as above and/or in the event of delay in excess of the above time limits arising from circumstances beyond the control of the Assured

NOTE — IT IS NECESSARY FOR THE ASSURED TO GIVE PROMPT NOTICE TO THESE ASSURERS WHEN THEY BECOME AWARE OF AN EVENT FOR WHICH THEY ARE "HELD COVERED" UNDER THIS POLICY AND THE RIGHT TO SUCH COVER IS DEPENDENT ON COMPLIANCE WITH THIS OBLIGATION.

PERILS CLAUSE: Touching the adventures and perils which this Company is contented to bear, and takes upon itself, they are of the seas, fires, assailing thieves, jettisons, barratry of the master and mariners, and all other like perils, losses and misfortunes (illicit or contraband trade excepted in all cases), that have or shall come to the hurt, detriment or damage of the said goods and merchandise, or any part thereof.

SHORE CLAUSE: Where this insurance by its terms covers while on docks, wharves or elsewhere on shore, and/or during land transportation, it shall include the risks of collision, derailment, overturning or other accident to the conveyance, fire, lightning, sprinkler leakage, cyclones, hurricanes, earthquakes, floods (meaning the rising of navigable waters), and/or collapse or subsidence of docks or wharves, even though the insurance be otherwise F.P.A.

BOTH TO BLAME CLAUSE: Where goods are shipped under a Bill of Lading containing the so-called "Both to Blame Collision" Clause, these Assurers agree as to all losses covered by this insurance, to indemnify the Assured for the Assured's proportion of any amount (not exceeding the amount insured) which the Assured may be legally bound to pay to the shipowners under such clause. In the event that such liability is asserted the Assured agree to notify these Assurers who shall have the right at their own cost and expense to defend the Assured against such claim.

MACHINERY CLAUSE: When the property insured under this Policy includes a machine consisting when complete for sale or use of several parts, then in case of loss or damage covered by this insurance to any part of such machine, these Assurers shall be liable only for the proportion of the insured value of the part lost or damaged, or at the Assured's option, for the cost and expense, including labor and forwarding charges, of replacing or repairing the lost or damaged part but in no event shall these Assurers be liable for more than the insured value of the complete machine.

LABELS CLAUSE: In case of damage affecting labels, capsules or wrappers, these Assurers, if liable therefor under the terms of this policy, shall not be liable for more than an amount sufficient to pay the cost of new labels, capsules or wrappers and the cost of reconditioning the goods, but in no event shall these Assurers be liable for more than the insured value of the damaged merchandise.

DELAY CLAUSE: Warranted free of claim for loss of market or for loss, damage or deterioration arising from delay, whether caused by a peril insured against or otherwise, unless expressly assumed in writing herein.

AMERICAN INSTITUTE CLAUSES: This insurance, in addition to the foregoing, is also subject to the following American Institute Cargo Clauses, current forms:

1. CRAFT, ETC.	4. GENERAL AVERAGE	8. INCHMAREE	12. WAR RISK INSURANCE
2. DEVIATION	5. EXPLOSION	9. CONSTRUCTIVE TOTAL LOSS	13. SOUTH AMERICA 60 DAY CLAUSE
3. WAREHOUSING & FORWARDING CHARGES, PACKAGES TOTALLY LOST LOADING, ETC.	6. BILL OF LADING, ETC.	10. CARRIER	
	7. MARINE EXTENSION CLAUSES	11. S.R. & C.C. ENDORSEMENT	

PARAMOUNT WARRANTIES: THE FOLLOWING WARRANTIES SHALL BE PARAMOUNT AND SHALL NOT BE MODIFIED OR SUPERSEDED BY ANY OTHER PROVISION INCLUDED HEREIN OR STAMPED OR ENDORSED HEREON UNLESS SUCH OTHER PROVISION REFERS SPECIFICALLY TO THE RISKS EXCLUDED BY THESE WARRANTIES AND EXPRESSLY ASSUMES THE SAID RISKS:

F.C. & S. (a) Notwithstanding anything herein contained to the contrary, this insurance is warranted free from capture, seizure, arrest, restraint, detainment, confiscation, preemption, requisition or nationalization, and the consequences thereof or any attempt thereat, whether in time of peace or war and whether lawful or otherwise; also warranted free, whether in time of peace or war, from all loss, damage or expense caused by any weapon of war employing atomic or nuclear fission and/or fusion or other reaction or radioactive force or matter or by any mine or torpedo, also warranted free from all consequences of hostilities or warlike operations (whether there be a declaration of war or not), but this warranty shall not exclude collision or contact with aircraft, rockets or similar missiles or with any fixed or floating object (other than a mine or torpedo), stranding, heavy weather, fire or explosion unless caused directly (and independently of the nature of the voyage or service which the vessel concerned or, in the case of a collision, any other vessel involved therein, is performing) by a hostile act by or against a belligerent power; and for the purposes of this warranty 'power' includes any authority maintaining naval, military or air forces in association with a power.

Further warranted free from the consequences of civil war, revolution, rebellion, insurrection, or civil strife arising therefrom, or piracy.

S.R. & C.C. (b) Warranted free of loss or damage caused by or resulting from strikes, lockouts, labor disturbances, riots, civil commotions or the acts of any person or persons taking part in any such occurrence or disorder.

This Certificate is issued in Original and Duplicate, one of which being accomplished the other to stand null and void. To support a claim local Revenue Laws may require this certificate to be stamped.

Not transferable unless countersigned

Countersigned _____

ADDITIONAL CONDITIONS AND
INSTRUCTIONS TO CLAIMANTS ON REVERSE SIDE

OM18

President _____   Secretary _____

SAMPLE   ORIGINAL

Fig. 4-14. Certificate of marine insurance

DATE:

REFERENCE: ACCOUNT NAME & ADDRESS
             PURCHASE ORDER NO. AND/OR
             CONTRACT NO.

BANK NAME AND LETTER OR CREDIT NO.

MERCHANDISE DESCRIPTION:

             INSPECTION CERTIFICATE

WE HEREBY CERTIFY THAT THE HEREIN DESCRIBED
MERCHANDISE HAS BEEN INSPECTED AND FOUND TO BE
OF HIGHEST QUALITY AND IN GOOD WORKING ORDER.

             PORTER INTERNATIONAL INC.

             BY:_____
                     (Original signature)

Fig. 4-15. Inspection certificate

providing statistical information to the Bureau of Census and to indicate the proper authorization to export. It is the basis for measuring the volume and type of exports leaving a country. The document requires complete information about the shipment, including description, value, net and gross weights, and relevant license information, thus closing the licensing information loop back to the OEA. (See Fig. 4-17.)

Bills of Lading. A *bill of lading* is a contract between the owner of the goods (exporter) and the carrier. It is both evidence that the shipment has been made, and your receipt for the goods that have been shipped. Figure 4-18 is a bill of lading for an air carrier, called an air waybill. Figure 4-19 is an ocean bill of lading.

Straight Bills of Lading. *Straight* bills of lading are non-negotiable bills that consign the goods to an importer or other party named on the document. Once consummated, the seller

To: Your Company   Date: _____
     2A1 Moon River
     Yokohama, Japan

Gentlemen:

Under your order No. <u>123</u> the material listed below was shipped
<u>1/1/18</u> via <u>Truck and vessel</u>

To: <u>Yokohama</u>

Via:

Shipment Consists of: Marks:

___ Cases ___ Packages   Your Company, Ltd.
                          2A1 Moon River
___ Crates ___ Cartons   Yokohama, Japan

___ Bbls   ___ Drums   Made in U.S.A.

___ Reels   #7235

Package Number	Weights (Lbs or Kilos)		Dimensions			Quality	Contents
	Gross	Legal Net	Ht.	Wth.	Lth.		
7235	45	40	35	25	15		Toys

Fig. 4-16. Packing list

and/or the seller's bank loses title control because the goods will be delivered to anyone who can be identified as the consignee.

Order Bill of Lading. This is a negotiable bill. Unlike the straight bill, the *order* represents the title to the goods in transit.

FORM **7525-V** (3-19-85)

U.S. DEPARTMENT OF COMMERCE — BUREAU OF THE CENSUS — INTERNATIONAL TRADE ADMINISTRATION

SHIPPER'S EXPORT DECLARATION

OMB No. 0607-0018

1a. EXPORTER *(Name and address including ZIP code)*

ZIP CODE

2. DATE OF EXPORTATION

3. BILL OF LADING/AIR WAYBILL NO.

b. EXPORTER EIN NO.

c. PARTIES TO TRANSACTION

☐ Related   ☐ Non-related

4a. ULTIMATE CONSIGNEE

b. INTERMEDIATE CONSIGNEE

NONE

5. FORWARDING AGENT

Porter International, Inc.
P.O. Box 41-A
San Ysidro, California 92173

6. POINT (STATE) OF ORIGIN OR FTZ NO.

7. COUNTRY OF ULTIMATE DESTINATION

MEXICO

8. LOADING PIER/TERMINAL

9. MODE OF TRANSPORT *(Specify)*

TRUCK

10. EXPORTING CARRIER

Truck Lic.:

11. PORT OF EXPORT

San Diego, (S.Y.), California

12. FOREIGN PORT OF UNLOADING

13. CONTAINERIZED *(Vessel only)*

☐ Yes   ☐ No

VALUE (U.S. dollars, omit cents) *(Selling price or cost if not sold)* **(20)**

14. SCHEDULE B DESCRIPTION OF COMMODITIES. *(Use columns 15 — 19)*

MARKS, NOS., AND KINDS OF PKGS. (15)	D/F (16)	SCHEDULE B NUMBER (17)	QUANTITY — SCHEDULE B UNIT(S) (18)	SHIPPING WEIGHT *(Pounds)* (19)

21. VALIDATED LICENSE NO./GENERAL LICENSE SYMBOL

22. ECCN *(When required)*

23. Duly authorized officer or employee

The exporter authorizes the forwarder named above to act as forwarding agent for export control and customs purposes.

24. I certify that all statements made and all information contained herein are true and correct and that I have read and understand the instructions for preparation of this document, set forth in the "**Correct Way to Fill Out the Shipper's Export Declaration.**" I understand that civil and criminal penalties, including forfeiture and sale, may be imposed for making false or fraudulent statements herein, failing to provide the requested information or for violation of U.S. laws on exportation (13 U.S.C. Sec. 305; 22 U.S.C. Sec. 401; 18 U.S.C. Sec. 1001; 50 U.S.C. App. 2410).

Signature

Confidential For use solely for official purposes authorized by the Secretary of Commerce (13 U.S.C. 301 (g)).

Title EXPORT CLERK

Export shipments are subject to inspection by U.S. Customs Service and/or Office of Export Enforcement

Date

25. AUTHENTICATION *(When required)*

THESE COMMODITIES LICENSED BY U.S. FOR ULTIMATE DESTINATION — MEXICO — DIVERSION CONTRARY TO U.S. LAW PROHIBITED.

Fig. 4-17. Shippers export declaration

Shipper's Name and Address	Shipper's Account Number	Not negotiable **Air Waybill** (Air Consignment note) Issued by

Copies 1, 2 and 3 of this Air Waybill are originals and have the same validity

Consignee's Name and Address	It is agreed that the goods described herein are accepted in apparent good order and condition (except as noted) for carriage SUBJECT TO THE CONDITIONS OF CONTRACT ON THE REVERSE HEREOF. THE SHIPPER'S ATTENTION IS DRAWN TO THE NOTICE CONCERNING CARRIERS' LIMITATION OF LIABILITY. Shipper may increase such limitation of liability by declaring a higher value for carriage and paying a supplemental charge if required. To expedite movement, shipment may be diverted to motor or other carrier unless shipper gives other instructions hereon.

Issuing Carrier's Agent Name and City	Accounting Information

SEE WARSAW NOTICE AND CONDITIONS OF CONTRACT ON REVERSE SIDE.

Agent's IATA Code	Account No.

Airport of Departure (Addr. of first Carrier) and requested Routing

By first Carrier	Routing and Destination			Currency	WT/VAL PPD COLL	Other PPD COLL	Declared Value for Carriage	Declared Value for Customs

Airport of Destination	Flight/Date	For Carrier Use only	Flight/Date	Amount of Insurance	INSURANCE - If Carrier offers insurance, and such insurance is requested in accordance with conditions on reverse hereof, indicate amount to be insured in figures in box marked amount of insurance.

Handling Information

These commodities licensed by the United States for ultimate destination .... Diversion contrary to United States law prohibited.

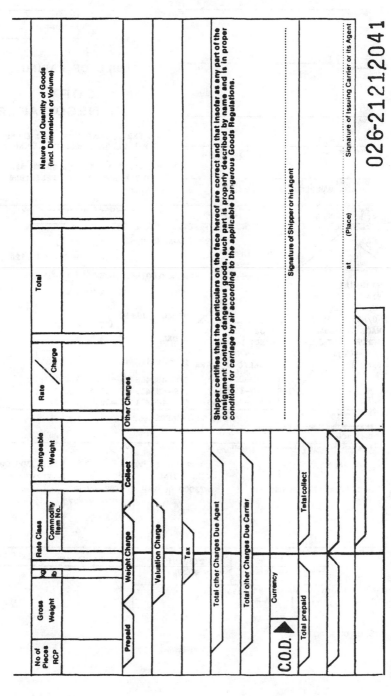

Fig. 4-18. Air waybill (bill of lading [air])

Shipper		B/L No.
		M132–11156

Consignee

BILL OF LADING

COPY
NON-NEGOTIABLE

Notify party

ALL TERMS, CONDITIONS AND EXCEPTIONS
AS PER ORIGINAL BILL OF LADING

Pre-carriage by	Place of receipt KAOHSIUNG CY

"SUBJECT TO ALL THE TERMS AND
CONDITIONS OF THE APPLICABLE
TARIFF"

Ocean vessel Voy. No. AMERICA MARU 55227B	Port of loading KAOHSIUNG

Port of discharge LOS ANGELES	Place of delivery TIJUANA CY	Final destination for the Merchant's reference

Container No.	Seal No. Marks and Numbers	No. of Cont- Kind of packages; description of goods ainers or pkgs.	Gross weight	Measurement
		''SHIPPER'S LOAD & COUNT''		
		3 CONTAINERS (677 CTNS)	9,014 KGS	120.32 M3

TIJUANA B.C. MEXICO
VIA LOS ANGELES CA.
MODEL: H260
C/NO. 1–235
MADE IN TAIWAN
REPUBLIC OF CHINA
—DO—BUT H667
C/NO.1

MODEL:
C/NO. 1–441
MADE IN TAIWAN
REPUBLIC OF CHINA

MODEL:H260,H670,H667
MODEL: JOB NO. & CODE NO.
MODEL: JOB NO.
        CODE NO.
MODEL: JOB NO. & CODE NO.
''FREIGHT COLLECT''

GSTU-8135538	C/S-480409 HS-41019	(192 C/T)
GSTU-8135939	C/S-480410 HS-41014	(192 C/T)
MOLU-2021646	C/S-480411 HS-41015	(293 C/T)

*Total number of Containers or other packages or units received by the Carrier (in words)

THREE CONTAINERS ONLY

Freight and charges	Revenue tons	Rate	per	Prepaid	Collect
BOX RATE		(40'x3)		US $2,100.00/VAN (INCLUDING D.D.C.)	US$6,300.00 vvvvvvvvvvvv
+ CY RECEIVING CHARGE				NT$900.00/VAN	NT$2,700.00 vvvvvvvvvvvv

Exchange rate (=	Prepaid at	Payable at TIJUANA	Place and date of issue TAIPEI TAIWAN JUL 30 1987
	Total prepaid in national currency	No. of original B(s)/L THREE/3	by

LADEN ON BOARD THE VESSEL
Date JUL 30 1987 Signature

Fig. 4-19. Bill of lading (ocean)

The original copy must be endorsed before it is presented to the bank for collection. In other words, the order bill can be used as collateral in financing—as documentation to discount or sell a draft. L/C transactions specify to whom the endorsement is to be made. Typically, they are made *in blank*, or to the order of a third party, a bank, or a broker. *Air bills of lading* are usually straight (i.e., nonnegotiable). Ocean shipping companies can issue straight or order.

Clean on Board. To verify shipping performance, the carrier indicates the condition of the goods upon acceptance. You should prefer to ship on a bill of lading marked *clean on board*. This means that the carrier accepted the cargo and loaded it on board the vessel without exception.

Foul Bill. A *foul bill* indicates an exception—that some damage is noted on the bill of lading. Discuss this with your carrier or freight forwarder to make sure you have an opportunity to exchange any damaged goods and obtain a clean on board bill.

Chapter 5 covers, from A to Z, how to build your company. It discusses how to decide on a name, how to go about getting start-up funds, and most important, how to think through and write a business plan.

5

Setting Up Your Own Import/Export Business

The language might be different, but in any country in the world you hear the same words, "I want my own business. How do I start?" The answer lies in these questions:

Have you done your homework?

What is your product?

Do you have contacts?

Who will buy it?

Is it profitable?

Do you have a marketing plan?

One person answered the question by stating, "My product is bead fringe."

"Why bead fringe?"

"Because I studied costume design in college and worked in the field. I know where the best bead fringe is and I want to get into the business."

It sounds like this person has done her homework and is ready to start her own import/export business. But she's not quite ready yet.

What she forgot was that an import/export business is a business and it takes capital, management, goals, and, above all, planning.

By incorporating what you've learned about the fundamentals of import/export in Chapters 2 through 4 along with the methods explained in this chapter, you should be ready to start your own import/export business.

The first part of this chapter describes the mechanics of start-up. The second part shows you how to develop a business plan so that you can raise capital and grow.

THE MECHANICS OF START-UP

The process for starting a small business is the same in any country in the world. You need capital, know-how, and management skills, but you do not need a fancy college degree. Anyone can operate a business.

Start-Up Capital

In the initial start-up stages, the funds needed to support the expenses of your own import/export business will most likely come from your own pocket. It is possible to begin an import/export business with as little as $1000 a year.

When your personal finances will not sustain the expenses of start-up until you reach break-even and begin to show a profit, you must look for outside financial assistance. Unfortunately, banks are seldom the source of start-up capital. Why? Banks do not take risks. They generally expect a track record and collateral. Catch-22? Where can you go for financing? Most often, the best sources are relatives and/or friends—people who know you and believe in you. Even they might want a description of your intended business, so from the beginning you should develop a written business plan. You might want to skip to the second part of this chapter to learn how to write that plan. You might return to this section when you complete your business plan.

Business Name

Think of a name for your business. The company's name should reflect what your business does. For example, you might easily visualize the business of a company called "Southeast U.S.A. Furniture

Import." This name gives a more accurate picture of what that company does than would, "Kim Yee and Son." If the name you choose does not contain your surname, a request to use a fictitious name, or doing-business-as (DBA) name is required in most places. If the name of your business includes your last name, you might not be required to file for approval to use a fictitious name. The cost for registering your fictitious name is about $10 in most counties. There is also a requirement that you publish your fictitious company name in a newspaper for several days. That cost is usually between $20 and $30.

The Business Organization

Next, decide how your business will be organized. The three common legal business forms are sole proprietorship, partnership, or corporation. Most new import/export businesses begin as sole proprietorships or partnerships. In the beginning, the owners find little need to take on the extra paperwork and reporting requirements of a corporation. Select the form for your business based on the intent, complexity, tax implications, and liability requirements of your business. If in doubt, consult a lawyer. Partnership agreements and incorporation papers can be expensive, requiring as little as a few hundred dollars or as much as several thousand.

Business License

Some countries require licenses to do international trade, but in the United States there is no requirement to do so. That is, there is no regulatory body that requires you to show special qualifications in order to hold yourself as an importer or exporter. However, like any other business, you probably must meet local and state business licensing requirements. It is possible that the foreign country you are doing business with will require a license as well. Check with your freight forwarder.

Seller's Permit

Most nations and states have a sales tax. In order to ensure collection, a seller's permit is often required. These permits are usually state controlled, so as you begin your own import/export business, you should investigate your local laws.

Financial Records

Open a separate bank account in the name of your business. Keep accurate records, and pass all business income and expenses through your business account. Do not pay personal expenses from this account or otherwise mix personal income or expenses with business income and expenses. You may list personal "capital contributions" and "capital withdrawals," but keep these infrequent and in reasonably large sums—don't take out money in dribs and drabs.

Accounting

From the beginning, learn to keep a simple set of books to feed into your Internal Revenue Service (IRS) forms at tax time. Keep a careful record (all receipts) of all business expenses, and invoice all work on your letterhead paper. At a minimum, you will need a general ledger organized into four sections: expenses, income, receivables (sales invoiced), and payables (bills received). For example, expenses like the cost of your trip to Hong Kong or Paris, should be listed chronologically, by month, down the left margin of the expense section. Across the page, the categories should correspond to the tax categories. Check current IRS publications. Some examples of categories are:

- Stationery and business cards
- Telephone, answering machine, adding machine, copier, typewriter, facsimile, and teletypewriter
- Rent, utilities, and office furniture
- Inventory
- Business checking account
- Salaries and other staff expenses
- Travel

Table 5-1 shows an example of the expense categories that should be shown in the expense section of your general ledger. The other sections of your ledger should be set up similarly.

Your Office

You might set up an office in your home or elsewhere. The location and outfitting will be determined by the volume and complexity of

Table 5-1. Expenses.

Date	Utilities	Telephone Fax	Travel Air	Travel Auto	Office Expense
January					
February					
March					

your firm. In the beginning, you might do business by letter and only use a telex and occasional part-time employees. However, as your import/export business grows, you might need warehouse space for inventory and a larger office for a growing staff.

Employees

As your office and trading staff grows, the complexity of paperwork and recordkeeping also will grow. Prior to hiring anyone, you must obtain an employers identification (ID) number from the IRS. You'll then need to consider worker's compensation and benefits insurance.

Business Insurance

Other business insurance policies that you should consider on a case-by-case basis are liability, disability, and a Foreign Credit Insurance Association (FCIA) umbrella. You should also consider a customs bond.

Support Team

Early in the establishment of your import/export business, you should develop a relationship with your international support team. After a brief period of shopping around, settle on a long-term relationship with (a) an international banker, (b) a freight forwarder, (c) a customhouse broker, (d) an international accountant, and (e) an international attorney. Also, consider contacting the Small Business Administration (SBA) if you run into problems. Members of the SBA's Service Corps of Retired Executives (SCORE) are often available to provide free advice.

THE 10 COMMANDMENTS OF STARTING AN OVERSEAS BUSINESS

I have put together what I consider to be the 10 most important activities you can do to start and run a successful import/export business.

1. Limit the primary participants to people who not only can agree and contribute directly, but who also are experienced in some form of international business.

2. Define your import/export market in terms of what is to be bought precisely by whom, and why.

3. Concentrate all available resources on two or three products or objectives within a given time period.

4. Obtain the best information from your own industry.

5. Write down your business plan and work from it.

6. "Walk on two legs." Pick a good freight forwarder or customhouse broker to walk alongside your banker.

7. Translate your literature into the language(s) of the country(ies) in which you will do business.

8. Use the services of the U.S. Commerce and Treasury Departments.

9. Limit the effects of your inevitable mistakes by starting slowly.

10. Communicate frequently and well with your international contacts, and visit the overseas markets and manufacturers.

THE BUSINESS PLAN

In the beginning, you might have only a notion of your plan tucked away in your head. As the concept of your business grows, it will be necessary to formalize your plan and stick to it. Putting out brush fires in order to maintain marginal survival is hardly a wise use of anyone's time.

The underlying concept of a business plan is to write out your thoughts. By raising and then systematically answering basic operational questions, you force self-criticism. Once your business plan is on paper, others can read it and you can invite their opinions. Don't let your ego get in your way. Ask for constructive criticism from the most experienced people you can find. It is often better to ask strangers because friends and relatives tend to want to shield you from hurt. Explain to your readers that you want to hear both the bad news and the good news. The more eyes that see your plan, the more likely you will be able to identify hazards while you still can act or avoid them and spot opportunities while you can easily act to maximize them.

"The plan is nothing; planning is everything."
—*President (General) Dwight Eisenhower*

A business plan can be as brief as 10 pages or as long as 50. On average, business plans run about 20 pages. Every outline is usually about the same. Figure 5-1 suggests an outline format for your business plan.

How to Begin Your Business Plan

Where do you start your business plan? Stop everything, and begin writing. The first draft of your plan will contain about 80% of the finished draft and can usually be finished in less than two days. One measure of the success of the process is the amount of pain it causes you. By looking at your business as an onlooker might, you might find that some of your vision, a pet project for instance, might have to be abandoned. Often, the process is done in eight steps:

1. Defining long-term objectives
2. Stating short-term goals
3. Setting marketing strategies
4. Analyzing available resources (personnel, material, etc.)
5. Assembling financial data
6. Reviewing for realism
7. Rewriting
8. Implementing

Define Long-Term Objectives. Start with the objectives of your import/export business; think ahead. What do you want the business to be like in 3 years? 5 years? 20 years? How big a business do you want?

State Short-Term Goals. Define your import-export business in terms of sales volume and assets. Be precise. State your goals in measurable units of time and dollars.

Set Marketing Strategies. If you have done your homework as explained in Chapter 2, and if you have applied the marketing concepts offered in Chapter 3, this part of the business plan should be simple. If not, go back and review the marketing section in Chapter 3, because nothing will happen with your business until you make a sale. If sales aren't made, projections and other

Cover Sheet: Name, principals, address, etc.

International Costumes, Inc.
Business Plan
Fiscal year 19xx

Statement of Purpose:

Table of Contents: (corresponds to each exhibit)

A. Executive summary
B. Description of the business
C. Product-line plan
D. Sales and market plan
E. Operations plan
F. Organization plan
G. Financial plan
H. Supporting documents
 I. Summary

Exhibits:

Exhibit A   Executive Summary
   1. Written last, summarizes in global terms the entire plan;
      succinct expression of long- and short-term goals

Exhibit B   Description of the Business
   1. Long- and short-term goals
        Financial
        Nonfinancial

   2. Strategies
        Product line
        Sales and marketing
        Product development
        Operations
        Organizational
        Financial

   3. Location
        Reasons

Exhibit C   Product-line Plan
   1. Product line and products
        Description
        Price

Fig. 5-1. Pro forma sales projections

Costs
Historical volume
Future expectations

2. Competition's product line and product position
   Pricing
   Advertising and promotion

Exhibit D   Sales and Market Plan
1. Person(s) responsible for generation product line and product
   sales
2. Competition's approach to sales and marketing

Exhibit E   Operations Plan
1. Production and operations function
   Production scheduling
   Inventory (product line and product)
2. Capital expenditures (if required)

Exhibit F   Organization Plan
1. Organization's structure
   Organization chart
   Résumés of key personnel
   Managerial style

Exhibit G   Financial Plan
1. Summary of operating and financial schedules

2. Schedules (refer to Figs. 7-1, 7-2, 7-3 and 7-4)
   Capital equipment
   Balance sheet
   Cash flow (break-even analysis)
   Income projections
   Pro forma cash flow
   Historical financial reports for existing business
   (Balance sheets for past three years; income statements
   for past three years, tax returns)

Exhibit H   Supporting Documents
1. Personal résumés
2. Cost of living budget
3. Letters of reference
4. Copies of leases
5. Anything else of relevance to the plan

Exhibit I   Summary

plans fall apart. Profitable sales support your business, so be prepared to spend 75% of your planning time on marketing efforts. Ultimately, the best marketing information comes through your own industry, here or overseas. Talk to those with experience. Talk to manufacturers as well as other importers/exporters. Don't overlook the data that can be found in libraries.

Make your marketing plan precise. Describe your competitive advantage. Outline your geographical and product-line priorities. Write down your sales goals. List your alternatives for market penetration. Will you sell direct or through agents? What is your advertising budget? Travel in an import/export business is a must. What is your travel budget? How much will it cost to expand your markets? What will be the cost of communications? Don't minimize your cost projections. It is not unusual to underestimate expenses. They are often three times more than you think.

Analyze Available Resources. Now for the pain. You must now ask yourself whether you have the resources to make the plan work. Take a management inventory. Do you have the skills to market your products? Do you need administrative or accounting skills? Will you need warehouse space? Will you need translators? How much cash will you need?

Assemble Financial Data. After all the dreaming and reality testing of the first four steps, you must now express your business plan in terms of cash flow, profit and loss projections, and balance sheets. Figure 5-2 shows a pro forma sales projection with a three-year summary, detailed by the month for the first year and detailed by the quarter for the second and third years. Figure 5-3 is a pro forma income (profit and loss) statement with details by month for the first year and details by the quarter for the second and third years.

Figure 5-4 is a pro forma balance sheet, and Fig. 5-5 is a pro forma cash flow statement with details by the month for the first year and details by the quarter for the second and third years. The use of *pro forma* financial statements enables you to estimate information in advance in a prescribed form.

The cash flow and the profit and loss projections serve double duty. They quantify the sales and operating goals, including personnel and other resources expressed in dollars and time. As a guide to the future, they can be used as control documents and to measure progress toward your goals. The balance sheet shows what your business owns, what it owes, and how those assets and liabilities are distributed.

Pro forma Sales (Shipments) Projection
Fiscal Year 19xx

Product Line(s) Product(s)	Jan	Feb	March	April	May	June	July	Aug	Sept	Oct	Nov	Dec	Year
A. Product Line A													
1. Product 1													
Shipments (Units)													
x Ave. Price/Unit													
Gross Sales	$___	$___	$___	$___	$___	$___	$___	$___	$___	$___	$___	$___	$___
2. Product 2													
3. Product 3													
—													
—													
n. Product N													
Product Line A— Gross Sales	$___	$___	$___	$___	$___	$___	$___	$___	$___	$___	$___	$___	$___
B. Product Line B													
C. Product Line C													
—													
—													
N. Product Line N													
Total Gross Sales	$___	$___	$___	$___	$___	$___	$___	$___	$___	$___	$___	$___	$___

Fig. 5-2. Pro forma income (Profit/Loss) statement

Pro forma Income Statement
Fiscal Year 19xx

	Jan	Feb	March	April	May	June	July	Aug	Sept	Oct	Nov	Dec	Year
Gross Sales													
less: Discounts, allowances, etc.													
Net Sales													
less: Variable costs													
Manufacturing:													
Material													
Labor													
Variable overhead													
Other													
Variable costs (manufacturing)													
Operating:													
Commissions													
Other													
Variable costs (operating)													
Variable costs (total)													
Contribution													
Percent of net sales	(%)												
less: Fixed costs													
Manufacturing													
Engineering													
Selling													
General and Administrative													
Financial													
Fixed costs (total)													
Profit before taxes													
less: Taxes													
Net Income													

Fig. 5-3. Pro forma balance sheet

Pro forma Balance Sheet Fiscal Year 19xx	Actual Dec	Jan	Feb	March	April	May	June	July	Aug	Sept	Oct	Nov	Dec
A. *Assets Employed*													
1. *Current Assets*													
Cash													
Accounts receivable (net)	—	—	—	—	—	—	—	—	—	—	—	—	—
Inventory	—	—	—	—	—	—	—	—	—	—	—	—	—
Prepaids	—	—	—	—	—	—	—	—	—	—	—	—	—
Other	—	—	—	—	—	—	—	—	—	—	—	—	—
Subtotal	—	—	—	—	—	—	—	—	—	—	—	—	—
2. *Current Liabilities* (excluding debt)													
Accounts payable	—	—	—	—	—	—				—	—	—	—
Accrued liabilities	—	—	—	—	—	—				—	—	—	—
Taxes payable	—	—	—	—	—	—				—	—	—	—
Other	—	—	—	—	—	—				—	—	—	—
Subtotal	—	—	—	—	—	—				—	—	—	—
Working capital (1–2)													
3. *Property, Plant, and Equipment*													
Land	—	—	—	—	—	—	—	—	—	—	—	—	—
Building	—	—	—	—	—	—	—	—	—	—	—	—	—
Equipment	—	—	—	—	—	—	—	—	—	—	—	—	—
less: Accumulated depreciation	—	—	—	—	—	—	—	—	—	—	—	—	—
Subtotal	—	—	—	—	—	—	—	—	—	—	—	—	—
4. *Other Assets*													
Investments	—	—	—	—	—	—	—	—	—	—	—	—	—
Other	—	—	—	—	—	—	—	—	—	—	—	—	—
Subtotal	—	—	—	—	—	—	—	—	—	—	—	—	—
Assets Employed													

Fig. 5-4. Pro forma cash flow statement

Pro forma Balance Sheet Fiscal Year 19xx	Actual Dec	Jan	Feb	March	April	May	June	July	Aug	Sept	Oct	Nov	Dec
Assets Employed													
B. *Capital Structure*													
1. *Debt*													
Short-term Notes													
Long-term (current portion)													
Long-term Debt													
Other													
Subtotal													
2. *Deferred Taxes*													
3. *Shareholders Equity*													
Paid in Capital													
Retained Earnings													
Subtotal													
Capital Structure													

Fig. 5-4. Continued

Pro forma Cash Flow Statement (Operational)
Fiscal Year 19xx

	Jan	Feb	March	April	May	June	July	Aug	Sept	Oct	Nov	Dec	Year
Cash Receipts													
Collection of accounts receivable													
Sale of assets													
Borrowings													
Equity financing													
Other													
Cash receipts													
Cash Expenditures													
Material													
Freight													
Wages and salaries													
Commissions													
Fringe benefits													
Manufacturing expenses													
Selling expenses													
General and administrative expenses													
Financial expenses													
Subtotal													
Capital expenditures													
Debt repayment													
Dividends													
Other													
Cash expenditures													
Cash flows													
Cumulative cash flows													

Fig. 5-5. Pro forma cash flow statement

Review for Realism. Your plan must not set contradictory goals. A coherent plan fits together. You cannot be expanding the introduction of goose liver from China at the same time you are getting out of animal products and into irrigation machinery. Look at your plan as a whole and ask, "Does this make good business sense?"

Rewrite. Now that the first draft is complete, let at least 10 experienced people look at it. Ask them to be critical and to tell you the truth. Let them know up front that you have a lot of ego in this project, but that because you want to be a success, you want their criticism—no matter how much it hurts.

Implement. Your business plan provides a road map, but the acid test is whether it will work. Like a map, you might have to take a detour to get where you are going, so don't put the map on the shelf and forget about it. Use it as an operating document, and review it and revise it as experience dictates.

Now you're ready to go. You've done your homework and written your business plan. If you've gotten this far, you have the style and determination to make it work.

By now, you have written your first letter and made your first contact. As an importer, you've asked for literature and samples or as an exporter you've sent them. You want early orders, and if you have done your homework, they should start rolling in. Be patient. Everything takes a little longer in international business.

SUCCESS STORY: Most tropical fruits must be imported to Japan. Thinking through her business plan, Sono Hikichi decided to start her business with avocados, and if that succeeded, she would expand to other fruits such as wild cherry, mango, and papaya. She chose avocados because Mexican dishes are becoming popular in Japan where they are used in sushi because they taste like tuna and are very profitable. Her plan called for buying 4 tons (20,000 units) a month at $2.50/unit and selling them at $3.50. She did just that, making a whole lot of money.

As you have learned in the previous three chapters, most of the fundamentals of international trade are common to both importing and exporting, but some major elements are specific to one or the other. The next chapters explain the elements of international trade that are unique to exporting or to importing, such as government support systems, information systems, tax considerations, tariffs, and private-sector support organizations.

6

Exporting from the United States

THE EARLIER CHAPTERS OF THIS BOOK EXPLAINED THE COMMONALITIES
of import/export, but some aspects of the transaction are not the
same. For example, government controls are unique to exporting
and tariffs are a characteristic of importing.

This chapter explores the basics of the international trade
transaction that are unique to *exporting* from the United States.
Among other things, you'll learn which public and private organizations support the export function and where to go for export information. The topics specific to export are:

- Export counseling
- World Trade Centers
- Information sources
- Freight forwarding
- Export controls
- Tax incentives
- Unfair import practices

GOVERNMENT EXPORT COUNSELING

All governments promote exporting because it brings needed foreign exchange and stimulates job expansion. Therefore, every national and many state and provincial governments provide a wide range of export counseling and assistance programs.

Most countries have an organization similar to that of the United States' International Trade Administration (ITA), a division of the Department of Commerce. ITA's importance to the United States is emphasized by the fact that it gets approximately 75% of that department's budget. The ITA is organized basically into arms that are external, internal, and central to the territorial boundaries of the United States.

External to the United States

The external arm of the ITA is the Foreign Commercial Service (FCS). The FCS maintains offices in more than 69 major foreign cities in the 69 countries that are the United States' principal trading partners. To help U.S. firms compete, these offices provide a full range of business, investment, and financial counseling services. These services include political and credit risk analysis, advice on market-entry strategy, sources of financing, and major project identification, tracking, and assistance. FCS officers identify and evaluate importers, buyers, agents, distributors, and joint-venture partners. They can introduce you to local business and government leaders and assist in trade disputes. These services are available to anyone who wants them; all you have to do is call or write either your local Department of Commerce district office or the offices listed in Appendix B.

The FCS Senior Commercial Officer in each country is a principal advisor to the U.S. Ambassador. The FCS staff gathers data on specific export opportunities, country trends affecting trade and investment, and prospects for specific industries. They also monitor and analyze local laws and practices that affect business conditions.

Internal to the United States

The United States offers a broad range of trade-related information, as well as one-on-one counseling by experienced trade specialists.

Commercial Services. The domestic or *internal* arm of ITA, Commercial Services, operates 47 district offices and 22 branch offices in industrial and commercial centers throughout the United States. (Call [800] USA-TRADE or see the district office addresses listed in Appendix C.) The district offices can provide exporters and other prospective businesses with information on the following:

- Trade and investment opportunities abroad
- Foreign markets for U.S. products and services
- Financial aid
- Insurance from the Foreign Credit Insurance Association (FCIA)
- Tax advantages of exporting
- International trade exhibitions
- Export documentation requirements
- Economic facts on foreign countries
- Export licensing requirements

District Export Councils. Commercial Service district offices work closely with experienced regional international business persons through 51 District Export Councils (DECs). The 1700 volunteer DEC members are available to counsel prospective exporters on the how-tos of international trade. They also cosponsor seminars and workshops with the district offices, address business groups on international business opportunities, and promote awareness of the trade-assistance programs of the Department of Commerce.

Export Assistance Centers. Besides the district offices and export councils, ITA has established Export Assistance Centers (USEACs) in several cities (four pilot USEACS are located in Baltimore, Chicago, Long Beach, and Miami). These are customer-focused offices designed to streamline export marketing and trade finance assistance by integrating in a single location the councilors and services of the Commercial Service, Export-Import Bank, the Small Business Administration (SBA), and in some cities, the U.S. Agency for International Development.

Small Business Development Centers. Small Business Development Centers (SBDCs) provide a full range of export assistance services to small businesses, particularly those new to export, and offer counseling, training, managerial, and trade finance assistance. Call (800) U-ASK-SBA; (202) 205-6720; (202) 205- 6766; fax: (202) 205-7272; or call (202) 205-7727.

SCORE. The Service Corps of Retired Executives (SCORE), usually collocated with your local SBA office, provides one-on-one counseling and training seminars. To reach the office nearest you, call (800) 634-0245 or fax (202) 205-7636.

Central to the United States

The U.S. Department of Commerce also has approximately 165 desk officers at their headquarters in Washington, DC whose job is to be experts in assigned countries from Afghanistan through Zimbabwe. These desk officers are resources who not only support the Secretary of Commerce and the Secretary's legislative responsibilities, but also provide specific information about the laws and products of their countries to American businesses. Desk officers are organized into two groups: the International Economic Policy Country Desk Officers (IEP) and the Trade Development Industry Officers (TD).

IEP desk officers are specialists who can examine the needs of an individual firm wishing to sell in a particular country in the full context of that country's economy, trade policies, and political situation.

TD officers are industry specialists who work with manufacturing and service industry associations and firms to identify trade opportunities and obstacles by product or service, industry sector, and market.

Exporters who are planning to visit Washington and would like to schedule appointments with either desk officers or program specialists within the Department of Commerce (and/or other agencies involved in international marketing) should contact the nearest district office or USEAC.

Office of Export Trading Company Affairs

This office, located at the Department of Commerce in Washington, DC, promotes the use of Export Trading Companies (ETCs), export management companies (EMCs), and the intermediary industry in general. They administer the Export Trade Certificate of Review that permits an antitrust *insurance policy* under the Export Trading Company Act (ETCA). This law, passed on October 8, 1982, permits bankers' banks and holding companies to invest in ETCs, reduces the restrictions on export financing provided by financial institutions, and modifies the application of the antitrust laws to certain export trade. For more information, call (202) 482-5131 or fax (202) 482-1790.

INFORMATION SOURCES

Information needed for exporting is easier to obtain than for domestic sales. Why? Because most governments subsidize the gathering and analysis of international trade data. A wealth of information, both on paper and computerized, exists to promote exporting. In fact, more information is available on exporting than one could digest in a lifetime, and the U.S. Department of Commerce has made it easy to acquire. For example, the Trade Opportunities Program (TOP) and the Export Contact List Service files are available in both printed form and up-to-the-minute computer-resident databases.

The following sections describe the export services offered by your nearest Department of Commerce district office, ITA office, or the various USEACS.

Trade Information Center. The Trade Information Center (TIC) is the single comprehensive resource for information on all governmentwide export assistance programs. The center's staff advises exporters on how to locate and use government programs, guides exporters through the export process, supplies general market information, and provides basic export counseling. Call (800) USA-TRADE, (202) 482-0543, or fax (202) 482-4473. A special line is available for those who are deaf or hearing impaired using a TDD machine, (800) TDD-TRADE. Ask for a free copy of their excellent pamphlet *Export Programs: A Business Directory of U.S. Government Services.*

National Trade Data Bank. The National Trade Data Bank (NTDB) is a one-stop source for export promotion and international trade data collected by 17 U.S. government agencies. Updated each month and released on two CD-ROMs, the NTDB enables exporters with IBM-compatible personal computers equipped with a CD-ROM reader to access more than 100,000 trade-related documents. For more information, call (800) USA-TRADE.

The Economic Bulletin Board. The Economic Bulletin Board (EBB), a personal computer-based electronic bulletin board, is your online source for trade leads as well as for the latest statistical releases from the Bureau of the Census, the Bureau of Economic Analysis, the Bureau of Labor Statistics, the Federal Reserve Board, and other federal agencies. For more information, call (202) 482-1986 or fax (202) 482-2164.

The Economic Bulletin Board/Fax. You can use your fax machine to receive trade leads and the latest trade and economic information from the federal government. Access the Economic Bulletin Board/Fax by dialing (900) RUN-A-FAX or call (202) 482-1986 for the EBB/FAX help-line; fax (202) 482-2164.

Other Sources of Export Information

In addition to the counseling and data products offered by the Department of Commerce, several excellent books are on the market from both the government and private sector.

International Market Research (IMR) Surveys. These provide in-depth analyses of the market for a given product category in a given country and range up to 400 pages in length. IMRs cost $50 to $200.

Country Market Surveys. The more detailed information in IMR surveys is abstracted into convenient, 10- to 15-page reports on a single industry in a single country. The cost of a single report is about $10.

Global Market Surveys. This survey is a compilation of individual country market surveys (ICMS) for a given product category. Prices vary depending on the number of ICMSs within each Global Market Survey (GMS).

World Traders Data Reports. This is a background report on individual foreign firms. It contains information about each firm's business activities, its standing in the local business community, its creditworthiness, and its overall reliability and suitability as a trade contact to U.S. exporters. World Traders Data Reports (WTDRs) are designed to help U.S. firms locate and evaluate potential foreign customers before making a business commitment. WTDRs cost $75 per report.

Monthly FT 410 Data. Every export valued at more than $2500 is accompanied by a Shipper's Export Declaration (SED). This is the document that you or your freight forwarder present to customs as the shipment leaves. When customs is finished with the document, it is sent to the Department of Commerce's Bureau of Census in Anderson, IN where it is entered into a computer database. Every month, the bureau publishes a book titled *U.S. Exports, Schedule E, Commodity by Country* or the *Monthly*

FT 410. In minutes, a great deal can be learned from a simple analysis of this data. Most important, the data is shown country by country so that the user learns where the potential markets are and how many units were shipped in each case.

HOT TIP: 43,535 smoke detectors valued at $750,000 left the United States during the month of June 1984. 310,502 smoke detectors valued at $6,022,000 left the United States from January to June 1984 (½ year). Multiplying by two, the estimated annual sales will be $12 million. Divide $6,022,000 by 310,502 units shipped, and learn that the average declared value of each unit was $19.39.

This data is invaluable if you are in the smoke detector business, but it is also available for an amazing list of products; everything from fruits to shoe laces, from fish to golf clubs, to integrated circuits. The cost for a monthly issue of the FT 410 is about $10 and an annual subscription is about $100.

Export Contacts

Most governments have programs to help exporters make cross-border contacts. The U.S. government is no exception. As a matter of fact, they have a full range of programs you should take advantage of.

Agent Distributor Service. The Agent Distributor Service (ADS) performs a custom overseas "search" for interested and qualified foreign representatives on behalf of a U.S. client. Foreign Commercial Services (FCS) officers abroad conduct the search and prepare a report identifying up to six foreign prospects that have personally examined the U.S. firm's product literature and expressed an interest in representing the firm. ADS costs about $250 per market or specific area. Contact your local district office or call (800) USA-TRADE.

Trade Opportunities Program. These are individual messages sent directly to subscribers. They can be sent via computer, fax, or printed hard copy. Each message contains detailed information regarding a current foreign trade lead, typically including the specifications, quantities, end-use, and delivery and bid deadlines for the product or service desired by the foreign customer. The Trade Opportunities Program (TOP) requires a $25 fee to set up the subscriber's interest file. Each block of 50 leads, up to 5 blocks, costs $37.50, prepaid.

> **HOT TIP:** TOP matches product interests of foreign buyers with those of U.S. subscribers.

Export Contact List Service. All trade leads are received at the computer center in Washington, DC. Trade leads include direct sales opportunities and foreign government tenders. Contact your nearest district office for more information.

Overseas Promotion

The ITA, U.S. Department of State, and our embassies and consulates collaborate to help companies gain foreign market exposure for their product or service through many publications and activities.

Overseas Trade Promotions Calendar. Revised quarterly, this calendar provides a 12-month schedule of U.S. Trade Center exhibitions and international trade fairs in which U.S. participation is planned. It also includes other overseas promotional activities that are planned and will be organized by the U.S. Department of Commerce. You can order the calendar free from the Office of International Marketing, International Trade Administration, U.S. Department of Commerce, Washington, DC 20230.

How to Get the Most from Overseas Exhibitions. This publication contains helpful planning tips and details the steps you should take to participate in an overseas exhibition. To obtain a copy, contact the Office of Export Development, International Trade Administration, U.S. Department of Commerce, Washington, DC 20230. There is no charge for this publication.

Export Statistics Profiles. These profiles provide a variety of export statistics by product and present the data in ways that make market analysis easy. It provides multiyear coverage, percentage of market shares, and top markets for products in rank order. The price ranges from $30 to $70 depending on the depth and specification.

Customs Service Statistics. This statistical service provides customs statistics in four export and/or import tables:

1. Up to 10 selected products showing trade to 9 major, world-market areas

2. Up to 10 selected products showing trade to every country worldwide in rank order

3. Up to 10 selected countries showing trade in individually specified products in rank order

4. The top 30 countries showing trade in up to 10 individually specified products in rank order.

Prices for these statistical reports range from $50 to $150 depending on the complexity.

Trade Lists. A list of all foreign manufacturers, wholesalers, agents, distributors, retailers, and other purchasers in a given industry or country is included in the Department of Commerce's automated Foreign Traders Index (FTI). The information provided for each firm includes the name, address, key contact, telephone number, cable number, type of business, and age of the information. Trade lists are priced from $12 to $40.

Understanding U.S. Foreign Trade Data. This publication explains the different foreign trade classifications, valuation systems, and other factors that complicate the understanding of U.S. foreign trade data. The cost is $7.50, and you can order it from the Superintendent of Documents, Government Printing Office, Washington, DC 20402, or by calling (202) 783-3238.

SUCCESS STORY: Mario Pepe is a young Italian who knows the younger generation. He gambled they were ready for an alternative to croissants, so his import plan introduced frozen waffles from the United States into Italy's frozen food market. His penetration was so successful that he opened a small production company in Genova and has expanded sales to other cities in the European Community.

The *United States Government Information: Publications, Periodicals, and Electronic Products* catalog annotates almost 1000 popular government publications by subject area. It can be ordered at no charge from any of the 24 bookstores operated by the Government Printing Office (GPO). (See Appendix F for bookstore addresses and telephone numbers.)

A Basic Guide to Exporting. Published by the U.S. Department of Commerce, this publication can be obtained by writing the Superintendent of Documents, GPO, Washington, DC 20402 or by calling (202) 783-3238. You also can contact any of the bookstores listed in Appendix F. This booklet is designed to show, step-by-step, how to expand an existing manufacturing business into the international marketplace. It is also an excellent resource for the small importer/exporter. The cost is about $8.

The EMC—Your Export Department. This publication describes the services provided to exporters by export management companies as well as how to go about selecting a suitable EMC. You can obtain a copy from the Office of Export Development, International Trade Administration, U.S. Department of Commerce, Washington, DC 20230.

The U.S. Export Management Companies (EMCs) Directory. This directory emphasizes the marketing capability of the EMCs. You can order the directory from Directory of Publishers, Inc., P.O. Box 9449, Baltimore, MD 21228.

Exporter's Encyclopedia (Annual). This is a valuable publication for the serious trader's library. It is chock-full of fingertip information. The publication can be found in most libraries or ordered from Dun & Bradstreet International, 99 Church Street, New York, NY 07054 or call (800) 526-0651; in New Jersey call (800) 624-0324. The cost is about $450.

An Introduction to the Overseas Private Investment Corporation (OPIC). This free publication reviews how the Overseas Private Investment Corporation (OPIC) can assist firms interested in investing in developing nations. It can be ordered from the Overseas Private Investment Corporation, 1129 20th Street, N.W., Washington, DC 20527.

Export-Import Bank of the United States. This free publication explains U.S. export financing programs and can be ordered from the Export-Import Bank of the United States, 811 Vermont Avenue, N.W., Washington, DC 20571.

Carnet. This publication explains what a carnet is and how it can benefit exporters. Application forms for applying for a carnet are included. Order free of charge from the United States Council for International Business, 121 Avenue of the Americas, New York, NY 10036.

FREIGHT FORWARDING

A *freight forwarder* is a private service company licensed to support shippers and the movement of their goods. These specialists in international physical distribution act as an agent for the exporter (shipper) in moving cargo to an overseas destination. They are familiar with the import rules and regulations of foreign countries, methods of shipping, U.S. government export regulations, and the documents connected with foreign trade.

From the beginning, freight forwarders can assist with the order by advising on such things as freight costs, consular fees, and insurance costs. They can recommend the degree of packing, arrange for an inland carrier, find the right airline, and even arrange for the containerization of your cargo. They quote shipping rates, provide information, and book cargo space. These firms are invaluable because they can make all shipping arrangements from the factory to the final destination, including all documentation, storage, and shipping insurance, as well as the routing of your cargo at the lowest customs charges.

Shipper

Any person whose primary business is the sale of merchandise can, without a license, dispatch and perform freight forwarding services on behalf of their own shipments, or on behalf of shipments or consolidated shipments of a parent, subsidiary, affiliate, or associated company. You cannot, however, receive compensation from the common carrier.

A large manufacturer usually has its own shipping department that serves as its own freight forwarder, but smaller manufacturing firms and small importers/exporters seldom have either the staff or the time to make their own arrangements. There are two types of freight forwarders: ocean and air. Most freight forwarding businesses can do both.

Often freight forwarders are called upon to help an exporter put together the final price quotation to a distributor. For example, when quoting C.I.F. (cost, insurance, freight), in addition to the manufacturer's price and the commission, the freight forwarder can provide information on dock and cartage fees, forwarder's fees, marine insurance, ocean freight costs, duty charges, consular invoice fees, and packing charges. It's not unusual (and can be quite prudent) to review a price quotation with the freight forwarder before putting it on the telex or fax.

How to Become a Freight Forwarder

An *ocean* freight forwarder must be licensed by the Federal Maritime Commission (FMC). To receive a freight forwarding license, an individual must have three years experience in ocean freight forwarding duties, have the necessary character to render forwarding services, and possess a valid surety bond.

For more information on how to submit an application, contact the Office of Freight Forwarders, Bureau of Tariffs, Federal Maritime Commission, Washington, DC 20573.

Air cargo agents are administered by the International Air Transportation Association (ITAT), headquartered in Montreal, Canada. This organization, through its subsidiary Cargo Network Services, Inc. (CNS), administers the qualifications and certification of agents in the United States. Additional information can be obtained by writing CNS, 300 Garden City Plaza, Suite 400, Garden City, NY 11530.

HOT TIP: You can become a licensed freight forwarder, but you do not have to be one to arrange movement of goods on behalf of your own shipments. Caution, don't act as a forwarder for someone else before being issued a license.

EXPORT CONTROLS

Another area in which exporting differs from importing is the licensing required to control exports. The history of export controls in the United States is based on the presumption that all exported goods and technical documentation are subject to regulation by the government. This presumption is fundamentally different than most nations, which often presume the freedom to export unless there is an explicit statement of a need to control. Therefore, the public regulation of international sales in the United States are often more onerous than elsewhere.

The exercise of controls by the United States varies from nonexistent (as is the case with Canada) to total embargoes (as in the cases of North Korea and Cuba). Several departments have legal authority to control exports. Arms, ammunition, implements of war, technical data relating thereto, and certain classified information are licensed by the Department of State. Narcotics and dangerous drugs are licensed by the Department of Justice. Nuclear material is licensed by the Nuclear Regulatory Commission. There are other exceptions, but in general, the Department of Commerce control system affects most exporters. The current law (Export Administration Act of 1979) is designed to promote the foreign policy of the United States, protect the national security, and protect the domestic economy from the excessive drain of scarce materials.

The law provides for three basic types of export licenses.

1. A *general license* authorizes export without application by the exporter. This license is usually for low dollar and low technology items and does not require pre-approval. All that is required is to place the symbol for general license on the documentation.

2. A *qualified general license* authorizes multiple exports to the specified purchaser and is issued pursuant to an application by the exporter.

3. A *validated license* authorizes a specific export to a specified country and purchaser. It is issued pursuant to an application by the exporter. Each type of validated export license—individua, project, periodic, distribution, time limit, and technical data—is good for one total transaction. You have two years to complete the shipment.

Export controls are organized on the Commodity Control List (CCL) according to country or by item. Some, however, have a more general focus, such as advancing human rights causes or those prohibiting doing business with those who boycott for ethnic or political reasons. With few exceptions, an exporter must complete a SED (Commerce Form 7525-V) and deposit it with the exporting carrier regardless of whether a shipment is exported under a validated or general license.

The vast majority of all exports *do not* require a validated export license and require only the appropriate general license notation on the SED. If you determine that you require a validated license for a specific export, however, you should submit an application for a license to the Bureau of Export Administration (BXA), P. 0. Box 273, Washington, DC 20044. An application consists of a completed Form ITA-622P, "Application for Export License," and required supporting information. Figure 6-1 is the application form for an export license.

Within 10 days after the date BXA receives the application, the office will either issue the license, deny it, send the application to

Form ITA-622P (REV. 4-85)
Form Approved OMB No. 0625-0001

Information furnished herewith is subject to the provisions of Section 12 (c) of the Export Administration Act of 1979, 50 U.S.C. app. 2411 (c), and its unauthorized disclosure is prohibited by law.

U.S. DEPARTMENT OF COMMERCE
INTERNATIONAL TRADE ADMINISTRATION

APPLICATION FOR
EXPORT LICENSE

DATE RECEIVED (Leave Blank)

APPLICATION/CASE NO. (Leave Blank)

1. DATE OF APPLICATION

2. APPLICANT'S REFERENCE NUMBER

3. APPLICANT'S TELEPHONE NO.

4. SPECIAL PURPOSE

5. APPLICANT

EXPORTER S.I.D. NO.

ADDRESS

CITY, STATE, ZIP CODE

6. PURCHASER IN FOREIGN COUNTRY
(If same as ultimate consignee, state "SAME AS ITEM 7." If same as intermediate consignee, state "SAME AS ITEM 8.")

OEA USE ONLY

NAME

ADDRESS

CITY AND COUNTRY

7. CONSIGNEE IN COUNTRY OF ULTIMATE DESTINATION

OEA USE ONLY

NAME

ADDRESS

CITY AND COUNTRY

8. INTERMEDIATE CONSIGNEE IN FOREIGN COUNTRY
(If none, state "NONE"; if unknown, state "UNKNOWN.")

OEA USE ONLY

NAME

ADDRESS

CITY AND COUNTRY

9(a) QUANTITY

(b) DESCRIPTION OF COMMODITY OR TECHNICAL DATA (When appropriate, use Commodity Control List descriptions and include characteristics such as basic ingredients, composition, type, size, gauge, grade, horsepower, model number, etc.)(Attach separate sheet if more space is needed.)

(c) EXPORT CONTROL COMMODITY NUMBER AND PROCESSING CODE

(d) NET VALUE U.S. DOLLARS

UNIT PRICE

TOTAL PRICE

TOTAL $

10. FILL IN IF PERSON OTHER THAN APPLICANT IS AUTHORIZED TO RECEIVE LICENSE.

NAME

ADDRESS

CITY, STATE, ZIP CODE

11. IF APPLICANT IS NOT THE PRODUCER OF COMMODITY TO BE EXPORTED, GIVE NAME AND ADDRESS OF SUPPLIER. (If unknown, state "UNKNOWN.")

12. SPECIFIC END-USE OF COMMODITIES OR TECHNICAL DATA BY CONSIGNEE IN ITEM 7 ABOVE. IF KNOWN, GIVE NAME AND ADDRESS OF END-USER IF DIFFERENT FROM ITEM 7.

13. IF APPLICANT IS NOT EXPORTING FOR HIS OWN ACCOUNT, GIVE NAME AND ADDRESS OF FOREIGN PRINCIPAL AND EXPLAIN FULLY.

14. FOREIGN AVAILABILITY (Completion Optional) This(These) ☐ commodity(ies) or similar commodities ☐ technical data ☐ is ☐ is not available outside the U.S. If available, give names and addresses of foreign producers and distributors and appropriate descriptive technical information on a separate attachment to this application. ☐ Foreign availability not known.

15. ADDITIONAL INFORMATION (Attach separate sheet if more space is needed.)

Fig. 6-1. Export license application form

16. **APPLICANT'S CERTIFICATION:** I hereby make application for a license to export, and I certify that (a) to the best of my knowledge, information and belief all statements in this application, including the description of the commodities or technical data and their end-uses, and any documents submitted in support of this application are correct and complete and that they fully and accurately disclose all the terms of the export transaction; (b) this application conforms to the instructions accompanying this application and the Export Administration Regulations; (c) I obtained the order from the order party who has completed item 17, or I negotiated with and secured the export order directly from the purchaser or ultimate consignee, or through his or their agent(s); (d) I will retain records pertaining to this transaction and make them available as required by §387.13 of the Export Administration Regulations; (e) I will report promptly to the U.S. Department of Commerce any material changes in the terms of the order or other facts or intentions of the export transaction as reflected in this application and supporting documents, whether the application is still under consideration or a license has been granted; and (f) if the license is granted, I will be strictly accountable for its use in accordance with the Export Administration Regulations and all the terms and conditions of the license.

Type or Print _____

SIGN HERE IN INK

_____ (SIGNATURE of person authorized to execute this application.)

(APPLICANT) (Same as Item 5.)

Type or Print _____

(NAME and TITLE of person whose signature appears on the line to the left.)

17. **ORDER PARTY'S CERTIFICATION** (See § 372.6(b) of the *Export Administration Regulations*).— The undersigned order party certifies to the truth and correctness of item 16(a) above, and that he has no information concerning the export transaction that is undisclosed or inconsistent with representations made to the Department of Commerce and agrees to comply with Items 16(d) and 16(e) above.

Type or Print _____

SIGN HERE IN INK

_____ (SIGNATURE of person authorized to sign for the Order Party.)

(Order Party)

Type or Print _____

(Name and title of person whose signature appears on the line to the left.)

This license application and any license issued pursuant thereto are expressly subject to all rules and regulations of the Department of Commerce. Making any false statement or concealing any material fact in connection with this application or altering in any way the validated license issued, is punishable by imprisonment or fine, or both, and by denial of export privileges under the Export Administration Act of 1979, and any other applicable Federal statues. No export license will be issued unless this form is completed and submitted in accordance with Export Administration Regulation 372.4 (50 U.S.C. app. Sec. 2403: 15 CFR Sec. 372.4)

FOR DEPARTMENT OF COMMERCE USE ONLY

ACTION TAKEN	VALIDITY PERIOD	AUTHORITY	RATING		DV	TECH DATA
☐ APPROVED			END-USE CHECK	REEXPORT	SUPPORT DOCUMENT	TYPE OF LICENSE
☐ REJECTED	MONTHS					
DOCUMENTATION		POLICY				

(Licensing officer) _____ (No.) _____ (Date) _____

(Review officer) _____ (Date) _____

ORIGINAL
OEA FILE COPY

NOTE: Submit the first five copies of this application, Form ITA-622P (with top stub attached), to the Office of Export Administration, P.O. Box 273, Washington, D.C. 20044, retaining the sextuplicate copy of the form for your files. Remove the long carbon sheet from in front of the sextuplicate copy. Do not remove any other carbon sheets. Reproduction of this form is permissible, providing that content, format, size, and color of paper and ink are the same.

Fig. 6-1. Continued

the next step in the license process, or, if the application is improperly completed or additional information is required, return the application without action. Once the approved license is received, the exporter keeps the validated license on file. Although all you submit is the SED, all information on the SED must conform with that found in the validated license.

To avoid export control violations and shipping delays, contact your local ITA District Office or the Exporter's Service Staff, Office of Export Administration, International Trade Administration for assistance.

HOT TIPS TO AVOID EXPORT CONTROL VIOLATIONS: Determine whether a validated export license is required. When in doubt, contact the Export License Application and Information Network (ELAIN) at (202 482-4811 or Expert Licensing Voice Information System (ELVIS) (202) 482-2753, BXA for assistance.

Fully describe your commodities or technical data on export shipping documents. Use the applicable destination control statement on commercial invoices, air bills, and bills of lading as required by Section 386.6 of the Export Administration Regulations. Avoid overshipments by maintaining an accurate account of the quantity and value of goods shipped against a validated export license.

Be mindful of the expiration date on validated export licenses to avoid shipments after the applicable license has expired. Enter the applicable validated export license number or general license symbol on the SED. Make certain that shipping documents clearly identify the exporter, intermediate consignee, and ultimate consignee.

Mail your completed form ITA-622P by private courier express to the Office of Export Administration, Room 1099, U.S. Department of Commerce, 14th & Pennsylvania Avenue, N.W., Washington, DC 20230.

TAX INCENTIVES FOR EXPORTING

A prominent tax attorney once said, "Business in America? It's all about taxes." International business is no exception. Taxes on income derived from international trade are in accordance with current laws for other income except that tax incentives for exporting are substantial; there are no tax incentives for importing.

Tax incentives for exporters amount to approximately a 15% exclusion of the combined taxable income earned on international sales. The tax law provides for a system of tax deferrals for Domestic International Sales Corporations (DISCs) and Foreign Sales Corporations (FSCs).

Prior to December 31, 1984, DISC was the only medium for distributing export earnings. DISCs don't require a foreign presence, and, in fact, are legal entities established only on paper. The DISC incentive was created by the Revenue Act of 1971 and provides for deferral of federal income tax on 50% of the export earnings allocated to the DISC with the balance treated as dividends to the parent company. Since its enactment, DISC had been the subject of an ongoing dispute between the United States and certain other signatories of the General Agreement on Tariffs and Trade (GATT). Other nations contended that DISC amounted to an illegal export subsidy because it allowed indefinite deferral of direct taxes on income from exports earned in the United States.

Under new rules put into effect on January 1, 1985, to receive a tax benefit that is designed to equal the tax deferral provided by DISC, exporters must establish an office abroad. The FSC must also be a foreign corporation, maintain a summary of its permanent books of account at the foreign office, and have at least one director resident outside of the United States.

Meeting the requirement of the new regulations isn't difficult for large U.S.-based multinational firms with overseas offices and ample resources, but thousands of small businesses involved in international commerce are concerned about administrative costs and other overhead expenses. Actually, small exporters have several options for their foreign sales operations. They can continue to export through a DISC and pay an interest charge on the deferred income or they can join with other exporters to own an FSC. Another alternative is that they individually can take advantage of relaxed, small FSC rules under which they need not meet all of the tests required of large FSCs. A small FSC, one with up to $5 million of gross receipts during the taxable year, is excused from the foreign management and foreign economic process requirements.

The mechanics of setting up a DISC or FSC are somewhat complex, but within the capability of most accountants. Some 23 foreign countries, those that have an agreement to exchange tax information with the United States, and U.S. possessions like the

Virgin Islands, Guam, and Saipan have established offices that are capable of providing direct assistance in setting up a FSC.

Exporters with up to $10 million of annual exports may continue to operate through DISCs, generally under the present rules, but they must pay an annual interest charge on the amount of tax that would be due if the post-1984 accumulated DISC income were included in the shareholder's income. This interest is imposed on the shareholders and paid to the Treasury of the United States.

Up to 25 exporters can jointly own an FSC and through the use of several classes of common stock can divide the profits of an FSC among shareholders.

SUCCESS STORY: Ben Martin, a San Diego, California surfer and businessman knows a bargain when he sees it. He discovered that new major-brand surfboards sell for $1200 in Japan. He could buy surfboards from a new U.S. manufacturer at $120 and sell them to retailers at about half the going rate. That's when he got serious about international trade. His first-year sales topped $780,000, and he paid back his initial capital (borrowed from friends, parents, and relatives) in less than three years.

HOW TO GAIN RELIEF FROM UNFAIR IMPORT PRACTICES

Remaining competitive in world markets is an internal management problem. The underlying elements are quantity, quality, and price. Nevertheless, government intervention is sometimes necessary when you learn about foreign firms that are not competing on what has become known as a "level playing field."

The U.S. International Trade Committee's (ITC) *Rules of Practice and Procedure*, which set forth the procedures for the filing and conduct of investigations, is available by writing the Docket Section, U.S. International Trade Commission, 500 E Street S.W., Washington, DC 20436 or calling (202) 205-1802.

The ITC, Congress, and/or the U.S. Trade Representative can investigate the following allegations:

- Countervailing duties imposed by a foreign country
- Antidumping
- General investigations of trade and tariff matters

- Investigations of costs of production
- Alleged unfair practices in import trade
- Investigations of injury from increased imports
- Workers adjustment assistance
- Firms adjustment assistance
- Enforcement of U.S. rights under trade agreements and in response to certain foreign trade practices
- U.S. response to foreign trade practices that restrict or discriminate against U.S. commerce
- Investigations of market disruptions by imports from Communist countries

Points of contact for instituting investigations are:

Office of Investigations
Office of the Assistant Secretary for Trade Administration
U.S. Department of Commerce
Washington, DC 20230
(202) 482-5497

Trade Remedy Assistance
U.S. International Trade Commission
500 E Street S.W.
Washington, DC 20436
(202) 205-2200 or (800) 343-9822

Office of Trade Adjustment Assistance
U.S. Department of Labor
Washington, DC 20213
(202) 219-5555

Chairman
Section 301 Committee
Office of the U.S. Trade Representative
600 17th Street N.W.
Washington, DC 20506
(202) 395-7305

Chapter 7 explains those things that are unique to importing, such as customs, tariffs, and quotas.

How to Import into the United States

SOME ASPECTS OF IMPORTING DON'T APPLY TO EXPORTING. FOR EXAMPLE, the tariff schedule applies only to importing and the Customs Service is concerned only with goods coming into a country. The basics unique to importing are gathered in this chapter for easy learning:

- Government support
- Information sources
- Customhouse brokers
- Getting through the customs maze
- How to use the tariff schedule
- Import quotas
- Special import regulations
- Free trade zones
- Customs bonded warehouses

GOVERNMENT SUPPORT

Although the Customs Service of the Department of Treasury cannot be thought of as the supporting government organization for importing in the way that the Department of Commerce is for exports, it is nevertheless responsible for enforcement of the relevant trade.

The Bureau of Customs is one of the nation's oldest public institutions. Provision for the service was probably the second thing the First Congress did after forming the new nation. Created in 1789, it provided most of the federal government's revenue for almost 130 years. After the income tax became the nation's primary revenue source, the major responsibility of the Customs Service shifted to the administration of the Tariff Act of 1930, as amended. These duties include enforcing laws against smuggling and collecting all duties, taxes, and fees due on the volumes of goods moved through the United States's more than 300 ports of entry. A Customs Court, consisting of nine judges appointed by the President, reviews and settles disputes between importers and exporters and those that collect duties for the Bureau of Customs.

Like the Department of Commerce, the Customs Service is organized with an external as well as an internal arm.

The *internal* arm is organized into 5 Strategic Trade Centers (STC); 20 Customs Management Centers (CMCs); and 300 plus ports-of-entry offices. Figure 7-1 illustrates the Customs Service organization.

Although not as extensive as Commerce's Foreign Commercial Service (FCS), Customs attaches (Custom's *external* arm) are attached to the embassies or missions in the countries listed below:

Belgium	Hong Kong	Mexico
Canada	Italy	Pakistan
England	Japan	Thailand
France	Korea	West Germany

IMPORT INFORMATION SOURCES

The Customs Service does provide considerable information related to the importing function in the form of booklets, newsletters, and seminars available through the CMCs or the U.S. Government Printing Office (GPO). Most of this information amounts to extractions from and simplification of customs regulations.

Information about how to make contacts and/or perform the import function must be obtained through private sector publishers and organizations such as chambers of commerce (COC) or

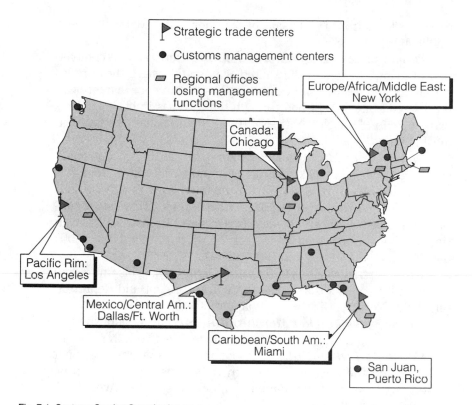

▶ Strategic trade centers

● Customs management centers

▱ Regional offices
  losing management
  functions

Europe/Africa/Middle East:
New York

Canada:
Chicago

Pacific Rim:
Los Angeles

Mexico/Central Am.:
Dallas/Ft. Worth

Caribbean/South Am.:
Miami

● San Juan,
  Puerto Rico

Fig. 7-1. Customs Service Organization U.S. Department of the Treasury, *Journal of Commerce,* Val Hernandez-Rhodes.

trade associations. Several sources are helpful for learning more about importing.

Importing into the United States. This excellent booklet, published by the Department of the Treasury and available from GPO outlines the requirements that must be met by the importer to enter goods. The cost is less than $10.

Encyclopedia of Associations. This publication, which costs approximately $250, can be found at most libraries. It provides a complete list of American and international manufacturers' associations. Order it from Gale Research Company, Brook Tower, Detroit, MI 48226 or call (800) 223-GALE.

Directory of the United States Importers (Edition). This directory serves as a guide to the people, products, and marketing opportunities in the U.S. import industry. It costs about $250 and can be ordered from The Journal of Commerce, 445 Marshall Street, Phillipsburg, NJ 08865.

Thomas Register of American Manufacturers. A compilation of manufacturers in the United States and where they are located, the Thomas Register can be used as a source for marketing in the United States. Published through the Thomas Publishing Company, 1 Penn Plaza, New York, NY 10001. It can usually be found in most libraries.

Directory of Manufacturers Agents. This excellent publication can be used to make contact with industrial distributors. It is published by McGraw-Hill, 11 West 19th Street, New York, NY 10011.

Market Guide of Mass Merchandisers. This list of contacts for salespeople is published by Dun and Bradstreet International, 99 Church Street, New York NY 07054; telephone (800) 536-0651; in New Jersey call (800) 624-0324.

Manufacturers Agents Annual Directory. This up-to-date listing of U.S. agents is available through the Agent and Representative, 626 North Garfield Ave., Alhambra, CA 91802.

Major Mass Market Merchandisers. This is published by The Salesman's Guide, Inc., 1182 Broadway, New York, NY 10001.

Contacts Influential. This book identifies businesses, what they do, and the decision-makers in those businesses. It can be leased from Contacts Influential, 12395 West 53rd Ave. #G-7, Arvada, CO 80002; telephone (303) 420-1212.

CUSTOMHOUSE BROKERS

The *customhouse broker* is a private, for-profit liaison between the Customs Service and the importing public. Customhouse brokers will be needed as long as there are legal requirements and regulations pertaining to the movement of merchandise.

Like the freight forwarder for exporting, the customhouse broker is licensed to assist importers in the movement of their goods. Formal entries of foreign-made goods representing many billions of dollars in duty collections are filed each year with the Customs Service, and virtually all of them are prepared by customhouse brokers on behalf of importers. Some brokers are sole proprietors with a single office at one port of entry, while others are large corporations with branches in many ports throughout the country. All are licensed and regulated by the Department of the Treasury.

The importer employs the customhouse broker as his or her agent, who frequently is his or her only point of contact with the

Customs Service. It is not necessary to employ a customhouse broker to enter goods for your own behalf; however, as an importer, you must post a bond if you don't employ a custom house broker.

Most experienced importers will recommend the services of a broker because of the extras they offer, including the comfort of knowing that a professional is supporting your project. A broker provides advice on the technical requirements of importing, preparing and filing entry documents, obtaining the necessary bonds, depositing U.S. import duties, securing release of the product(s), arranging delivery to the importer's premises or warehouse, and obtaining drawback refunds.

The broker often consults with the Customs Service to determine the proper rate of duty or bases of appraisement. If the broker is dissatisfied with either rate or value, he or she usually will pursue appropriate administrative remedies on behalf of the importer.

Another good reason to use a customhouse broker is that at some point, your time will become more valuable to you in managing your company and marketing your product(s) than it might be in handling the paperwork of an entry. Consult the yellow pages of your local phone book for a listing of customhouse brokers in your area.

Bonds

All importers must post a *surety bond* with the Customs Service to ensure payment of the proper amounts of duties, taxes, and other charges associated with entry. Bonds can be for single entry or continuous (*term*). Based on the value of the shipment, the Customs Service determines the value of the required bond. Often, they require a bond three times the value of the shipment. A surety company usually requires 100% collateral in the form of an irrevocable letter of credit (L/C), trust deed, or cashiers check. Bond premiums are about 2% of the value with a minimum of about $100. The premium for a term bond is usually higher (5%). Collateral depends on the financial condition of the importer.

Drawback

Drawback is the refunding of duties paid on imported goods and their derivatives if they are subsequently exported. For example, suppose you simply re-export goods that were originally imported; or you export items that contain imported merchandise; or you export items that contain whole imported components. For each of these you might claim a drawback of tariffs paid when imported. The key to drawback is good inventory tracking and record-keeping procedures. Make application for drawbacks with your local Customs Service port-of-entry office.

Automated Brokerage Interface

The Automated Brokerage Interface (ABI) is for those large-volume importers who file many simple entries and wish to avoid the cost of a broker. ABI permits importers (and brokers) to electronically file preliminary entry data in advance of the arrival of cargo.

How to Become a Customhouse Broker

You can become a customhouse broker by (a) studying the Customs Service Regulations and learning the application of the tariff schedules, and then (b) passing an examination given several times a year. This license is not necessary to act on your own behalf, but it is needed if you act as an agent for others. The cost to take the examination is approximately $400. Details about the examination can be obtained from any Customs Service Office. Figure 7-2 shows the application form required to gain a license.

GETTING THROUGH THE CUSTOMS MAZE

A *tariff* is a schedule of duties. It is also the duty or tax imposed by a country and the duty or tax within the tariff schedule. As a tax, a tariff is placed on goods as they cross the border between two countries.

At one time, tariffs were the primary way the United States raised money to support the federal government. However, in the early 1900s, when the income tax was introduced, revenue-raising tariffs took on less importance. Since then, tariffs have been predominantly used to protect home industries.

The Entry Process

When a shipment of goods intended for commercial use reaches the United States, it may not be legally entered until after (a) it enters the port of entry, (b) estimated duties have been paid, and (c) Customs authorizes delivery of the merchandise. During this process only the owner (or his or her agent) is responsible for the entry—the Customs Service simply checks each step to ensure correctness. Table 7-1 lists the steps of the commercial entry process.

Form Approved: O.M.B. No. 1515-0076

DEPARTMENT OF THE TREASURY
UNITED STATES CUSTOMS SERVICE

APPLICATION FOR CUSTOMHOUSE BROKER'S LICENSE
19 U.S.C. 1641; 111.12 C.R.

Privacy Act Statement on Reverse of Form

1. APPLICANT'S NAME AND ADDRESS *(Principal Office OR Home Address,*

INSTRUCTIONS: Applicants must be United States citizens. Submit application in duplicate to the District Director of the District named in Block 3. All additional continuation sheets, if required, and attachments should also be in duplicate.

2. TYPE OF LICENSE APPLIED FOR	3. CUSTOMS DISTRICT FOR WHICH LICENSE IS APPLIED
☐ Individual ☐ Corporation ☐ Partnership ☐ Association	

4. HAVE YOU EVER APPLIED FOR A CUSTOMHOUSE BROKER'S LICENSE? ☐ NO ☐ YES *(Explain in item 17)*

5. HAS THE APPLICANT *(OR ANY OFFICER OR MEMBER THEREOF)* EVER HAD A LICENSE SUSPENDED, REFUSED, REVOKED, OR CANCELED? ☐ NO ☐ YES *(Explain in item 17)*

6. IF APPLICANT HAS A CURRENT LICENSE, STATE WHEN AND FOR WHAT DISTRICT ISSUED.

7. IS THE APPLICANT *(OR ANY OFFICER OR MEMBER THEREOF)* AN OFFICER OR EMPLOYEE OF THE UNITED STATES? ☐ NO ☐ YES *(Explain in item 17)*

SECTION I — INDIVIDUALS ONLY

8. DATE OF BIRTH	9. BIRTHPLACE *(City & State)*	10. SOCIAL SECURITY NO.	11. HOME PHONE NO.	12. BUSINESS PHONE NO.

13. U.S. CITIZENSHIP
☐ NATURAL-BORN ☐ NATURALIZED-Give Date & Place ▶

14. HAVE YOU EVER BEEN A DEFENDANT IN A CRIMINAL PROSECUTION? *(You may exclude minor traffic violations where the fine was $50 or less.)* ☐ NO ☐ YES *(Explain in item 17)*

15. DO YOU PROPOSE TO ENGAGE IN THE BUSINESS OF A CUSTOMHOUSE BROKER:

(More than one may apply. Explain answer(s) in Item 17.)

(a) ☐ ON YOUR OWN INDIVIDUAL ACCOUNT? *(State name in which business is to be conducted; if trade name, state authority for use of the name and attach evidence of such authority.)*

(b) ☐ AS A MEMBER OF A PARTNERSHIP? *(State name of partnership and list names of all the partners.)*

(c) ☐ AS AN OFFICER OF AN ASSOCIATION? *(State name of the association, the title of the office you hold, and the general nature of your duties.)*

(d) ☐ AS AN OFFICER OF A CORPORATION? *(State name of the corporation, the title of the office you hold, and the general nature of your duties.)*

(e) ☐ AS AN EMPLOYEE? *(State name and address of your employer (if different than item 1)and the nature of your employment.)*

16. LIST THE NAMES AND ADDRESSES OF SIX REFERENCES.

SECTION III — CERTIFICATION *(ALL APPLICANTS)*

INDIVIDUAL	ASSOCIATION, CORPORATION, OR PARTNERSHIP
I, _____ certify that the statements contained in the foregoing application and supporting attachments thereto are true and correct to the best of my knowledge and belief. Written notice of any change in my mailing address, any business connection, or the name and style under which I conduct my business will be given to the Commissioner of Customs.	I, _____, certify that I am an officer or partner of the applicant; that I am a licensed customhouse broker; and that the statements contained in the foregoing application and supporting attachments thereto are true and correct to the best of my knowledge and belief. The officers or partners who are licensed customhouse brokers are aware of the requirements for the exercise by them of responsible supervision and control of the transaction of the customs business of the applicant. Written notice of any change in the applicant's mailing address, name, licensed officers or partners, or the charter, certificate, articles, or other instrument of organization of the applicant will be given to the Commissioner of Customs.

23. SIGNATURE	24. DATE

Customs Form 3124 (03-03-81)

Fig.. 7-2. Application for customhouse broker license

HISTORY NOTE: The word tariff presumably comes from the Arabic term for inventory, which is ta'rif. The French word, *tarif*, as well as the Spanish word *tarifa*, means price list or rate book. An alternate version has it that the word originated sometime after 700 A.D. At that time, near Gibraltar, there was a village called Tarifa, where a small band of thieves lived. They stopped every merchant ship and forced the captain to pay a handsome sum of money before the vessel could proceed through the strait. Seamen began calling the money they were forced to pay a tariff.

Table 7-1. Commercial Entry Process.

Who is Responsible?	What does Customs do?
Owner; Agent; Purchaser	
Step	Step
1. Entry: Arrives within port	1. Check and verify. Store in general warehouse?
a. Decide consumption or bonded warehouse/FTZ	
b. If consumption, file entry documents	
c. Documents required	Check
1. Entry manifest	
2. Right to make entry	
3. Invoices	
4. Packing lists	
5. Entry summary	
6. Evidence of bond	Verify
2. Valuation	
3. Classify/appraise	
4. Estimate and pay tariff (check or cash)	2. Examine
	3. Validate
	a. Classification
	b. Appraisement
	4. Authorize entry
	5. Liquidate transaction

Owner/Agent Responsibilities

The process, in its simplest form, has four essential steps.

Step One: Entry. Within five working days after a shipment of goods arrives at a U.S. port of entry, the owner/agent must decide whether to *enter* the goods for consumption or place them into a bonded warehouse or free (foreign) trade zone (FTZ) (explained in detail later in the chapter). If the decision is made to enter for consumption, the following entry documents must be filed:

- Entry Manifest, Customs Form 7533; or Application and Special Permit for Immediate Delivery, Customs Form 3461

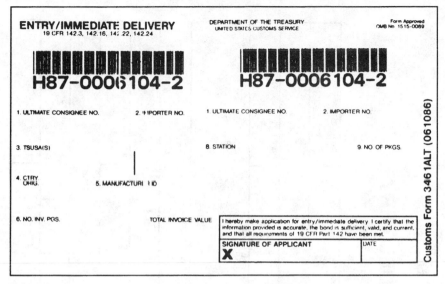

Fig. 7-3. Special immediate entry permit (land)

- Evidence of right to make entry
- Commercial invoice or a pro forma invoice
- Packing list(s) if appropriate
- Entry Summary, Customs Form 7501, and other documents necessary to determine merchandise admissibility
- Evidence of bond

Customs Form 3461 is a special permit for immediate delivery and is an alternative procedure that provides for the immediate release of a shipment. Figure 7-3 shows the form used for land shipments, and the form shown in Fig. 7-4 is used for ocean and air shipments. Application should be made before the arrival of the goods, so that, if approved, the goods won't have to sit on the dock or in a warehouse and will be released on arrival. You are allowed 10 working days to file a proper entry summary (Form 7501) and deposit estimated duties. Release under this provision is limited to:

- Merchandise arriving from *Canada* or *Mexico*
- Fresh fruits and vegetables for human consumption arriving from Canada or Mexico
- Articles for a trade fair

DEPARTMENT OF THE TREASURY
UNITED STATES CUSTOMS SERVICE

Form Approved
OMB No. 1515-0069

ENTRY/IMMEDIATE DELIVERY

19 CFR 142.3, 142.16, 142.22, 142.24

1. ARRIVAL DATE	2. ELECTED ENTRY DATE	3. ENTRY TYPE CODE/NAME	4. ENTRY NUMBER
5. PORT	6. SINGLE TRANS. BOND	7. BROKER/IMPORTER FILE NUMBER	
	8. CONSIGNEE NUMBER		9. IMPORTER NUMBER
10. ULTIMATE CONSIGNEE NAME		11. IMPORTER OF RECORD NAME	
12. CARRIER CODE	13. VOYAGE/FLIGHT/TRIP	14. LOCATION OF GOODS—CODE(S)/NAME(S)	
15. VESSEL CODE/NAME			
16. U.S. PORT OF UNLADING	17. MANIFEST NUMBER	18. G.O. NUMBER	19. TOTAL VALUE
20. DESCRIPTION OF MERCHANDISE			

21. IT/BL/AWB CODE	22. IT/BL/AWB NO.	23. MANIFEST QUANTITY	24. TSUSA NUMBER	25. COUNTRY OF ORIGIN	26. MANUFACTURER NO.

27. CERTIFICATION

I hereby make application for entry/immediate delivery. I certify that the above information is accurate, the bond is sufficient, valid, and current, and that all requirements of 19 CFR Part 142 have been met.

SIGNATURE OF APPLICANT

X

PHONE NO.   DATE

29. BROKER OR OTHER GOVT. AGENCY USE

28. CUSTOMS USE ONLY

☐ OTHER AGENCY ACTION REQUIRED, NAMELY:

☐ CUSTOMS EXAMINATION REQUIRED.

☐ ENTRY REJECTED, BECAUSE:

DELIVERY AUTHORIZED: SIGNATURE   DATE

Paperwork Reduction Act Notice: This information is needed to determine the admissibility of imports into the United States and to provide the necessary information for the examination of the cargo and to establish the liability for payment of duties and taxes. Your response is necessary.

Customs Form **3461** (112085)

Fig. 7-4. Special immediate entry permit (air and ocean)

- Tariff-rate quota merchandise and, under certain circumstances, merchandise subject to an absolute quota
- Merchandise specifically authorized by customs because of perishability or inconvenience to the importer, carrier, or agent.

Step Two: Valuation. *Valuation* determines the value of the goods for purposes of applying any tariffs or duties. Generally, the customs value will be the transaction value or the price actually paid or payable for the merchandise when sold for exportation to the United States, plus amounts for the following items if not included in the price:

- The packing costs incurred by the buyer
- Any selling commission paid by the buyer
- The value of any assist (Note: An example of an assist would be tools, dies, molds, engineering, artwork, etc.)
- Any royalty or license fee that is required from the buyer as a condition of the sale
- The proceeds from the sale of the imported goods that accrue to the seller

If the transaction value for the goods cannot be used, then secondary bases are used in the following order of precedence: transaction value of identical merchandise, transaction value of similar merchandise, deductive value, and computed value.

Step Three: Classification. The responsibility for *classification* rests with the importer, customhouse broker, or other person preparing the entry papers. The importance of this step cannot be overemphasized because it determines the *ad valorem* (percentage) tariff rate that should be applied to the valuation of the goods. Familiarity with the Tariff Schedule of the United States (TSUS) and the Harmonized System (HS) Tariff Schedule of the United States facilitates the process.

> **HOT TIP:** First rule of importing—always get an advance ruling from Customs!

Step Four: Payment. Payment of duties is made by cash or check payable to the Treasurer of the United States.

Customs Service Responsibilities

The Customs Service involvement in the entry process can be characterized by five steps: assist and check, examination, validation, authorize entry, and liquidation.

Step One: Check and Verify. For this step, Customs officers check the entry documents and verify evidence of a bond. Of course, when the goods arrive at the port of entry the owner or agent is responsible for immediately making arrangements for the shipment and storage of the goods. Those goods that are not claimed are stored in a general warehouse. Storage is billed to the owner when the goods are retrieved or when they are sold at auction.

Step Two: Examination. Examination is the step during which the Customs officer examines the goods to determine their value and suitability for entering. It also has five sub-steps:

1. Valuing the goods for customs and their dutiable status
2. Checking the proper markings of the goods with the country of origin
3. Determining whether the shipment contains prohibited items
4. Determining whether the goods are correctly invoiced
5. Taking an inventory to determine whether there are excesses or shortages of the invoiced quantities

Step Three: Validation. The validation step consists of checking the classification of the goods and appraising the goods to ensure correct valuation.

Step Four: Authorize Entry. After the classification and valuation, as well as other required import information have been reviewed for correctness, proper appraisement, and agreement of the submitted data, the merchandise may be *authorized* for actual import.

Step Five: Liquidation. If the goods are accepted without changes, they are *liquidated as entered*. This step is finalized in the traditional way of posting a notice on the public bulletin board at the customs house. The bulletin board is now a computer printout. After the liquidation, an importer can pursue claims for adjustment or refund by filing, within 90 days, a protest on Customs Form 19. Time limits do not begin to run until the date of posting. If, after further review, the importer is still not satisfied, a summons can be filed with the U.S. Customs Court of International Trade.

SUCCESS STORY: Angelica Pfleger's opportunity came when she discovered a market for German crystal tableware in California. Her company "Crystal Treasures" grossed her $85,000 the first year by buying at a discount 5% below the wholesale price and gaining a 3% discount on the total sales price by making payment within 10 days. By ensuring all shipments were above the $1000 threshold noted in HTS 7013.31, she was able to take advantage of only a 3.4 % ad valorem duty (tariff) rate. Thus, she was able to become profitable by her second year in business.

THE HARMONIZED TARIFF SYSTEM

The Harmonized Schedule (HS) is an international, multipurpose classification system designed to improve the collection of import and export statistics, as well as for Customs purposes. Intended to serve as a core for national systems, it promotes a high degree of international uniformity in the presentation of Customs tariffs and foreign trade statistics. The HS replaced the TSUS and the Tariff Schedule of the United States Annotated (TSUSA) as the United States' import schedule. It also replaced Schedule B as the United States' export code.

How to Use the Harmonized Schedule

The HS is about the size of a major city's telephone book and is available from GPO in three-hole, loose-leaf form for about $70. It is a complete product classification system, organized in a framework that employs a numbering system. To assist the user, a section in the front of the book gives instructions known as General Notes and General Rules of Interpretation (GRI), which explain the use and interpretation of the schedule and a table of contents.

At the international level, about 5000 article descriptions are grouped in 21 sections and arranged in 97 chapters. The U.S. version has 22 sections and 99 chapters. Chapter 98 includes information from the "old" TSUSA Schedule 8 (articles 806.20, 806.30, and 807) related to offshore assembly. Chapter 99 contains information transformed from the TSUSA Schedule 9. The 22 sections and their chapter headings are listed in a table of contents in the front of the HS.

HISTORY NOTE: For decades, the international trading community was confronted with problems caused by the number of differing classification systems covering the movement of goods in international trade. In 1970, representatives of the Customs Cooperation Council (CCC), formerly known as the Brussels Tariff Nomenclature (BTN), undertook a study of commodity descriptions and coding with a view to developing a system capable of meeting the principal requirements of customs authorities, statisticians, carriers, and producers. The result of the study was that the development of such a system was not only feasible, but imperative.

Some 13 years later the Harmonized Commodity Description and Coding system and a convention for its implementation was completed. Forty-eight countries and more than a dozen private and public organizations participated in its development.

HOT TIP: When you read the HS codes, remember the chapter is the first two digits (example: 44), the heading is the first four digits (example: 4409), the subheading is the first six digits (example: 4409.10), and the item is the first eight digits (example: 4409.10.10).

Case Study—Guitars

Let's hypothesize that you are an importer of guitars valued at less than $100. Your order from Germany arrives. Assuming you wish to enter them immediately into Commerce, you must present the documents listed in step one of the entry process to the Customs Service within five working days.

Note: If the guitars were perishable or you had a special scheduling problem, you could have applied (in advance) for their immediate delivery using Special Entry Permit Form 3461. In this case, let us assume there was no need for immediate entry, so we proceed as a normal, formal entry.

Let's further assume you used an L/C to make payment, so you can only pick up your entry documents after you square your account with your banker. The invoice shows 1000 guitars at $89 each, for a total of $8900. This is the transaction value for purposes of valuation. Because the value of your goods is more than $1250, you must make a formal entry. Had the value been under $1250, the informal entry process would have been much simpler, you could easily have done your own paperwork, and a bond would not have been required. Figure 7-5 shows an Entry Summary, the basic form used for both formal and informal entry. Table 7-2 shows the difference between a formal and an informal entry.

Table 7-2. Entry Process.

	Informal	*Formal*
Value	Less than $1250*	$1250 or greater
Bond	No	Yes
Duties	Pay on entry	Pay within 10 days**
Liquidation	On the spot	Liquidation notice
Forms required	7501, invoice, B/L, check ($$$ duties), packing list	7501, invoice, B/L, packing list, check ($$$ duties), other agency, documents, bond

*For some articles, formal entry is specified regardless of value (check your local Customs Service office or customhouse broker).
**An example of a good that might require immediate payment would be an item under quota.

Had the goods been for your personal use and you had been out of the country for more than 48 hours, the first $400 ($800 when returning from a U.S. insular possession) would have been exempt, the next $1000 dutied at 10%, and the remainder at the ad valorem rate from the TSUSA.

Beginners sometimes ask, "What if I entered the goods for personal use in small quantities and then sold them?" In answer, one Customs agent told me "They might get away with it the first time, but we (the computers) remember, and sooner or later we'll catch them. The penalty is at least a $5000 fine."

Full, complete, and honest disclosure is the responsibility of the importer. The penalties are severe and not worth the gamble. Make your money and pay your duties.

DEPARTMENT OF THE TREASURY
UNITED STATES CUSTOMS SERVICE

ENTRY SUMMARY

1. Entry No.	2. Entry Type Code	3. Entry Summary Date
4. Entry Date	5. Port Code	
6. Bond No.	7. Bond Type Code	8. Broker/Importer File No.
9. Ultimate Consignee Name and Address		
10. Consignee No.	11. Importer of Record Name and Address	12. Importer No.
	State	
13. Exporting Country		14. Export Date
15. Country of Origin		16. Missing Documents
17. I.T. No.		18. I.T. Date
19. B L or AWB No.	20. Mode of Transportation	21. Manufacturer I.D.	22. Reference No.
23. Importing Carrier	24. Foreign Port of Lading	25. Location of Goods/G.O. No.
26. U.S. Port of Unlading	27. Import Date	

Fig. 7-5. Sample entry summary

(28) Line No.

(29) Description of Merchandise

30. (A) T.S.U.S.A. No. (B) ADA CVD Case No.

31. (A) Gross Weight (B) Manifest Qty.

(32) Net Quantity in T.S.U.S.A. Units

33. (A) Entered Value (B) CHGS (C) Relationship

34. (A) T.S.U.S.A. Rate (B) ADA/CVD Rate (C) I.R.C. Rate (D) Visa No.

(35) Duty and I.R. Tax — Dollars — Cents

(36) Declaration of Importer of Record (Owner or Purchaser) or Authorized Agent

I declare that I am the ☐ importer of record and that the actual owner, purchaser, or consignee for customs purposes is as shown above. OR ☐ owner or purchaser or agent thereof.

I further declare that the merchandise ☐ was obtained pursuant to a purchase or agreement to purchase and that the prices set forth in the invoice are true. OR ☐ was not obtained pursuant to a purchase or agreement to purchase and the statements in the invoice as to value or price are true to the best of my knowledge and belief.

I also declare that the statements in the documents herein filed fully disclose to the best of my knowledge and belief the true prices, values, quantities, rebates, drawbacks, fees, commissions, and royalties and are true and correct, and that all goods or services provided to the seller of the merchandise either free or at reduced cost are fully disclosed. I will immediately furnish to the appropriate customs officer any information showing a different state of facts.

Notice required by Paperwork Reduction Act of 1980. This information is needed to ensure that importers/exporters are complying with U.S. Customs laws, to allow us to compute and collect the right amount of money, to enforce other agency requirements, and to collect accurate statistical information on imports. Your response is mandatory.

▼ U.S. CUSTOMS USE ▼

TOTALS

A. Liq. Code
B. Ascertained Duty
C. Ascertained Tax
D. Ascertained Other
E. Ascertained Total

(37) Duty
(38) Tax
(39) Other
(40) Total

(41) Signature of Declarant, Title, and Date

Customs Form 7501 (030984)

Fig. 7-5. Continued

In this example, because the value is $1250 or greater ($8900), a formal entry is required. For the formal or informal entry process, you need to classify the product. Begin by scanning the table of contents for the general category within which your product fits. In this case, "Musical Instruments" is in Section XVIII, Chapter 92.

If you have a copy of the HS available, turn to page 92-2. If not, flip to Fig. 7-6 of this book. Figure 7-6 is a copy of page 92-2 from the HS related to our case study about guitars.

HARMONIZED TARIFF SCHEDULE of the United States (1993)

Annotated for Statistical Reporting Purposes

XVIII

92-2

Heading/ Subheading	Stat. Suf- fix	Article Description	Units of Quantity	Rates of Duty 1 General	Rates of Duty 1 Special	2
9201		Pianos, including player pianos, harpsichords and other keyboard stringed instruments:				
9201.10.00	00	Upright pianos	No.	5.3%	Free (A, E, IL, J) 2.6% (CA)	40%
9201.20.00	00	Grand pianos	No.	5.3%	Free (A, E, IL, J) 2.6% (CA)	40%
9201.90.00	00	Other	No.	5.3%	Free (A, E, IL, J) 2.6% (CA)	40%
9202		Other string musical instruments (for example, guitars, violins, harps):				
9202.10.00	00	Played with a bow	No.	4.9%	Free (A, E, IL, J) 2.4% (CA)	37.5%
9202.90		Other: Guitars:				
9202.90.20	00	Valued not over $100 each, excluding the value of the case	No.	6.8%	Free (A, E, IL, J) 3.4% (CA)	40%
9202.90.40	00	Other	No.	10%	Free (A, E, IL, J) 6.5% (CA)	40%
9202.90.60	00	Other	No.	7%	Free (A, E, IL, J) 3.5% (CA)	40%
9203.00		Keyboard pipe organs; harmoniums and similar keyboard instruments with free metal reeds:				
9203.00.40	00	Keyboard pipe organs	No.	Free		35%
9203.00.80	00	Other	No.	5.3%	Free (A, CA, E, IL, J)	40%
9204		Accordions and similar instruments; mouth organs:				
9204.10		Accordions and similar instruments:				
9204.10.40	00	Piano accordions	No.	4.7%	Free (A, CA, E, IL, J)	40%
9204.10.80	00	Other	No.	5.1%	Free (A, CA, E, IL, J)	40%
9204.20.00	00	Mouth organs	Doz.	4.7%	Free (A, E, IL, J) 2.3% (CA)	40%
9205		Other wind musical instruments (for example, clarinets, trumpets, bagpipes):				
9205.10.00		Brass-wind instruments		5.8%	Free (A, E, IL, J) 2.9% (CA)	40%
	40	Valued not over $10 each	No.			
	80	Valued over $10 each	No.			
9205.90		Other: Woodwind instruments:				
9205.90.20	00	Bagpipes	No	Free		40%
9205.90.40	00	Other		4.9%	Free (A, E, IL, J) 2.4% (CA) 1/	40%
	20	Clarinets	No.			
	40	Saxophones	No.			
	60	Flutes and piccolos (except bamboo)	No.			
	80	Other	No.			
9205.90.60	00	Other	No.	3.4%	Free (A, E, IL, J) 1.7% (CA)	40%
9206.00		Percussion musical instruments (for example, drums, xylophones, cymbals, castanets, maracas):				
9206.00.20	00	Drums	No.	4.8%	Free (A, CA, E, IL, J)	40%
9206.00.40	00	Cymbals	No.	Free		40%
9206.00.60	00	Sets of tuned bells known as chimes, peals or carillons	No.	2.5%	Free (A, CA, E, IL, J)	50%
9206.00.80	00	Other	No.	5.3%	Free (A, CA, E, IL, J)	40%

1/ See subheading 9905.92.10.

Fig. 7-6. Sample page from harmonized tariff schedule

Run your finger down the page until you find guitars valued at less than $100. In this case, the classification of guitars is straightforward, but keep in mind that classifying a product is usually the most difficult part of using any tariff schedule. The correct classification can save you money and heartache. Consult with the Customs Service or your customhouse broker if you have any doubts.

The heading for this product is 9202.90.20. The first two digits refer to the chapter, in this case Chapter 92. The next two refer to the heading, the next two to the international subdivision, then the U.S. subdivision, and finally the U.S. statistical subdivision.

Now, draw your finger across the page. Note that there are three vertical columns, each with an ad valorem duty rate. In Column 1 "General," the rate is 6.8%. This is the rate for Most Favored Nations (MFNs) such as England, France, or Germany. Thus, because your guitars came from Germany, you will pay 6.8% of $8900, or $605.20 ad valorem duty.

Note that the duty rate shown in column 1, "Special," is free (pay no tariff) for country groups A, E, IL, J and only 3.4% for Canada. The countries in these groups are listed in the "special" category programs in the front of the Tariff Schedule under head notes. Table 7-3 shows these special programs.

Table 7-3. Special Tariff Treatment Programs.

General System of Preferences	A or A*
Automotive Products Trade Act	B
Agreement on Trade in Civil Aircraft	C

North American Free Trade Agreement:
  Goods of Canada, under the terms of
  general note 12 of this schedule.
  Goods of Mexico, under the terms of
  general note 12 of this schedule.
	
	CA
	
	MX

Caribbean Basin Economic Recovery Act	E or E*
United States-Israel Free Trade Area	IL
Andean Trade Preference Act	J or J*

*Extracted from the Harmonized Tariff Schedule of the United States.

The third column labeled "2," shows a rate of 40% for guitars valued under $100. This column shows the ad valorem duty rate for countries under "Communist domination or control," such as North Korea, Cuba, etc. If the guitars had come from North Korea instead of Germany, the ad valorem duty paid to the Department of the Treasury would be 40% of $8900, or $3560.

Having estimated your duties as $605.20, the next step is to fill out the required entry documents and post surety in the form of cash or evidence of having a bond (minimum of $10,000). If a customhouse broker makes the entry for you, the broker may use their bond. This is not automatic. In many cases, they will help you obtain your own bond. There are three types of bonds: *term*, which covers entry through only one port of entry; *general*, which covers all U.S. ports; and *continuous*, which can substitute for both.

After filling out the commercial customs invoice, the special (consular) customs invoice, the bill of lading, and the entry form, the goods may now be picked up from the carrier.

Remember, you or your agent (customhouse broker) originally classified and estimated the duties owed. Final liquidation of this transaction by the Customs Service could take as much as several months but must be finalized (with exceptions) within one year. You will receive notice of the date of liquidation and what amounts are due, if any.

Generalized Systems of Preference

The Generalized Systems of Preference (GSP) includes those countries designated by the United Nations as *developing*. To assist in their economic growth, these countries get special preference and, therefore, pay no tariff.

IMPORT QUOTAS

The importation of certain products is controlled by quantity. *Quotas* for this control are established by specific legislation, usually to protect infant industries or established industries under marketing pressure from foreign countries. Therefore, the Commissioner of Customs has no right to change or modify them.

The status of quotas are maintained by a central Customs Service computer in Washington, DC. Access to current quota status can be obtained by taped telephone message. These telephone numbers are available from your local Customs Service office.

U.S. import quotas are divided into two types: absolute and tariff-rate. Absolute quotas are *quantitative quotas*: no more than the amount specified may be permitted during the quota period. Some are global; others apply only to certain countries. When an absolute quota is filled, further entries are prohibited during the remainder of the quota period.

Tariff-rate quotas provide for the entry of a specified quantity at a reduced rate of duty during a given period. Quantities entered in excess of the quota for the period are subject to higher duty rates.

SPECIAL IMPORT REGULATIONS

Many countries require a license to import, but the United States does not. Thousands of products are imported freely with no restrictions. Although the importation of goods does not require a license from the Customs Service, certain classes of merchandise might be prohibited or restricted by other agencies to protect the economy and the security of the country, to safeguard health, or to preserve domestic plant and animal life.

The importer is wise to inquire (complete with samples and specifications) with the regulatory body involved well before entering into any business arrangements. There have been cases where an importer ended up with a warehouse full of products unfit or prohibited from entering the United States.

Agricultural Commodities. The U.S. Food and Drug Administration and the Department of Agriculture control or regulate the importation of most animals, animal foods, insects, plants, and poultry products.

Arms, Ammunition, and Radioactive Materials. The Bureau of Alcohol, Tobacco, and Firearms of the Department of the Treasury prohibits the importation of implements of war except when a license is issued. Even temporary importation, movement, and exportation is prohibited unless licensed by the Office of Munitions Control, Department of State. Of course, the Nuclear Regulatory Commission controls all forms of radioactive materials and nuclear reactors.

Consumer Products. Consumer products, such as refrigerators, freezers, dishwashers, water heaters, television sets, and furnaces (and other energy-using products) are regulated by the Consumer Products Efficiency Branch of the Department of Energy.

Food, Drugs, Cosmetics, and Medical Devices. The Federal Food, Drug, and Cosmetic Act governs the importation of food, beverages, drugs, devices, and cosmetics. This Act is administered by the Food and Drug Administration of the Department of Health and Human Services.

Gold, Silver, Currency, and Stamps. Provisions of the National Stamping Act, enforced by the Department of Justice, regulate some aspects of importing silver and gold.

Pesticides and Toxic and Hazardous Substances. Three acts control the importation of these substances: the Insecticide, Fungicide, and Rodenticide Act of 1947; the Toxic Substances Control Act of 1977; and the Hazardous Substances Act. Further information can be obtained from the Environmental Protection Agency, Washington, DC 20460.

Textile, Wool, and Fur Products. Textile fiber products must be stamped, tagged, and labeled as required by the Textile Fiber Products Identification Act. Similarly, wool products must be clearly marked in accordance with the Wool Products Labeling Act of 1939. Fur must be labeled as required by the Fur Products Labeling Act. Regulations and pamphlets containing the text of these labeling acts can be obtained from the Federal Trade Commission, Washington, DC 20580.

Trademarks, Trade names, and Copyrights. The Customs Reform and Simplification Act of 1979 strengthened the protection afforded trademark owners against the importation of articles bearing counterfeit marks. In general, articles bearing trademarks or marks that copy or simulate a registered trademark of a U.S. or foreign corporation are prohibited from importation. Similarly, the Copyright Revision Act of 1976 provides that the importation into the United States of copies of a work acquired outside the United States without authorization of the copyright owner is an infringement of the copyright.

Wildlife and Pets. The U.S. Fish and Wildlife Service, Department of Interior, controls the importation of wild or game animals, birds, and other wildlife or any part or product made thereof and the eggs of wild or game birds. The importation of birds, cats, dogs, monkeys, and turtles is subject to the requirements of the U.S. Public Health Service, Center for Disease Control, Quarantine Division, Atlanta, Georgia.

FREE TRADE ZONES

Special zones for free trade, sometimes called in-bond regions, did not develop in any significant way until the nineteenth century. Some of the more notable zones worldwide are the port regions of Hamburg, Hong Kong, Koushieng in Taiwan, and Jurong Port in Singapore.

Inland free zones also exist, most notable of which are the in-bond, free zones surrounding the Mexican Maquiladoras. Even Russia is establishing free zones to promote interchange of business with market economies.

Free zones, under legislation of the sovereign nation where they are located, are considered outside the customs territory of that country. The concept is an ancient one dating back to Egyptian times. Goods entering the zone pay no tariff or other taxes under a guarantee (bond) that they will not be entered into the domestic market. Should they enter the domestic market, all duties must be routinely paid. While in these free zones, goods can be altered, assembled, manufactured, and manipulated. Thus, they become areas where barriers to free trade are circumvented.

U.S. Foreign Trade Zones

Everywhere in the world special tariff zones are called free zones, but in the United States, they are called Foreign Trade Zones (FTZ). FTZs are restricted areas considered outside customs territory under the supervision of the Customs Service.

Typically, an FTZ is a large warehouse, fenced and alarmed for security reasons, that tenants lease in order to bring in merchandise—foreign or domestic—to be stored, exhibited, assembled, manufactured, or processed in some way. They are usually located in or near customs ports of entry, usually in industrial parks or in terminal warehouse facilities.

The usual customs entry procedures and payment of duties are not required on foreign merchandise in the FTZ unless it enters the customs territory for domestic consumption. The importer has a choice of paying duties either on the original foreign material or the finished product. Quota restrictions do not normally apply to foreign merchandise in an FTZ.

Local governments in the United States build FTZs for the purpose of stimulating international trade and thus contributing to the economic growth of the region by creating jobs and income. From the importer/exporter point of view, FTZs are all about profits.

HISTORY NOTE: The success of free zones like the "freeport of Hamburg" stimulated interest in the United States and culminated in the passage of the Foreign Trade Zones Act of 1934 and its amendment in 1950. The early history of FTZ is not glamorous. Growth was slow and profits modest. Until the early 1970s, the number of FTZs authorized and in operation in the United States was less than 25, a number that had not changed appreciably since the enabling legislation was passed in 1934. Since 1975, the number of FTZs has grown at an almost exponential rate. At last count, the number of authorized FTZs was more than 110, with 56 special subzones and 50 applications pending.

FTZ SUCCESS STORIES

Using an FTZ is not advantageous for every business, but those that do not take the time to do some simple calculations might find that they are paying significantly higher costs than their competitor. These success stories saved millions of dollars.

Leather Boot/Roller Skates. An importer found high-quality boots manufactured in China, but the tariff at the time was too high. Cleverly, he shipped the boots into an FTZ, attached wheels to the bottoms, and entered the boots as roller skates. Now at practically no duty, this businessperson made a ton of money.

Maritime Subzone. The National Ship Building Company in San Diego, California, discovered a quirk in U.S. import laws that says a vessel is "an intangible" and not subject to tariff. The company applied and received permission to become a subzone of the Long Beach FTZ. Foreign parts were brought into the FTZ duty free, incorporated into the hull of the vessel, and then sailed away duty free. More than $1 million was saved due to this clever use of the law.

The Computer Chip. Computer chips were manufactured offshore in Singapore. Before they were entered into U.S. Customs territory, they were brought into an FTZ for QA inspection. Those found below standard were crushed, ground, and sorted. The gold used in the chips was reclaimed but never entered into the United States. Instead, the gold was shipped back to the plant in Singapore. The remainder of the waste materials were entered as trash, duty

free. Only those chips that passed QA were entered for duty purposes. This firm avoided drawback, and thus kept their money
working for the company, not Uncle Sam.

CUSTOMS BONDED WAREHOUSES

A bonded warehouse is a building or other secure area within customs territory where dutiable foreign merchandise can be placed
for a period up to five years without payment of duty. Only cleaning, repacking, and sorting is allowed. The owner of the bonded
warehouse incurs liability and must post a bond with the Customs
Service and abide by those regulations pertaining to control and
declaration of tariffs for goods on departure. The liability is canceled when the goods are removed.

Types of Bonded Warehouses

Customs regulations authorize eight different types of bonded
warehouses.

1. Storage areas owned or leased by the government to store
   merchandise undergoing Customs inspection, under seizure,
   or unclaimed goods.
2. Privately owned warehouses used exclusively for the storage
   of merchandise belonging or consigned to the proprietor.
3. Publicly bonded warehouses used exclusively to store imported goods.
4. Bonded yards or sheds for the storage of heavy and bulky
   imported merchandise such as pens for animals—stables
   and corrals, and tanks for the storage of imported fluids.
5. Bonded grain storage bins or elevators.
6. Warehouses used for the manufacture in bond, solely for
   exportation, of imported articles.
7. Warehouses bonded for smelting and refining imported
   metal-bearing materials.
8. Bonded warehouses created for sorting, cleaning, repacking, or otherwise changing the condition of imported merchandise, but not manufacturing.

How to Establish a Bonded Warehouse

Your local Customs district office has all the information you will need to get started, but in general, the following five items must be fulfilled:

1. An application to the Customs district office giving the location and stating the class of warehouse to be established. Your application should describe the general character of the merchandise, the estimated maximum duties and taxes that could become due at any one time, and whether the warehouse will be used for private storage or treatment, or as a public warehouse.
2. A fee of about $80.
3. A certificate that the building is acceptable for fire insurance purposes.
4. A blueprint of the building or space to be bonded.
5. A bond of $5000 or greater on each building depending on the class of the bonded area.

Bonded Warehouse or Foreign Trade Zone?

Table 7-4 shows a comparison of an FTZ to a bonded warehouse. Being aware of all the possibilities is a vital part of competing and winning the trade game. Not every importer/exporter will need countertrade or to make use of an FTZ or a Customs' bonded warehouse, but proper and advanced planning is essential if you want to take advantage of the subtleties of the trade laws. An appreciation for the capabilities of each of the business tools presented in this chapter might lead to the recognition of a winning opportunity.

The preceding two chapters have presented those things that are different about the export/import transaction. The remaining three chapters of the book are dedicated to understanding the basics of doing business in the major regions of the world: the Americas, Europe, and Asia.

Table 7-4. Comparison of FTZ to Bonded Warehouse.

Function	Bonded Warehouse	Zone
Customs Entry	A bonded warehouse is within U.S Customs territory; therefore a Customs Entry must be filed to enter goods into the warehouse.	A Zone is not considered within customs territory. Customs entry is, therefore, not required until removed from a Zone.
Permissible Cargo	Only foreign merchandise may be placed in a bonded warehouse.	All merchandise, whether domestic or foreign, may be placed in a Zone.
Customs Bonds	Each entry must be covered by either a single entry, term bond or general term bond.	No bond is required for merchandise in a Zone.
Payment of duty	Duties are due prior to release from bonded warehouses.	Duties are due only upon entry into U.S. territory.
Manufacture of goods	Manufacturing is prohibited.	Manufacturing is permitted with duty payable at the time the goods leave the Zone for U.S. consumption. Duty is payable on either the imported components or the finished product, whichever carries a lower rate.
Appraisal and Classification	Immediately.	Tariff rate and value may be determined either at the time of admission into a Zone or when goods leave a Zone, at your discretion.
Storage periods	Not to exceed 5 years.	Unlimited
Operations on merchandise destined for domestic consumption	Only cleaning, repackaging and sorting may take place and under Customs supervision.	Sort, destroy, clean, grade, mix with foreign or domestic goods, label, assemble, manufacture, exhibit, sell, repack.
Customs Entry Regulations	Apply fully.	Only applicable to goods actually removed from a Zone for U.S. consumption.

8

Doing Business in the Americas

OF COURSE, TRADE GOES ON CONTINUOUSLY AMONG THE 35 NATIONS OF the Americas, and each international business must frequently assess the impact of tariffs and other barriers on profitability. The following is a list of the nations of the Americas.

Antigua	Dominica	Nicaragua
Argentina	Dominican Republic	Panama
Bahamas	Ecuador	Paraguay
Barbados	El Salvador	Peru
Barbuda	Grenada	St. Kitts-Nevis
Belize	Grenadines	St. Lucia
Bolivia	Guatemala	St. Vincent
Brazil	Guyana	Surinam
Canada	Haiti	Trinidad & Tobago
Chile	Honduras	United States
Columbia	Jamaica	Urugray
Costa Rica	Mexico	Venezuela
Cuba		

Table 8-1 shows the potential of the American market. Central and Latin American markets, although having smaller gross domestic products, nevertheless have a growing middle class and offer excellent trade potential.

Table 8-1. American Trade Potential.

Country	Population (millions)	National Income (bn $)	National Income (per head $)
Canada	27.8	521	18,741
United States	250	5,950	23,895
Mexico	88	195	2,242
NAFTA Totals	363.8	6,666	18,065
Central/Latin America	369.2	788	2,135
Totals	733	7,454	10,669

Source: *Journal of Commerce*, Tuesday, December 8, 1994.

Each nation of the Americas has its own tariff schedule and each belongs to one or more regional trade arrangements that dictate the bloc tariff. This chapter deals with the three major elements of doing business in the Americas: NAFTA, other existing trade arrangements, and NAFTA enlargement.

NAFTA

The North American Free Trade Area (NAFTA) is composed of Canada, the United States, and the Americas. With a combined population of 360 million people and high per capita incomes of more than $18,000 a year (about $2500 in Mexico), NAFTA is the richest market in the world and has always been the first target for anyone doing international business.

NAFTA, which went into effect on January 1, 1994, offers preferential tariff treatment for business trading within the newly created single market. It is a major step toward stimulating regional trade. NAFTA rules are clear and understandable, but require thought as they apply to a given firm's products. The tactical implications of NAFTA depend on a product-by-product analysis as well as whether the firm is an insider or outsider.

Key Provisions

The NAFTA document is more than 1000 pages and its companion tariff schedule is even longer. Obviously, over the years changes will be negotiated by the three countries, but those changes will be the result of users (exporters and importers) shoring up loopholes and finding better ways of doing business. The intent of the basic document will remain as follows:

- Phase out tariffs from applied rates in effect on July 1, 1991, including the U.S. General System of Preferences (GSP) and Canadian General Preference Treatment (GPT) rates
- Eliminate all tariffs between the United States and Canada by 1998
- Phase out and eliminate duties on U.S. and Canadian trade with Mexico within 15 years
- Prevent third-country intrusion through the use of certificates of origin
- Eliminate customs user fees and duty drawbacks
- Eliminate quotas unless grandfathered
- Prohibit product standards as a barrier to trade
- Eliminate agricultural tariffs and subsidies
- Eliminate Mexican tariffs on all U.S. exports within 10 years except for corn and beans, which will have a 15-year phaseout
- Expand government procurement markets
- Eliminate discrimination on laws related to service providers

National Treatment

NAFTA incorporates the fundamental *national treatment* obligation of the General Agreement on Tariffs and Trade (GATT). This commitment means that goods of other parties will be treated, in terms of tariffs and laws, as if they were domestic goods. The commitment extends to provincial and state measures.

> **SUCCESS STORY:** Taking note of Mexico's entry into GATT and then the potential success of NAFTA, Joao Perez Allende intuitively saw an opportunity for increased sales of heavy machinery. His research proved him right. The industries' growth rate was 15% with most of the sales by U.S. manufacturers. His initial sales were the popular CATs D5H and D6H tractors into the states of Oaxaca and Chiapas. He then expanded into Guatemala, Belize, and Honduras.

Temporary Entry of Business Persons

Taking into account the preferential trading relationship between the NAFTA countries, the agreement commits, on a reciprocal basis, to temporary entry into their respective territories of businesspersons who are citizens of Canada, Mexico, or the United States. Each country will grant temporary entry to four categories of businesspersons.

Business Visitors. Individuals engaged in international business activities for the purpose of conducting activities related to research and design, growth, manufacture and production, marketing, sales, distribution, after-sales service, and other general services.

Traders and Investors. Individuals who carry on substantial trade in goods or services between their own country and the country they wish to enter, provided that such persons are employed or operate in a supervisory or executive capacity or one that involves essential skills.

Intra-Company Transfers. Individuals employed by a company in a managerial or executive capacity or those who have specialized knowledge and who are transferred within that company to another NAFTA country.

Certain Categories of Professionals. Individuals who meet minimum educational requirements or who possess alternative credentials and who seek to engage in business activities at a professional level in that country.

HOT TIP: Temporary Entry Rules

**Ordinary Business
(non-NAFTA)**

U.S. Citizens	No papers up to 72 hours and 48 miles. For longer stays, a tourist card or Visa.
Mexican Citizens	Valid border crossing card (USINS) up to 72 hours and 25 miles. For longer stays, a visa.

NAFTA Business Visitors

Proof of Citizenship

Purpose Documentation, i.e., must be international in scope.

Employment outside territory of grantor

Each party grants temporary entry visa

Duty-Free Temporary Admission of Goods

The agreement allows businesspersons covered by NAFTA's *temporary entry* provisions to bring into a NAFTA country *professional equipment* and *tools of the trade* on a duty-free, temporary basis. These rules also cover the importation of commercial samples, certain types of advertising films, and goods imported for sports purposes or for display and demonstration.

Other rules provide that by 1998 all goods that are returned after repair or alteration in another NAFTA country will reenter duty-free.

Country of Origin Marking

Under NAFTA, *country of origin markings* are designed to minimize unnecessary costs and, to this end, any reasonable marking method can be used, including stickers, labels, tags, paint, etc. Markings must be conspicuous and permanent.

Marking exemptions are made for items that are incapable of being marked, cannot be marked prior to exportation without injury to goods, cannot be marked except at great expense, which would discourage exportation, a crude substance, and an original work of art.

Certificates of Origin

Each of the three countries have their own certificates for goods entering from non-NAFTA countries; however, Fig. 8-1 shows the common NAFTA *certificate of origin*. Note the key elements of the certificate are items 5, Description of goods; 6, HS tariff classification number; 7, preference; 8, producer; 9, net cost; and 10, country of origin. Figures 8-2 and 8-3 show the NAFTA certificate of origin continuation sheet and instruction sheet respectively.

Rules of Origin

Over a 15-year transition period, NAFTA eliminates all tariffs on goods originating in Canada, Mexico, and the United States. This is often of such financial benefit that foreign traders attempt to defeat preferential treatment by going around the free trade area and importing through the state that has the least external tariff. The solution is a rigorous set of *Rules of Origin* (ROOs) that define which goods are eligible.

DEPARTMENT OF THE TREASURY
UNITED STATES CUSTOMS SERVICE

Aproved through 12/31/96
OMB No. 1515-0204
See back of form for Paperwork Reduction Act Notice.

NORTH AMERICAN FREE TRADE AGREEMENT

CERTIFICATE OF ORIGIN

Please print or type 19 CFR 181.11, 181.22

1. EXPORTER NAME AND ADDRESS TAX IDENTIFICATION NUMBER:	2. BLANKET PERIOD *(DD/MM/YY)* FROM TO
3. PRODUCER NAME AND ADDRESS TAX IDENTIFICATION NUMBER:	4. IMPORTER NAME AND ADDRESS TAX IDENTIFICATION NUMBER:

5. DESCRIPTION OF GOOD(S)	6. HS TARIFF CLASSIFICATION NUMBER	7. PREFERENCE CRITERION	8. PRODUCER	9. NET COST	10. COUNTRY OF ORIGIN

I CERTIFY THAT:

• THE INFORMATION ON THIS DOCUMENT IS TRUE AND ACCURATE AND I ASSUME THE RESPONSIBILITY FOR PROVING SUCH REPRESENTATIONS. I UNDERSTAND THAT I AM LIABLE FOR ANY FALSE STATEMENTS OR MATERIAL OMISSIONS MADE ON OR IN CONNECTION WITH THIS DOCUMENT;

• I AGREE TO MAINTAIN, AND PRESENT UPON REQUEST, DOCUMENTATION NECESSARY TO SUPPORT THIS CERTIFICATE, AND TO INFORM, IN WRITING, ALL PERSONS TO WHOM THE CERTIFICATE WAS GIVEN OF ANY CHANGES THAT COULD AFFECT THE ACCURACY OR VALIDITY OF THIS CERTIFICATE;

• THE GOODS ORIGINATED IN THE TERRITORY OF ONE OR MORE OF THE PARTIES, AND COMPLY WITH THE ORIGIN REQUIREMENTS SPECIFIED FOR THOSE GOODS IN THE NORTH AMERICAN FREE TRADE AGREEMENT, AND UNLESS SPECIFICALLY EXEMPTED IN ARTICLE 411 OR ANNEX 401, THERE HAS BEEN NO FURTHER PRODUCTION OR ANY OTHER OPERATION OUTSIDE THE TERRITORIES OF THE PARTIES; AND

• THIS CERTIFICATE CONSISTS OF ____ PAGES, INCLUDING ALL ATTACHMENTS.

11.				
	11a. AUTHORIZED SIGNATURE		11b. COMPANY	
	11c. NAME *(Print or Type)*		11d. TITLE	
	11e. DATE *(DD/MM/YY)*	11f. TELEPHONE NUMBER	*(Voice)*	*(Facsimile)*

Customs Form 434 (121793)

Fig. 8-1. NAFTA certificate of origin

ROOs are required because each country maintains its own external tariffs on imports from other countries. Disparities between each nation's tariffs make ROOs necessary to prevent imports from third countries being shipped through one NAFTA partner into another in order to escape a higher tariff.

DEPARTMENT OF THE TREASURY UNITED STATES CUSTOMS SERVICE NORTH AMERICAN FREE TRADE AGREEMENT **CERTIFICATE OF ORIGIN CONTINUATION SHEET** 19 CFR 181.11, 181.22					
5. DESCRIPTION OF GOOD(S)	6. HS TARIFF CLASSIFICATION NUMBER	7. PREFERENCE CRITERION	8. PRODUCER	9. NET COST	10. COUNTRY OF ORIGIN

Customs Form 434A (121793)

Fig. 8-2. NAFTA certificate of origin (Continuation Sheet)

NAFTA reduces tariffs only for goods made in North America. For duty-free treatment, the goods must contain substantial North American content. ROOs rewards companies using North American parts and labor. ROOs prevents "free riders" from benefiting through minor processing or transshipment.

Mexico and Canada cannot be used as export platforms into the U.S. market. Goods containing nonregional components qual-

Instructions for the CF 434, as found on the form:

PAPERWORK REDUCTION ACT NOTICE: This information is needed to carry terms of the North American Free Trade Agreement (NAFTA). NAFTA requires that, upon request, an importer must provide Customs with proof of the exporter's written certification of the origin of the goods. The certification is essential to substantiate compliance with the rules of origin under the Agreement. You are required to give us this information to obtain a benefit.

Statement Required by 5 CFR 1320.21: The estimated average burden associated with this collection of information is 15 minutes per respondent or recordkeeper depending on individual circumstances. Comments concerning the accuracy of this burden estimate and suggestions for reducing this burden should be directed to U.S. Customs Service, Paperwork Management Branch, Washington, DC 20229, and to the Office of Management and Budget, Paperwork Reduction Project (1515-0204), Washington, DC 20503.

NORTH AMERICAN FREE TRADE AGREEMENT CERTIFICATE OF ORIGIN INSTRUCTIONS

For purposes of obtaining preferential tariff treatment, this document must be completed legibly and in full by the exporter and be in the possession of the importer at the time the declaration is made. This document may also be completed voluntarily by the producer for use by the exporter. Please print or type:

FIELD 1: State the full legal name, address (including country and legal tax identification number of the exporter. Legal taxation number is: in Canada, employer number or importer/exporter number assigned by Revenue Canada; in Mexico, federal taxpayer's registry number (RFC); and in the United States, employer's identification number or Social Security Number.

FIELD 2: Complete field if the Certificate covers multiple shipments of identical goods as described in Field #5 that are imported into a NAFTA country for a specified period of up to one year (the blanket period). "FROM" is the date upon which the Certificate becomes applicable to the good covered by the blanket Certificate (it may be prior to the date of signing this Certificate). "TO" is the date upon which the blanket period expires. The importation of a good for which preferential treatment is claimed based on this Certificate must occur between these dates.

FIELD 3: State the full legal name, address (including country) and legal tax identification number, as defined in Field #1, of the producer. If more than one producer's good is included on the Certificate, attach a list of additional producers, including the legal name, address (including country) and legal tax identification number, cross-referenced to the good described in Field #5. If you wish this information to be confidential, it is acceptable to state "Available to Customs upon request." If the producer and the exporter are the same, complete field with "SAME." If the producer is unknown, it is acceptable to state "UNKNOWN."

FIELD 4: State the full legal name, address (including country) and legal tax identification number, as defined in Field #1, of the importer. If the importer is not known, state "UNKNOWN," if multiple importers, state "VARIOUS."

FIELD 5: Provide a full description of each good. The description should be sufficient to relate it to the invoice description and to the Harmonized System (H.S.) description of the good. If the Certificate covers a single shipment of a good, include the invoice number as shown on the commercial invoice. If not known, indicate another unique reference number, such as the shipping order number.

FIELD 6: For each good described in Field #5, identify the H.S. tariff classification to six digits. If the good is subject to a specific rule of origin in Annex 401 that requires eight digits, identify to eight digits, using the H.S. tariff classification of the country into whose territory the good is imported.

FIELD 7: For each good described in Field #5, state which criterion (A through F) is applicable. The rules of origin are contained in Chapter Four and Annex 401. Additional rules are described in Annex 703.2 (certain agricultural goods), Annex 300-B Appendix 6 (certain textile goods) and Annex 308.1 (certain automatic data processing goods and their parts). **NOTE: In order to be entitled to preferential tariff treatment, each good must meet at least one of the criteria below.**

Preference Criteria

A   The good is "wholly obtained or produced entirely" in the territory of one or more of the NAFTA countries as referenced in Article 415. **Note: The purchase of a good in the territory does not necessarily render it "wholly obtained or produced."** If the good is an agricultural good, see also criterion F and Annex 703.2 *(Reference: Article 401(a) and 415)*

B   The good is produced entirely in the territory of one or more of the NAFTA countries and satisfies the specific rule of origin, set out in Annex 401, that applies to its tariff classification. The rule may include a tariff classification change, regional value-content requirement, or a combination thereof. The good must also satisfy all other applicable requirements of Chapter Four. If the good is an agricultural good, wee also criterion F and Annex 703.2. *(Reference: Article 401(b))*

C   The good is produced entirely in the territory of one or more of the NAFTA countries exclusively from originating materials. Under this criterion, one or more of the materials may fall within the definition of "wholly produced or obtained," as set out in Article 415. All materials used in the production of the good must qualify as "originating" by meeting the rules of Article 401(a) through (d). If the good is an agricultural good, see also criterion F and Annex 703.2. *Reference: Article 401(c).*

D   Goods are produced in the territory of one or more of the NAFTA countries but do not meet the applicable rule of origin, set out in Annex 401, because certain non-originating materials do not undergo the required change in tariff classification. The goods do nonetheless meet the regional value-content requirement specified in Article 401 (d). This criterion is limited to the following two circumstances:

1. The good was imported into the territory of a NAFTA country in an unassembled or disassembled form but was classified as an assembled good, pursuant to H.S. General Rule of Interpretation 2(a), or

2. The good incorporated one or more non-originating materials, provided for as parts under the H.S., which could not undergo a change in tariff classification because the heading provided for both the good and its parts and its parts and was not further subdivided into subheadings, or the subheading provided for both the good and its parts and was not further subdivided.

NOTE: This criterion does not apply to Chapters 61 through 63 of the H.S. *(Reference: Article 401(d))*

E   Certain automatic data processing goods and their parts, specified in Annex 308.1, that do not originate in the territory are considered originating upon importation into the territory of a NAFTA country from the territory of another NAFTA country when the most-favored-nation tariff rate of the good conforms to the rate established in Annex 308.1 and is common to all NAFTA countries. *(Reference: Annex 308.1)*

F   This good is an originating agricultural good under preference criterion A, B, or C above and is not subject to a quantitative restriction in the importing NAFTA country because it is a "qualifying good" as defined in Annex 703.2, Section A or B (please specify). A good listed in Appendix 703.2B.7 is also exempt from quantitative restrictions and is eligible for NAFTA preferential tariff treatment if it meets the definition of "qualifying good" in Section A of Annex 703.2. **NOTE 1: This criterion does not apply to goods that wholly originate in Canada or the United States and are imported into either country. NOTE 2: A tariff rate quota is not a quantitative restriction.**

FIELD 8:   For each good described in Field #5, state "YES" if you are the producer of the good. If you are not the producer of the good, state "NO" followed by (1), (2), or (3), depending on whether this certificate was based upon; (1) your knowledge of whether the good qualifies as an originating good; (2) your reliance on the producer's written representation (other than a Certificate of Origin) that the good qualifies as an originating good; or (3) a completed and signed Certificate for the good, voluntarily provided to the exporter by the producer.

FIELD 9:   For each good described in Field #5, where the good is subject to a regional value content (RVC) requirement, indicate "NC" if the RVC is calculated according to the net cost method; otherwise, indicate "NO." If the RVC is calculated over a period of time, further identify the beginning and ending dates (DD/MM/YY) of that period. *(Reference: Articles 402.1, 402.5)*

FIELD 10:   Identify the name of the country ("MX" or "US" for agricultural and textile goods exported to Canada; "US" or "CA" for all goods exported to Mexico; or "CA" or "MX" for all goods exported to the United States) to which the preferential rate of customs duty applies, as set out in Annex 302.2, in accordance with the Marking Rules or in each party's schedule of tariff elimination.

For all other originating goods exported to Canada, indicate appropriately "MX" or "US" if the goods originate in that NAFTA country, within the meaning of the NAFTA Rules of Origin Regulations, and any subsequent processing in the other NAFTA country does not increase the transaction value of the goods by more than seven percent; otherwise "JNT" for joint production. *(Reference: Annex 302.2)*

FIELD 11:   This field must be completed, signed, and dated by the exporter. When the Certificate is completed by the producer for use by the exporter, it must be completed, signed, and dated by the producer. The date must be the date the Certificate was completed and signed.

Customs Form 434 (121793)(Back)

Fig. 8-3. NAFTA certificate of origin (Instruction Sheet)

ify if sufficiently transformed in a NAFTA region to warrant change of tariff classification.

NAFTA ROOs work like this:

- Each product has a ROO that applies to it (found in Volume II of the NAFTA Agreement).
- Rules are organized according to the Harmonized Commodity Description and Coding System (HS). The first six digits of the HS classify products using the internationally recognized commodity code. To determine the tariff elimination schedule for a particular product, exporters must find out the product's HS number.
- There are two types of rules: tariff-shift and value-content. See Table 8-2 for an explanation of these rules.

Table 8-2. Examples of NAFTA Origin Rule Types.

Rule type	Description	Example
Tariff-Shift	All non-NAFTA inputs must be of a different tariff class than final product.	Wood molding (HS #4409) made from (HS #4403) imported. Because manufacturing process results in required HS heading shift.
	Rules state level of tariff shift required.	
	May require non-NAFTA input be a different HS chapter, heading, or item number.	
Value-Content	Set percent of value must be North American (usually coupled with a tariff-shift requirement).	If medicaments (HS #3004), for example, fail tariff-shift rule, they must contain 50–60% North American content to get preferential treatment.
	Some goods subject to value-content rule only when they fail to pass tariff-shift test.	

Examples of specific ROOs are:

CHAPTER 44: Wood And Articles Of Wood/44.01–44.21. A change to heading 44.01 through 44.21 from any other heading, including another heading within that group.

CHAPTER 30: Pharmaceutical Products/30.04: A change to subheading 30.04.10 through 30.04.90 from any other heading, except from heading 30.03; or a change to subheading 30.04.10 through 30.04.90 from any other subheading within heading 30.04, whether or not there is a change from any other heading, provided there is a regional value of not less than:

    a. 60 percent; transaction value method

    b. 50 percent; net cost method

HOT TIP:
Question: What is a good?
Answer: Whatever crosses the border.
Question: What is material?
Answer: Material is the components (stuff) that makes up a good.

How to Claim NAFTA Tariff

Using the Customs Entry Document and the certificate of origin follow these steps.

1. Classify the good.
2. Determine its HS number.
3. Determine its Tariff Staging Category.
4. Determine its Tariff difference.
5. Determine its Preference Criteria.
   A through F
6. If Preference B
   A. Chapter 4 Rule
      1. Is there a Tariff Shift?
      2. What is an RVC? Tariff Shift + RVC?
      3. What is its Regional Value Content?

The Preference criteria definitions are:

A. The good is "wholly obtained or produced entirely" in the territory of one or more of the NAFTA countries. NOTE: The purchase of a good in one territory does not necessarily render it "wholly obtained or produced." If the good is an agricultural good, see also criterion F.

B. The good is produced entirely in the territory of one or more of the NAFTA countries and satisfies the specific ROO set out in Annex 401 that applies to its tariff classification. The rule might include tariff classification change, regional value content requirement, or a combination thereof.

C. The good is produced entirely in the territory of one or more of the NAFTA countries exclusively from originating materials. Under this criterion, one or more of the materials cannot fall within the definition of "wholly produced or obtained." All materials used in the production of the good must qualify as "originating."

D. Goods are produced in the territory of one or more of the NAFTA countries but do not meet applicable ROO because certain non-originating materials do not undergo the required change in tariff classification. The goods do nonetheless meet the regional value-content requirement specified.

- The good was imported into the territory of a NAFTA country in an unassembled or disassembled form, but was classified as an assembled good.

- The good incorporated one or more non-originating materials, provided for as parts under the Harmonized Tariff System (HTS). HTS, which could not undergo a change in tariff classification because the heading provided for both the good and its parts was not further subdivided into subheadings, or the subheading provided for both the good and its parts and was not further subdivided.

E. Certain automatic data processing goods and their parts that do not originate in the territory are considered originating upon importation into the territory of a NAFTA country from the territory of another NAFTA country when the most-favored-nation tariff rate of the good conforms to the rate common to all NAFTA countries. (This will go into effect when the NAFTA parties establish a Common External Tariff [CXT] Schedule.)

F. The good is an originating agricultural good under preference criterion A, B, or C and is not subject to a quantitative restriction in the importing NAFTA country because it is a "qualifying good" (as defined in the NAFTA agreement).

Content Calculation

The content calculation is defined as follows:

- Tariff-shift: According to HS instructions
- Regional Value-Content (RVC) calculation
- *Transaction-Value (TV) Method*: Based on price paid or payable for good.

$$RVC = \frac{TV - VNM}{TV} \times 100$$

- *Net-cost (NC) Method*: Based on total cost minus costs of royalties, sales promotion, and packing and shipping. (Sets limit on allowable interest.)

$$RVC = \frac{NC - VNM}{NC} \times 100$$

- May use either method but net-cost must be used where transaction value is not accepted under GATT Customs valuation code. Net-cost must also be used for certain products, such as automotive.
- de minimus rule: If good otherwise fails, eligibility may still be OK if non-NAFTA content no more than 7% of price or total cost of good.

NAFTA by Industry

The NAFTA agreement goes beyond tariff reduction of general goods and specifies treatment by specific industries. The following is a cursory treatment.

Automotive Goods. NAFTA eliminates barriers to trade in North American automobiles, trucks, buses, and parts ("automotive goods") within the free trade area and eliminates investment restrictions in this sector over a 10-year transition period.

Textiles and Apparel. NAFTA textiles and apparel provisions take precedence over Multi-Fiber Arrangement (MFA) and other arrangements between NAFTA countries and provide for the immediate elimination or phase-out of duties that meet ROOs over a maximum period of 10 years. In addition, the United States will immediately remove import quotas on Mexican goods and will gradually phase out import quotas that do not meet such rules. Mexico will immediately eliminate tariffs on 20% of textile and apparel exports to the United States. Immediate duty-free treatment, by Mexico, of denim, underwear, sewing thread, and many household furnishings.

Textile and Apparel ROOs. Specific NAFTA ROOs define when imported textile or apparel goods qualify for preferential treatment. For most products, the "yarn forward" rule applies: goods must be made from yarn made in a NAFTA country in order to benefit from such treatment. The *fiber forward* rule provides for certain goods such as cotton and synthetic fiber yarns. Fiber forward means that the goods must be produced from fiber made in a NAFTA country. Preferential treatment is allowed for fabrics in short supply, such as silk, linen, and certain shirting fabrics.

Energy and Basic Petrochemicals. NAFTA recognizes the desirability of strengthening the important role that trade in energy and basic petrochemical goods play in the North American region and the need to enhance its role by sustained and gradual liberalization. The energy provisions incorporate and build on GATT disciplines regarding quantitative restrictions on imports and exports.

- A country cannot impose minimum or maximum import or export price requirements, subject to the same exceptions that apply to quantitative restrictions.

- Each country can administer export and import licensing systems provided that the systems are operated in a manner consistent with the provisions of the agreement.

- No country can impose a tax, duty, or charge on the export of energy or basic petrochemical goods unless the same tax, duty, or charge is applied to such goods when consumed domestically.

- Any import and export restrictions on energy trade will be limited to certain specific circumstances, such as to conserve exhaustible natural resources, deal with a short supply situation, or implement a price stabilization plan.

- Imports and exports may be restricted for national security reasons.

- Mexico reserves to the Mexican State goods, activities, and investments in Mexico in the oil, gas, refining, basic petrochemicals, nuclear, and electricity sectors.

- Investment in nonbasic petrochemical goods is governed by the general provisions of the agreement.

Agriculture. NAFTA sets out separate bilateral undertakings on cross-border trade in agricultural products, one between Canada and Mexico, and the other between Mexico and the United States. Both include a special transitional safeguard mechanism. The rules of the Canadian-U.S. FTA will continue to apply to agricultural trade between Canada and the United States.

Technical Standards

NAFTA is designed to create a harmonization of technical standards in the three countries and prohibit countries from using technical standards as a barrier to market entry.

Government Procurement

NAFTA opens a significant portion of the government procurement market in each NAFTA country on a nondiscriminatory basis to suppliers from other NAFTA countries for goods, services, and construction services.

Investment

NAFTA removes significant investment barriers, provides fair treatment of investors, eliminates government requirements that distort business decisions, and provides a dispute settlement mechanism for investors.

Services

NAFTA establishes a set of principles governing services trade. Virtually all services are covered with the exception of aviation, transport, maritime, and basic telecommunications.

Telecommunications

NAFTA provides that public telecommunications networks ("public networks") and services are to be available on reasonable and nondiscriminatory terms and conditions for firms or individuals who use those networks for the conduct of their business. These uses include the provision of enhanced or value-added telecommunications services and intracorporate communications. However, the operation and provision of public networks and services have not been made subject to NAFTA.

Financial Services

NAFTA establishes a principles-based approach to disciplining government measures regulating financial services. This section covers measures affecting financial institutions in the banking, insurance, and securities sectors, as well as other financial services.

Intellectual Property

NAFTA embraces copyright, patent, and intellectual property laws, binding the three countries to existing international agreements and builds upon GATT and other international treaties.

Transformation: Maquiladoras, FTZ, and Bonded Ware-house

To claim NAFTA tariff, goods must in general have 60% North American content. Transformation of goods to obtain this content can be achieved in three ways: in a Maquiladora, a foreign trade zone, or a bonded warehouse (the later two were explained earlier in Chapter 7). The Mexican Maquiladora Program, created in 1966 and still in effect, creates free zones in any location in Mexico where labor may be added to a production-sharing process. It is a business form where goods and capital equipment can be imported into Mexico duty free. Duties on the exported product originally were imposed only on the value-added labor content. Now, all products must meet the 60% regional content (average) and duties are no longer assessed on value-added labor.

OTHER EXISTING TRADE ARRANGEMENTS

Trade among Central and Latin American nations has skyrocketed in recent years, rising threefold from $7 billion in 1983 to $26 billion in 1994. Much of the gains can be attributed toward the movement to reduce tariffs regionally. In addition to NAFTA, there already exists 10 regional trade arrangements, each of which is outlined in the following sections.

Andean Common Market. The Andean Pact, which began with the Cartagena Agreement in 1969, is one of the oldest free trade agreements in existence today. The original membership of Bolivia, Chile (since withdrawn), Columbia, Ecuador, and Peru now includes Venezuela. This market of $73 million, finalized in 1993, establishes a four-level CXT.

The Caribbean Basin Initiative (CBI). This trade arrangement is a 12-year-old program intended to stimulate trade with about 20 Caribbean nations. The centerpiece of the agreement is that almost all goods imported from the region without regard for quotas can enter the United States free of tariffs. Contact the Office of Latin America and Caribbean (OLAC) Facts in a Flash for CBI Information or call (202) 482-2521 or (202) 482-2527.

Association of Caribbean States. Launched on January 1, 1995, this 200-million-strong market provides preferential tariffs to Antigua and Barbuda, Cuba, Mexico, Dominca, Nicaragua, Bahamas, Dominican Republic, Barbados, Paraguay, Belize, El Salvador, Grenada, St. Kitts-Nevis, St. Lucia, Guyana, St. Vincent and The Grenadines, Haiti, Surinam, Columbia, Honduras, Trinidad and Tobago, Costa Rica, and Venezuela.

Caribbean Common Market (Caricom). This 5.5 million consumer market was created on July 4, 1973 and includes Antigua and Barbuda, Bahamas, Barbados, Belize, Dominica, Grenada, Guyana, Jamaica, St. Vincent and The Grenadines, and Trinidad and Tobago.

Caricom-Bolivia Free Trade Agreement. This free trade arrangement on selected products was launched January 1, 1995 and includes most of the same nations as Caricom plus Bolivia.

Caricom-Venezuela Free Trade Agreement. Again only applying to certain products, this arrangement is the same as Caricom with the addition of Venezuela.

Central American Common Market. This customs union composing a market of 28 million people began December 13, 1960 and includes Costa Rica, El Salvador, Guatemala, Honduras, and Nicaragua.

Group of Three. This free trade area of 141 million includes only Mexico, Columbia, and Nicaragua.

Latin American Integration Association (LAIA). This is a trade preference association formed in August 1980. Its 371 million strong market consists of Argentina, Bolivia, Brazil, Chile, Columbia, Ecuador, Mexico, Paraguay, Peru, Uruguay, and Venezuela.

Mercosur (Southern Cone Common Market). Composed of Brazil, Argentina, Paraguay, and Uruguay, this association was launched on March 26, 1991.

Organization of Eastern Caribbean States. This is a *Customs Union* of Antigua and Barbuda, Dominica, Grenada, Montserrat, St. Kitts-Nevis, St. Lucia, St. Vincent and The Grenadines.

NAFTA ENLARGEMENT

NAFTA is currently a single market composed of the three North American states. However, integration of the other 31 (less Cuba) states is moving ahead. At the "Miami Summit" in December 1994, the leaders of 34 of the 35 democratic nations of the Americas signed a declaration to negotiate by the year 2005 a *Free Trade Area of the Americas* (FTAA).

The area of no trade barriers would embrace a market of 750 million people and stretch from Alaska to the tip of Argentina. One method of achieving FTAA would be through the expansion of NAFTA. The first step would be the admittance of Chile. Another route would be the merger and linking of the other subregional trade arrangements with the FTAA.

9

Doing Business in New Europe

NEW EUROPE REFERS TO THE CHANGING EUROPEAN MARKET, INCLUDING the enlargement of the European Union (EU) and the opportunities offered by the newly independent states of Middle- and Eastern-Europe. The trade potential of the EU and the European Free Trade Area (EFTA) is shown in Table 9-1.

This chapter discusses the following important elements of doing business with the EU, EFTA, and the enlarging EU. It also looks at the trade potential of the newly independent states, how to do business in the single market, and how to do business with the New Russia. For additional information call (800) USA-TRADE.

THE EUROPEAN UNION

The 12-nation EU originally consisting of Belgium, France, West Germany, Italy, Luxembourg, United Kingdom, Spain, Netherlands, Denmark, Greece, Portugal, and Ireland established a single market when they agreed to a common external tariff (CXT) about 1968. Subsequently, they harmonized most internal tariff and non-tariff rules related to their so-called "four freedoms": free movement of goods, services, persons, and capital.

These four freedoms amount to a principle that individual EU member states may not adopt measures that have the effect of re-

Table 9-1. Western Europe Trading Potential.

Country	Population (millions)	National (income) (bn $)		National (income) (per head $)
		European Union		
Germany	61.2	1,059.4		17,310
France	55.9	773.5		13,837
United Kingdom	57.1	730.0		12,785
Italy	57.4	687.1		11,970
Spain	38.8	246.6		6,356
Netherlands	14.8	203.0		13,716
Belgium/ Luxembourg	9.9	128.9		13,020
Denmark	5.1	88.2		17,294
Greece	10.0	42.4		4,243
Portugal	10.4	33.2		3,192
Ireland	3.5	23.6		6,743
Total	324.1	4,015.9	Ave:	11,123
		European Free Trade Association		
Switzerland	6.5	161.3		24,815
Sweden	8.4	137.5		16,369
Austria	7.6	102.4		13,474
Finland	5.0	74.3		14,860
Norway	4.2	70.2		16,714
Iceland	0.25	3.3		13,200
Total	31.95	549.0	Ave:	16,572
			Total Ave Europe	12,940

Compiled using 1988 data found in International Monetary Fund, *International Financial Statistics*, April 1990, Washington.

stricting or interfering with intracommunity trade, subject to specific exceptions provided by EU law.

In practice, the EU is a modern evolution of a customs union that expanded to a common market then became a political union with the signing of the Maastricht Treaty in 1992.

EUROPEAN FREE TRADE ASSOCIATION

The EFTA is a regional grouping established in 1960 by the Stockholm Convention, headquartered in Geneva, and now comprising

HISTORY NOTE: The EU had its beginning in 1951 when the Treaty of Paris established the Coal and Steel Community between Belgium, France, the Federal German Republic, Italy, Luxembourg, and Holland. In 1957, the European Economic Community (ECC) was formed when the members of the Coal and Steel Community signed the Treaty of Rome. The more popular term *European Community* (EC) is the organization that resulted from the 1967 Treaty of Fusion that merged the secretariat (the "Commission") and the intergovernmental executive body (the "Council") of the older EEC with those of the European Coal and Steel Community (ECSC) and the European Atomic Energy Community (EURATOM), which was established to develop nuclear fuel and power for civilian purposes.

SUCCESS STORY: Caroline Rogers knew American products were very fashionable in France: Levis go for $80, Van's shoes for $100, Zippo lighters for $25, etc. The Harley Davidson motorcycle is also one of those very fashionable products. The price for a used Harley starts at $8000. Caroline started her business by buying used Harleys through the local city want ads for $2000 to $3000 (depending on model) and had a mechanic check them out. Her European import price was $3300 to $4500 with a retail price of $5700 to $7100. She sold 10 a month and was profitable in her first year.

Austria, Iceland, Norway, Sweden, and Switzerland. Finland is an associate member. Denmark and the United Kingdom were formerly members, but later withdrew from EFTA when they joined the EC in 1973. Portugal, also a former member, withdrew from EFTA in 1986 when it joined the EU. EFTA member countries have gradually eliminated tariffs on manufactured goods originating and traded within EFTA. Agricultural products, for the most part, are not included on the EFTA schedule for internal tariff reductions. Each member country maintains its own external tariff schedule and each has concluded a trade agreement with the European Community (EC) that provides for the mutual elimination of tariffs for most manufactured goods except for a few sensitive products. As a result, the EC and EFTA form what is now called the de facto European Economic Area (EEA).

TRADE POTENTIAL OF THE NEWLY INDEPENDENT STATES

The break-up of the Soviet Union offers practically virgin territory and excellent opportunities for market expansion. The peaceful revolution of 1989 saw the beginning of a movement from Marxism toward market theory. But in Central and Eastern Europe *perestroika* is suffering in its attempt to leap forward from state enterprise to private ownership. Because there are few entrepreneurs and little private capital, it is more likely that the immediate mechanism adopted by these nations will be a hybrid mixture of Marxist-market, which takes the best of the two theories for the good of the economic growth of the regional nations. The ultimate change to privatization could take three or more decades.

The year 1989 was one of the most significant years of the twentieth century. It was the year the Berlin Wall crumbled, signifying the peaceful revolution of central European nations retreating from the nonmarket economics. Even more significant was 1991 when the Soviet Union splintered into individual parts. It was also the year the world sifted into two worlds: the industrial "haves" and the underdeveloped "have nots."

Using statistics from the 1994 *The World Fact Book* (U.S. Central Intelligence Agency, Washington, DC) and my own comments, I have put together short descriptions of the newly independent states (NIS) of the former Soviet Union (FSU).

Central Europe

- **Poland:** per capita GNP—$4680; population 38.6 million; aggressive; continuing transition to market economy; racing to export; big debt mostly forgiven by Western banks; be creative
- **Czech Republic:** per capita GNP—$7200; population 10.4 million; now two countries; healthiest; some political turmoil; most industrial before WWII; has a capitalistic memory; aggressive; wants in the EU
- **Slovakia:** per capita GNP—$5800; population 5.4 million; wants Western goods; will import; privatizing more than 3000 large enterprises; welcomes all types of investment
- **Hungary:** per capita GNP—$5500; population 10.3 million; aggressive; big debt; racing for Western markets; will import; has currency in foreign banks

- **Romania:** Per capita GNP—$2700; population 23.2 million; cheap wages ($15/month); Western goods are scarce; making progress
- **Serbia and Montenegro:** per capita GNP—$1000; population 10.7 million; civil war; turmoil; no bank ranking
- **Croatia:** per capita GNP—$4500; population 4.7 million; civil war; turmoil; bank ranking slipping fast
- **Bosnia:** per capita GNP—not applicable; population 4.6 million; Civil war; turmoil; bank ranking low
- **Bulgaria:** per capita GNP—$3800; population 8.8 million; high debt load but has potential; joining EU
- **Albania:** per capita GNP—$1000; population 3.4 million; least opportunity, but with 20% unemployed, plenty of labor

Eastern Europe

- **Estonia:** per capita GNP—$5480; population 1.6 million; reform oriented; business minded; industrial; infrastructure; entrepot of high-tech services and industry
- **Latvia:** per capita GNP—$4810; population 2.7 million; corridor for former Soviet Union; enthusiasm for things Western; moving to privatize; attracting foreign investors for full ownership and repatriation of profits
- **Lithuania:** per capita GNP—$3240; population 3.8 million; moving toward Scandinavian-style economy; limited comprehension of market economy; some privatization
- **Belarus (Byelorussia):** per capita GNP—$5890; population 10.4 million; one of the most developed of the former Soviet states, strong machine building and agricultural sectors; privatizing just beginning
- **Ukraine:** per capita GNP—$3960; population 51.8 million; second most powerful new nation; fertile lands produce ¼ of former Soviet output; liberalizing quickly; diversified heavy industry
- **Georgia:** per capita GNP—$1390; population 5.7 million; tourism, citrus, industrial sector; Black Sea Access
- **Maldova:** per capita GNP—$3650; population 4.4 million; convertible currency; privatizing

- **Russia:** per capita GNP—$5190; population 150 million people on a land mass three times greater than the United States; see the section "Doing Business in Russia" later in this chapter
- **Azerbaijan:** per capita GNP—$2040; population 7 million; large oil producer; grows cotton, grapes, and silk
- **Kazakhstan:** per capita GNP—$3510; population 16.6 million; large oil and coal producer; grew one-third of former Soviet Union's wheat
- **Kyrgystan:** per capita GNP—$2440; population 4.3 million; mines coal and mercury ore; produces cotton
- **Tasikistan:** per capita GNP—$1180; population 5.1 million; produced 11% of the former Soviet Union's cotton
- **Turkmenistan:** per capita GNP—$3330; population 3.5 million; largest sulfur deposits in the world; largest cotton producer
- **Uzbekistan:** per capita GNP—$2430; population 19.9 million; grows 67% of the former Soviet Union's cotton

ENLARGEMENT OF THE EUROPEAN UNION

The four fundamental freedoms of the EU provide the framework for limitless boundary expansion and formation of a new Europe. Over the next decades, the EU will welcome new members, the alacrity depending on economic and political reforms in Eastern Europe and the republics of the former Soviet Union.

Standing in the wings to join the EU are many nations that see benefits to the economic integration. The EFTA members as well as nations of central Europe are all candidates.

The agreement forming the EEA between the EU and the EFTA countries signified the next step towards the economic integration of all Europe. Already three of the EFTA nations: Sweden, Finland, and Austria have formally joined the EU. Applications to join the EU are pending for Turkey (1987) and Switzerland (1992). The people of Norway have rejected joining. The EU has also entered into bilateral association agreements with Poland and Hungary, and is exploring the ways to integrate these nations as well as the Czech and Slovak republics into the EU. It is likely that the EU will expand to a customs union of at least 20 countries early in the next century. A "Greater Europe," stretching from the Atlantic to the Urals will only develop into an organized power if it is built around a stable nucleus capable of speaking and acting as one.

HOW TO DO BUSINESS IN THE SINGLE MARKET

The Single European Act (SEA) contained a series of amendments to the Treaty of Rome, which made it easier to negotiate the directives needed to make the single market work. The key innovation in the SEA was to extend the use of majority voting in place of unanimity in the EU's main decision-making body. Without majority voting, it would have been impossible to have passed the more than 280 separate items of legislation required to be enacted to eliminate internal EU frontiers and have the single market ready by the end of 1992. The measures already adopted relate to the:

- Liberalization of public procurement
- Harmonization of taxation
- Liberalization of capital markets
- Standardization, due to a new approach to certification and testing and recognition of the equivalence of national standards
- Abolition of technical barriers (freedom to exercise an activity and recognition of the equivalence of training qualifications) and physical barriers (elimination of border checks) to the free movement of individuals
- Creation of an environment that encourages business cooperation by harmonizing company law and approximating legislation on intellectual and industrial property

National Treatment

A White Paper issued in 1985 consolidated the principle of mutual recognition of national laws and regulations. This eliminated the need to create a new uniform body of EU regulations. Harmonization at the EU level was only necessary where basic health, safety, or the environment were too divergent.

Customs Duties

The EU established a common commercial policy towards third countries through adoption of a Common Customs Tariff (CCT), which applies equally to all nonEU goods entering any part of the EU for the first time. The imported product is eligible for *free circulation* within the Union once customs duties are paid and all customs formalities completed. Free circulation means the goods will be treated in the same manner as goods of EU origin and are able to move within the EU without incurring further customs import charges. Steps in assessing customs duties include:

- Identifying the tariff classification of the goods in the CCT and the rate that applies for that classification
- Establishing the value of the goods for customs purposes
- Applying the CCT rate to the customs value of the goods, subject to any preferential rates that might exist if the goods originate from particular countries

Valuation

EU valuation is based on the principles of the General Agreement on Tariffs and Trade (GATT) Valuation Code. The customs value is usually based on C.I.F. (cost, insurance, and freight) and should include all payments by the buyer made as a condition of the sale of the goods. This usually means that royalties, license payments, or sales commissions accruing to the exporter on resale of the goods by the importer are included in the valuation.

There are six methods of ascertaining the value, and each must be applied in turn until a suitable valuation is achieved. These alternative methods ensure that a value can be put on goods that are, for instance, sold at an undervalue, whether because the sale is part of a barter transaction or because it is between related companies.

Customs Procedures

The EU has adopted the international harmonized system of commodity description and coding and applies the annex on origin rules to the International Convention on the Simplification and Harmonization of Customs Procedures. The test, wherein two or more countries are involved in the manufacture of a product, is "origin," which is determined by where the substantial process or operation was performed. Proof of origin rests with the importer.

As of 1988, the free movement of goods meant goods were no longer subject to checks. Some 30 documents had been reduced to one—the so-called Single Administrative Document (SAD). However, on January 1, 1993, the SAD was no longer required for internal movement but will be required for goods crossing an EU external border with a nonmember country.

Nonmember Documentation

The usual documents on commercial shipments to the EU countries irrespective of value or means of transport are: the commercial invoice, bill of lading, certificate of origin (when requested by the importer or required for certain items), the packing list, and various special certificates (health, sanitary, etc.), depending on the nature of the goods being shipped or on the request of the importer.

Commercial invoices should provide a clear and precise description of the product, terms of sale, and all details necessary to establish the full C.I.F. price.

Rules of Origin

The EU has established rules of origin (ROOs) within the context of its common external commercial policy as a key to any differential treatment applied to imports from nonmember countries. For example, the origin of goods is a necessary concept to apply preferential tariff treatment, to charge antidumping duties, or to enforce quantitative quotas.

The question of origin is relevant for extra-Union trade, at importation as well as at exportation, but not for intra-Union trade, which is subject to specific rules (free circulation). In intra-Union trade, the question of origin can only be pertinent in the case where measures of commercial policy (surveillance or protective measures) are decided by the EU with regard to certain goods originating in third countries and put into free circulation in one of the member states.

The ROOs applicable at importation into the EU or at exportation of goods from the EU belong in two different categories: preferential and non-preferential.

Preferential. The EU has some 24 different preferential trading regimes covering more than 150 countries. Descriptions of the major groups follow.

- The six EEC-EFTA agreements (Iceland, Norway, Sweden, Finland, Austria and Switzerland) cover both exports and imports.

- The Mediterranean Agreements cover all the Mediterranean countries (including Jordan and the Occupied Territories), but exclude Libya and Turkey. All cover imports; three cover exports (Cyprus, Malta, and Israel).

- The Lome Convention and the linked arrangement for some overseas countries and territories cover most of Africa south of the Sahara (except the Union of South Africa), the Caribbean Islands (formerly dependent on Community Member States), and former dependencies in the Pacific— all of these in relation to imports.

- The Generalized System of Preferences is for the remaining developing countries.

Non-preferential. The non-preferential ROOs, which also have to be applied when preferential rules are not fulfilled in a preferential context of exchanges, are laid down in Regulation (EEC) No. 802/68. Goods wholly obtained or produced in one country are considered as originating in that country. For goods produced in more than one country, origin is established in the country in which *the last substantial process or operation* that is *economically justified* was performed, having been carried out in an *undertaking equipped for the purpose*, and *resulting in the manufacture of a new product or representing an important stage of manufacture*. These four italicized conditions are cumulative and are to be taken in conjunction with one another.

Certificates of origin are not required on most commercial and industrial goods exported from the United States to Europe. However, Spain requires certificates of origin on all products with the exception of motor vehicles, and other countries, such as France, require it on certain other goods (textile products).

Value-Added Tax Harmonization

Each EU member has a standard value-added tax (VAT) that is assessed on the sale of both domestic and imported products. The VAT is a sales or consumption tax imposed on buyers on the sale of goods, which includes the beginning of the production and distribution cycle to the final sale to the consumer.

The Union exporter and importer of any given item is required to file a declaration with their local VAT authority in their home country. VAT authorities in member states cooperate closely to ensure that frauds are not committed. A standard VAT rate is 15% to 25% with a range of exceptions for essential goods, such as food, medicines, books, transport, etc., which qualify for a lower rate. Table 9-2 shows these rates for the 12-member Union.

Currently, payment of VAT is made in the country where a product or service is finally sold. However, after 1996, it is to be paid in the country of origin. In other words, firms can now buy, sell, and invest in any member state without having to go through checks or formalities when crossing intra-Union borders.

Table 9-2. VAT Rates in the 12-Member Community.

	Standard[1] (%)	Reduced[2] (%)	Increased[3] (%)	Other[4] (%)
Belgium	19.5	12		
Denmark	25			
France	18.6	5.5		
Germany	15	7		
Greece	18	8		
Ireland	21	10		0
Italy	19	9	38	
Luxembourg	15	6		
Netherlands	17.5	6		
Portugal	16	5	30	
Spain	15	6	28	
United Kingdom	17.5			0

[1] A standard rate applies on most products. Exceptions are noted in other footnotes.
[2] Reduced rates are levied on basic necessities, such as foodstuffs, electricity, heat, lumber, books, etc., but items affected and rates vary among countries.
[3] Increased rates are generally levied on luxury items including perfumes, jewelry, hi-fi and stereo equipment, cameras, cars, etc.
[4] Zero rates of duty are applied by some EU countries on foodstuffs and medicines.

Citizens can obtain goods for their own use in any EU state and take them across borders without being subject to controls or held liable for tax. For importers from non-Union nations, the VAT should be applied on the C.I.F. value plus the duty charged on the particular good. Thus:

[C.I.F. + duty (C.I.F. × duty rate)] + [VAT] = total cost to importers

Recovery of VAT

In as much as the VAT must be paid on entry into the EU and again collected at the point of sale, nonmember exporters can (with exceptions) recover any VAT paid on entry.

Common Currency

Targeting 1999 at the latest, the EU expects to have a common currency. The composition of the ECU (1991) is a basket of the 12 currencies dominated by a 30% Deutsche mark share and 20% French franc share. All other currencies are represented, but in shares ranging from as much as 12% UK pound to as little as 1% Portuguese escudo.

How the EU Standards Process Works

The EU has developed hundreds of new product standards that are an important condition of sale. In fact, standards are one of the principal pieces of the internal market program. Europeanwide standards are replacing divergent national product standards. The advantage is that a manufacturer will only have to meet one Europeanwide standard and will not have to make costly changes to meet 12 different national standards.

Mutual recognition of national standards applies to nonsafety aspects of unregulated products (those not covered by EUwide directives, such as paper and furniture). Mutual recognition applies both for intra-European trade and trade among the EU and other countries.

The impetus for the harmonization of technical standards came in the mid-1980s and is detailed in the EU's *new approach* directives. As shown in Table 9-3, there are 15 new approach directives covering such areas as machinery, toy safety, construction products, personal protective equipment, and medical devices.

Markings

For products within their scope, EU's new approach directives require that an EU mark be affixed to the product (or its packaging, under certain circumstances) to signify that the product complies with all relevant EU legal requirements specified in appropriate directives. The EU Commission has proposed legislation to harmo-

Table 9-3. New EU Standards Approach Directives.

Adopted	Implementation date	Transition period
Toys	1/1/90	None
Simple pressure vessels	7/1/90	7/1/92
Construction products	6/27/91	Indefinite
Electromagnetic compatibility	1/1/92	12/31/95
Gas appliances	1/1/92	12/31/95
Personal protective equipment	7/1/92	12/31/92
Machinery	12/31/92	12/31/94 (except for ROPS, FOPS, & industrial trucks (12/31/96)
Nonautomatic weighing instruments	1/1/93	1/1/2003
Active implantable medical devices	1/1/93	12/31/94

nize EU marking requirements. However, until this legislation is adopted, manufacturers must continue to comply with the marking requirements in specific directives.

Products bearing EU marks are guaranteed free circulation within the EU market. It does not eliminate the need to obtain other marks for the product, however, which might be recognized or expected by purchasers. These marks might include performance marks, product or process quality marks, and marks indicating environmental friendliness or recyclability.

Quality System Registration

While the EU's new approach legislation focuses on product approval, there are many instances in which the independent assessment of a manufacturer's design and/or production process is also an important factor in marketing in the Union. Process approval in Europe generally means registration by an independent third party to the relevant standard in the ISO 9000 (series) (quality management and quality assurance standards).

ISO 9000 (series) registration is becoming increasingly important in EU markets, both in legal terms and as a competitive factor. Compliance with ISO 9000 (series) standards is referenced in specific EU product safety directives as a component of the product approval process. In a growing number of sectors, European purchasers can require suppliers to attest that they have an approved quality system in place as a condition for purchase. ISO 9000 (series) registration can also be a competitive factor in product areas where safety or liability are concerns.

To find out more about EU standards, testing, and certification, check the list of directives and business guides available through SIMIS; obtain copies of applicable EUwide directives or regulations; determine if EUwide regulations cover your product; check the EU technical requirements; check whether European national standards apply; check if any European standards are referenced; check international standards; and obtain copies of European Standards (see Chapter 7).

Distribution

Great care should be taken when selecting an importing distributor in Europe, because in many EU countries, statutory provisions or traditionally developed doctrines exist that restrict the freedom of contract in the distributorship area. One such restriction is the rule that a distributorship agreement cannot be terminated or renewed, even in accordance with its terms, without payment of special compensation to the distributor unless the distributor has been found to have committed certain statutorily defined breaches. EU law is clear in that it forbids absolute territorial limits and resale price maintenance provisions in distribution contracts.

A sales subsidiary is an alternative that should be considered in lieu of an importing distributor. With the advent of the single market, a foreign exporter need not be established in each European country; rather a sales subsidiary in one country can transship to the entire EU and might be more profitable in the long run.

DOING BUSINESS IN NEW RUSSIA

Russia is the most politically powerful of the independent states of the FSU. It has instituted sweeping economic reforms, including broad privatization. It is a nation of 148.6 million (1991) people, or

51.4% of the FSU, with precious natural resources, a huge consumer market, and an educated work force. With massive shortages of consumer as well as capital goods, it is seeking many joint-venture opportunities. Investors can now buy hard currency and repatriate profits and dividends. Foreign trade activity has not only been authorized, it is encouraged.

In 1992, Russia gained admission to the International Monetary Fund (IMF) and the World Bank. In practical terms, this means there is hard-currency credit available for imports. Nevertheless, many transactions involve barter trade.

Hot Tip: For U.S. exporters, the Department of Commerce has developed American Business Centers in Moscow and St. Peters-burg. To make use of these valuable assistance facilities, contact BISNIS Assistance, Room H-7413, U.S. Department of Commerce, 14th Street and Constitution Avenue, N.W., Washington, DC 20230; telephone (202) 482-4655 or fax (202) 482-2293.

Administration

Russia is divided administratively into provinces (Oblast and Krai), metropolitan cities (Moscow and St. Petersburg), 16 autonomous republics with their own independent governments, 5 autonomous regions, and 10 national republics.

Industrial Profile

Russia manufactures approximately 62% of all machinery made in the FSU and nearly 60% of the FSU's crude steel (Russia is the world's largest steel producer after Japan). Other key industries are chemicals, timber and wood products, paper, and nonferrous metals. State monopolies still dominate in all major industries. Nearly 15% of Russia's industries are defense related.

Importing into Russia

Foreign goods destined for Russia are potentially subject to three Russian levies, which are collected at Russian customs entry points: an import duty/tariff, a VAT, and an excise tax.

Tariffs are calculated at the good's customs value (CV), which includes any applicable shipping and handling terms that are included in the price of the shipment (e.g., C.I.F. or F.O.B.), in addition to the stated transaction price of the particular goods. The VAT is applied to nearly all goods imported into Russia and is calculated as a percentage (generally 23%) of the sum of the good's CV and, where applicable, the excise duty. An excise tax is calculated as a percentage of the CV of the goods.

Customs Fees. Every importer of goods into Russia must pay customs fees. Customs clearance fees depend on the customs regimes applicable to the commodity for imports and other factors. Customs fees are generally paid equal to 0.1% of the CV (paid in rubles). An additional 0.05% of the customs fee is to be paid in foreign currency for regimes of free circulation, reexport, duty-free shops, customs storage, and temporary import and export. Processing fees equal to 0.1% of CV under the regime of "commodity in transit."

Goods Transiting CIS Countries. The Commonwealth of Independent States (CIS) has established a CIS Customs Union so goods originating in one CIS country are not subject to import taxes upon import to another CIS country. Goods of any origin can transit through one CIS country to a destination in another CIS country without incurring customs fees in the country of transit. To establish CIS origin, goods must undergo "sufficient processing," which is essentially determined to be a change of the first four digits of the commodity code classification.

Packing. Special packing requirements for shipping goods to Russia are not required, but proper packing is essential to ensure the goods reach the destination in good condition. Containers should be locked, have heavy-duty seals, and include proper documentation noting that anyone opening at a point other than the point of customs clearance is responsible for breaking the original seal and must replace it with a valid new seal. Roads and highways can cause considerable damage if extra care is not taken to block and brace goods.

Labeling. In addition to any special handling instructions on packages, the exporter should include the shipper's mark, country of origin, weight marking in pounds and kilograms, number of packages and sizes of cases (in inches and centimeters), size (gross and net weights and dimensions), handling marks (international pictorial symbols), package number, cautionary marks, port of entry, and labels for hazardous materials.

Documention. Russians place a great deal of faith in official seals; therefore, you are encouraged to stamp documents with your company seal. In addition to the documents found in Chapter 4, you might be required to provide an import license, steamship certificate, certificate of quality, certificate of value, and certificate of safety.

Other Recommendations for Shippers. Consignees should be fully informed of the expected time of arrival and have all necessary documentation ready to clear customs. Do not expect truck drivers to know who is the rightful owner of the goods.

Import Licenses. In order to import goods into Russia, the company receiving the goods from abroad must have one of two types of import licenses issued on a "one commodity-one license" principle. A *general license* is valid for one year from the date of issuance regardless of the number of transactions. A *one-off license* is issued for a single transaction to be exercised within 12 months upon issue (in some cases lengthened). Licenses are approved through the Ministry of Foreign Relations (MFR).

Highest Potential Imports to Russia. Russia has an almost insatiable market for data processing machines, telecommunications equipment, medical supplies, pollution control equipment, agricultural machinery, and computer software. Of course, grain and other agricultural products such as animal feed, wheat, and maize are mainstays of their importing business. Goods imported from the United States receive most-favored-nation rates. The Russian government imposes a VAT on most goods sold in Russia, including imported goods. The VAT on imported goods is calculated as a percentage of the sum of the CV of the good, the imported tariff, and the excise tax. Exemptions are available for certain investors.

Exports from Russia

Russia is a nation rich in natural resources. Hydrocarbons, 40% of the world's natural gas, 50% of the world's timber, and inorganic chemicals are available, as well as iron ore, metals, and an excellent machinery production capacity. Companies exporting from Russia are required to pay an average export tariff of about 20% on a number of goods and services sold in cash transactions and an average of about 30% for those sold on noncash (barter) transactions.

Russia has a harmonized system for export licensing on "strategic raw materials" and products that are of long-term importance to the country. All quotas were removed as of January 1, 1995. Russian exporters are required to sell 50% of their export earnings on one of the interbank currency exchanges within seven days.

Banks

Banking activities are regulated by the Russian Central Bank (RCB), which currently has more than 2300 commercial banks licensed with the RCB. About 20 to 30 of these, including Vnesheconombank, the former state bank of the Soviet Union are considered sound, professional banks.

Many foreign banks have received a "general license" allowing them to accept deposits and make loans to both Russian and foreign clients with minimal limitations. Banks now certified and having offices in Moscow are Bank of America, Chase Manhattan, NorWest Bank, Citicorp/Citibank, Chemical Bank, Bank of New York, Credit Lyonnais (France), Italian Commerica, Societe General, Generale Bank, Dresden Bank (Germany), and ING (Netherlands).

Import/Export Platforms

To assist investors and joint venturers, Russia has established two major free trade (economic) zones: Kaliningrad and Nakhodka. Those contemplating exporting to Russia and anticipating special rates might consider shipping through the free zones or bonded warehouses to ensure expeditious processing.

Imported goods can remain in a bonded warehouse for up to two years without paying duties. A third year can be arranged.

Travel Information

A passport and a visa are required for business travel. Without a visa, travelers cannot register at hotels and will be required to leave the country immediately via the route by which they entered. For visa applications, contact the Russian Consulate at 1825 Phelps Place, N.W., Washington, DC 20008 or telephone (202) 939-8907, 8911, 8913, 8918 or contact the consulates in New York, San Francisco, or Seattle for current information on tourist or business visa requirements.

Medical care in Russia is limited and doctors and hospitals often expect immediate payment for health services. Travelers have found that in some cases supplemental medical insurance with specific overseas coverage has proven useful. Further information on health matters can be obtained from the Centers for Disease Control's international travelers hotline (404) 332-4559.

Because crime against foreigners continues to increase, travelers are encouraged to stay in groups. Traders might find it necessary to hire security services to protect warehoused inventory and any transfer of funds.

The next chapter discusses how to do business in Asia.

10

Doing Business in Asia

ASIA IS BY FAR THE LARGEST TRADING REGION IN THE WORLD, COVERING more than 17 million miles with a population of more than 3 billion people. Asia includes Japan and Australia/New Zealand to the East and stretches as far West as Turkey and Israel. China and India are the most populous nations with 1.2 billion people and 900 million people respectively. Japan is the richest. This chapter concentrates only on three areas: Japan, China, and the Pacific Basin, including the Tigers of Asia (South Korea, Taiwan, Hong Kong, and Singapore). Additional information is available by calling (800) USA-TRADE or the PACRIM hotline at (202) 482-3875.

JAPAN

Japan is a dynamic nation of people with a population of about 125 million and a per capita gross national product (GNP) of more than $24,000, which makes Japan a prime target for international market expansion.

Import Policies

The average Japanese tariff is low—about 3.4%, but on certain items such as foodstuffs and leather goods, tariffs and quotas are quite trade restrictive. Duties are assessed on the C.I.F. (cost, insurance, freight) value at ad valorem or specific rates and, in a few instances, are charged on a combination of both.

Taxes

Since April 1989, the commodity tax has been replaced with a general consumption tax of 3% (6% on autos), which is levied on the c.i.f. plus duty value.

Marketing Strategy

The key to marketing success in Japan is commitment and persistence. You must ensure your product is of the highest quality and has excellent after-sales service. Without these two qualities, a product that might sell satisfactorily in other countries will not do well in Japan.

Japan's External Trade Organization

Japan has established a nonprofit, government-supported organization dedicated to promoting mutually beneficial trade with businesses of other nations. The *Japan External Trade Organization* (JETRO) is headquartered in Tokyo but maintains a network of 30 offices in Japan, as well as in 77 overseas offices in 57 countries. JETRO's services are free of charge and should be the first stop for any firm contemplating doing business in or with Japan. To contact JETRO, call the offices nearest you:

New York, NY	Chicago, IL
(212) 997-0400	(312) 527-9000
Houston, TX	Denver, CO
(713) 759-9595	(303) 629-0404
Los Angeles, CA	San Francisco, CA
(213) 624-8855	(415) 392-1333
Atlanta, GA	
(404) 681-0660	

Distribution and Sales Channels

The Japanese distribution system is as inefficient as it is complex. Multiple layers of middlemen typically are involved in a system of highly institutionalized marketing channels linking producers, retailers, and end-users.

If the market for your product is one in which there are a large number of end-users, it might be better to rely on an existing network of wholesalers. On the other hand, if your buyers are con-centrated, a single intermediary might be your best marketing method. To set up your own distribution system is very expensive initially but more efficient over the long-term.

Information

The U.S. Department of Commerce has set up a special Japan Export Information Center; call (202) 482-2425 or use the Japan Export Promotion Hotline fax: (202) 482-4565.

CHINA

The People's Republic of China (PRC) is one of the fastest growing economies in the world and the driving force has been world trade. Foreign trade as a percentage of GNP has risen from about 10% in the late 1970s to 38% in 1992.

China is a nation moving toward a market system. State-owned enterprises, banking, taxation, social security, and foreign trade are all in a state of reform.

In the past, trade with China was conducted by the former Ministry of Foreign Trade within the overall plans and guidelines es-tablished by the relevant economic policy-making bodies, such as the State Economic and Financial Commission, the State Planning Commission, and the State Energy Commission. Since 1979, China's foreign trade structure has undergone significant change and is still fluid. In recent times, there's been a significant shift to private en-terprise. A large number (about 6000) trading corporations (FTCs) have been granted trading rights. About 300 specialized FTCs re-main under the direct control of the Ministry of Foreign Trade and Economic Cooperation (MOFTEC), which still formulates central-ized plans for a small portion of state critical products.

Development Zones and Free Trade Zones

Over the years of reform, the government has promoted foreign trade by establishing special economic zones (SEZs) in about 20 coastal provinces and, since 1990, free zones in most coastal cities. These zones provide preferential treatment including tax holidays, import/export duty exemption, low income tax rates, and other incentives to induce technology and export-oriented foreign investment.

Hong Kong-China

Hong Kong has long been noted as an international trade player because of its huge reexport trade. More than 38,000 trading companies are registered on the tiny island, all of which are eager to do business with outsiders who wish to trade with China. These companies are typically small and tend to specialize in importing or exporting or reexporting. Many companies that wish to foray into the China market begin by establishing operations in Hong Kong.

In 1997, Hong Kong will become a "Special Administrative Region" of China, but the government has stated the system will not change for 50 years.

Establishing Contact

The best way to make contact with trading officials is to write or phone the Chinese consulate nearest your city. Address your inquiry to the Foreign Trade Officer and ask to be put in contact with the appropriate office in China. See the list of key contacts in *The China Business Guide*. This excellent publication can be obtained by calling (202) 512-1800, order number 003-009-00637-6; the cost is approximately $4. You can also call (202) 482-3583 and ask for the fax "Everything you want to know about exporting to China," or call the PacRim Flashfax at (202) 482-3875.

Negotiating a Contract

Negotiations with China tend to be more technical, more detailed, and more time-consuming than with other countries. For Western time-conscious people, the pace of Chinese negotiations is extremely frustrating. Their approach to negotiating is characterized by patience and attention to the greatest detail. The Chinese are excellent negotiators and are well aware of the ploys and tactics used by negotiators around the world. The Chinese use these tactics with varying degrees of subtlety. The Chinese emphasize getting to know their trading partners and maintaining relationships with "old friends."

Payment

Chinese sellers prefer to be denominated in their own currency—renminbi (RMB). Most sales and purchase transactions in the

China trade typically call for payment by irrevocable letters of credit (L/C) against presentation of sight draft and shipping documents. Chinese end-users must be able to acquire foreign currency for imports, which can be done in one of three ways: (a) government allocates hard currency for a specific deal, (b) the importer can use retained foreign currency from previous deals, or (c) a Chinese importer can request assistance from an FTC, which would buy the goods using its own foreign currency and then sell the product to the end-user in RMB.

China's New Value-Added Tax

As of January 1, 1994, exporters to China are subject to China's new value-added tax (VAT), which together with the new consumption tax, replaces the 1958 consolidated industrial and commercial tax. Customs duty is first calculated, then consumption tax (if applicable) is determined, and last, VAT is computed.

PACIFIC BASIN

The Pacific Basin is the fastest growing region of the world, but it is also the most widely dispersed. As a coherent trade area, it is weakened by its geography (Fig. 10-1). The economic gap is even more formidable. For instance, Indonesia's per capita GNP is about $500, while Singapore's is about $10,000.

Made up mainly of islands strung North and South across the Pacific Ocean, the Pacific Basin region includes Australia, Brunei, Cambodia, China, Canada, Chile, Hong Kong, Indonesia, North Korea, South Korea, Laos, Malaysia, Mexico, New Zealand, The Philippines, Singapore, Papua New Guinea, Taiwan, Thailand, Vietnam, and the United States.

The Four Tigers are Hong Kong, South Korea, Singapore, and Taiwan and are best known for their extraordinary economic progress during the second half of the twentieth century. Of course, Japan stands alone as the major trading nation of Asia, but since 1960, South Korea's economy has grown by about 1500% and its per capita income has risen nearly eightfold.

The entire Pacific Basin region, which already accounts for 40% of world trade, is now poised to grow at the rates previously attributed only to the Tigers.

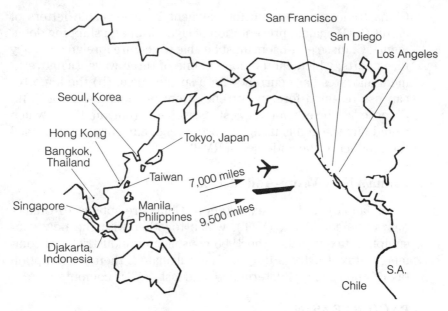

Fig. 10-1. Dispersement of potential Asian bloc

Regional Integration

The idea of a single Pacific Basin trade bloc similar to the North American Free Trade Area (NAFTA) and the European Union (EU) is difficult to grasp, but there is the distinct possibility that a third major trade bloc will be formed. The Asian bloc would then become the largest trade area in the world, with a total population of more than 2 billion, compared to the EU with about 350 million people and NAFTA with about 400 million. The Association of South East Asian Nations (ASEAN), formed in 1975, has considered expanding to become the Asia-Pacific Economic Cooperation (APEC) trade bloc or possibly the East Asia Economic Caucus (EAEC), which is similar to APEC but would exclude Canada, New Zealand, Australia, and the United States. Until an Asian regional trading area is formed, however, business practices continue to be conducted on a nation-by-nation basis.

APEC

At the APEC summit held in November 1994, 18 Pacific Rim nations agreed to remove trade and investment barriers by the year 2010 for industrialized countries and 10 years later for developing economies. Table 10-1 lists the members of the Asia-Pacific Economic Cooperation:

Table 10-1. APEC (Asia-Pacific Economic Cooperation).

ASEAN (Association of South East Asian Nations)

Indonesia	Singapore
Malaysia	Thailand
Philippines	

Plus

Australia	Japan
Brunei	Mexico
Canada	New Zealand
Chile	Papua New Guinea
China	South Korea
Chinese Taipei (Taiwan)	United States
Hong Kong	

The following are helpful publications and information sources:

- Japan Export Promotion (JEP) hotline: (202) 482-4565
- *Destination Japan: A Business Guide for the 90s—Second Edition,* U.S. Government Printing Office (see Appendix F for the GPO office nearest you)
- Pacific Basin hotline and flashfax documents: (202) 482-3875
- Vietnam Post-Embargo Document Index: (202)482-3875
- Africa and Near East and South Asia documents: (202) 482-0878
- South Asia automated information: (202) 482-4453
- China and Hong Kong business publications: (202) 512-1800
- *The China Business Guide*, U.S. Government Printing Office (see Appendix F for the GPO office nearest you); $4; order number 003-009-00637-6

The next chapter offers 20 tips for export/import success and how to make big profits.

11

Twenty Keys to Import/Export Success

SUCCESS IN THE INTERNATIONAL MARKETPLACE IS MEASURED IN PROFITS and market share. It is also measured in the satisfaction you feel in reaching new horizons and visiting places that previously were only dreams. You and your firm can be successful if you act on the 20 crucial keys presented in this chapter:

1. The most important key to success is commitment by you, the decision maker, to enter the global market. You'll reap tax advantages, sales volume advantages, the excitement of the international experience, and lots of profit. Change your game and get into the global competition. Get to work and earn a share of the more than $250 billion that is out there waiting for enthusiastic entrepreneurial Americans.

2. Go beyond cultural obstacles. Accept that the rest of the world isn't exactly like the United States. Other cultures have their way of doing things or they would change them. Get used to the idea that cultural differences exist, but be assured that the differences can be understood and even learned. At a minimum, the differences can be appreciated and respected. Remember that there are more similarities among people of the world than there are differences.

The Japanese like cars, and they don't dislike American cars. The problem is that American car manufacturers just haven't figured out how to satisfy the Japanese car consumer, who is used to a different style and, above all, different service considerations. The world is becoming more and more internationalized.

3. Plan, plan, plan, but don't treat international trade as a stand-alone process. Plan for success. Assuming that your initial market research effort revealed some demand for your product as it is or with minor redesign, develop a strategic plan for your business. From the beginning, *write* out your plan. What is your competitive advantage? What are your geographical and product line priorities? How are you going to penetrate the market?

4. The market, the market, the market. An early investigation of the market is the key that leads to success. Get an estimate of the demand for the products that you already manufacture. The best information will come from your own industry—here and overseas. Talk to those who have experience. Don't overlook available statistics and library resources. Lay out a map of the world and apply some logic. If you plan to export, divide the world into export regions and prioritize the regions based on broad assumptions of their need for your product and their ability to pay. Based on your common understanding of the various countries, regions, their languages, the environment, and their cultures, select one or more target countries for start-up. Do consider the political and financial stability of the country.

Use the same logic for imports. Examine a map of the United States or your region and divide the map into target segments. Do not try to sell to all of America, the entire world, or even one entire foreign country immediately, but remember that nothing happens until you sell something.

5. Information is crucial. Research is crucial to the success of your marketing plan. Begin with a list of the information you will need to support your analysis. What do you need to know about the regions of the United States (imports) or the foreign country (exports) you have selected? What level of detail will you require? Next, organize a list of the potential sources of your research. Classify your sources and begin the process of doing a logical sort of the material. You can gain the most accurate and meaningful information by traveling to the potential market.

6. What are your marketing goals? Develop a well researched, solidly reasoned marketing plan. It should include a background review, an analysis of the market environment, and a description of your goals in terms of your company.

7. Where there are competitors there is a market. Take a close look at the competition. It will be to your favor to discover that there is competition. Why? Because, where there is competition there is a market!

8. Be persistent; don't give up. Don't become discouraged if you find that your product is ahead of its time in the international marketplace. Don't give up on exporting. WD-40 and Coca-Cola created a global market for their product. Search for products that do have an overseas market and are similar to yours.

9. Adapt the product to the market. Learn what products your market likes and how they like the products, whether you are importing an article for American tastes or exporting a product for a foreign market. Be ready to adapt your product to the market. Redesign your product and compete.

10. Budget for success. Include international goals in your financial plan. Treat import/export start-up as you would any other entrepreneurial venture. Budget from the beginning and keep good books. Watch your costs and cash flow. Like any new business, expect short-term losses but plan for long-term gains.

11. You gotta manage. Manage for success. Develop the tactical plans that implement your overall strategic plan, such as a personnel plan, an advertising policy, a market entry, and a sales approach. Motivate your personnel by emphasizing team work.

12. Be patient; international trade takes longer. International trade takes a little longer than domestic trade to get off the ground. After all, there are oceans in between, and the transportation systems are slower. Every transaction will require financing. International financing and banking methods are sophisticated and generally excellent, but negotiations and transactions across borders take more time than domestic business.

13. The best long-term investment is a well planned trip. Those things that go right are those that the boss checks. And, in international business, that means international travel. After you have developed your strategic plan, visit the overseas sources or markets you have chosen. There is no substitute for first-hand information. You will find it interesting, rewarding, and essential to meet the people with which you will be doing business. Even after you have established a successful sales and distribution network, it will be necessary for you or your company representatives to visit your international contacts at least twice a year.

14. Walk on two legs. Carefully choose a good international banker, freight forwarder, and customhouse broker. Talk with them to learn the language of international business—pricing, quotations, shipping, and getting paid. Establish a good relationship and then stick with it. Deal with a bank that has personnel who are experienced in the international marketplace.

15. Proper communication gets sales results. Provide customer service the international way by communicating often, clearly, and simply. Keep your overseas business partners on the team by being particularly sensitive to communications, letters, telexes, and phone calls.

16. Expert counsel saves money. Minimize your inevitable mistakes by asking for help. Banks, customhouse brokers, freight forwarders, and the U.S. Department of Commerce are sources of free information. And most private consultants charge reasonable fees.

17. Selecting distributors is crucial. Your objective is to get your product in front of your buyer. The wrong distributor can stifle your market efforts and tie you up legally.

18. Stick to a marketing strategy. Don't chase orders. Of course, fill the over-the-counter orders, but be proactive rather than reactive. Establish an effective marketing effort according to your marketing plan.

19. International partners and customers should be treated the same as their domestic counterparts. It might surprise some people that the foreign ratio is less than half of the United State's bad debt ratio. The reason is that in the United States, credit is a way of life. In overseas markets, credit is still something to be earned as a result of having a record of prompt payment. Use common sense when extending credit to overseas customers, but don't use tougher rules than you use for your U.S. clients.

20. Don't fret about the international business cycle. Don't worry about booms or busts—just do it. International trade is exciting and profitable because there are so many side-benefits. Think of traveling to such exotic places as Hong Kong or Vienna and writing off the trip as a company expense.

Ok, you've found the sources, developed the markets, written the business plan, and have the entrepreneurial spirit to make your own import/export business a success. The time to get into the import/export market is now. I hope you earn a million dollars!

Glossary

acceptance The act of a drawee acknowledging in writing on the face of a draft payable at a fixed or determinable future date, that he or she will pay the draft at maturity.

acceptance draft A sight draft document against acceptance. *See also* **sight draft documents against acceptance**.

ad valorem Literally, according-to-value. *See* **duty**.

advisory capacity A term indicating that a shipper's agent or representative is not empowered to make definitive decisions or adjustments without approval of the group or individual represented. Compare **without reserve**.

affreightment (contract of) An agreement between steamship line (or similar carrier) and an importer or exporter in which cargo space is reserved on a vessel for a specified time and at a specified price. The importer/exporter is obligated to make payment whether or not the shipment is made.

after date A phrase indicating that payment on a draft or other negotiable instrument is due a specified number of days after presentation of the draft to the drawee or payee. Compare **after date, at sight**.

after sight A phrase indicating that the date of maturity of a draft or other negotiable instrument is fixed by the date on which it was drawn a specified number of days after presentation of the draft to the drawee or payee. Compare **after sight, at sight**.

agent *See* **representative**.

A.I.D. (Agency for International Development) A U.S. government institution that administers economic aid to foreign countries, makes long-term loans for expansion programs in less-developed countries, and guarantees loans made by private enterprise. These loans often provide the funds to pay for U.S. products.

air waybill   The carrying agreement between shipper and air carrier that is obtained from the airline used to ship the goods. Technically, it is a nonnegotiable instrument of air transportation that serves as a receipt for the shipper, indicating that the carrier has accepted the goods listed therein and obligates itself to carry the consignment to the airport of destination according to specified conditions. Compare inland bill of lading, ocean bill of lading, through bill of lading.

all risks clause   An insurance provision that provides additional coverage to an Open Cargo Policy usually for an additional premium. Contrary to its name, the clause does not protect against all risks. The more common perils it does cover are theft, pilferage, nondelivery, fresh water damage, contact with other cargo, breakage and leakage, inherent vice, loss of market, and losses caused by delay are not covered.

alongside   A phrase referring to the side of a ship. Goods to be delivered alongside are to be placed on the dock or lighter within reach of the transport ship's tackle so that they can be loaded aboard the ship.

amendment—letter of credit   A change in the terms, amount, or expiration date of a letter of credit.

antidiversion clause   *See* **destination control statement**.

arbitrage   The process of buying foreign exchange, stocks, bonds, and other commodities in one market and immediately selling them in another market at higher prices.

ATA   Admission Temporary Admission.

ATA Carnet   A customs document that enables one to carry or send goods temporarily into certain foreign countries without paying duties or posting bonds.

at sight   A phrase indicating that payment on a draft or other negotiable instrument is due upon presentation or demand. Compare **after sight, after-date**.

authority to pay   A document comparable to a revocable letter of credit but under whose terms the authority to pay the seller stems from the buyer rather than from a bank.

balance of trade   The balance between a country's exports and imports.

banker's bank   A bank that is established by mutual consent by independent and unaffiliated banks to provide a clearinghouse for financial transactions.

barratry   Negligence or fraud on the part of a ship's officers or crew resulting in loss to the owners. *See* **open cargo policy**.

barter   Trade in which merchandise is exchanged directly for other merchandise without use of money. Barter is an important means of trade with countries using currency that is not readily convertible.

beneficiary The person in whose favor a letter of credit is issued or a draft is drawn.

bill of exchange *See* **draft**.

bill of lading A document that provides the terms of the contract between the shipper and the transportation company to move freight between stated points at a specified charge.

blocked exchange Exchange that cannot be freely converted into other currencies.

bonded warehouse A building authorized by Customs authorities for the storage of goods without payment of duties until removal.

booking An arrangement with a steamship company for the acceptance and carriage of freight.

broker *See* **export broker**.

Brussels Tariff Nomenclature *See* **Nomenclature of the Customs Cooperation Council**.

buying agent An agent who buys in this country for foreign importers, especially for such large foreign users as mines, railroads, governments, and public utilities. Synonymous with "purchasing agent."

carnet *See* **ATA Carnet**.

carrier A transportation line that hauls cargo.

cash against documents (c.a.d.) Payment for goods in which a commission house or other intermediary transfers title documents to the buyer upon payment in cash.

cash in advance (c.i.a.) Payment for goods in which the price is paid in full before shipment is made. This method usually is used only for small purchases or when the goods are built.

cash with order (c.w.o.) Payment for goods in which the buyer pays when ordering and in which the transaction is binding on both parties.

CCCN (The Customs Cooperation Council Nomenclature) The customs tariff used by many countries worldwide. It is also known as the Brussels Tariff Nomenclature. Compare **standard industrial classification, standard international trade classification, tariff schedule, commodity groupings**.

certificate of free sale A certificate, required by some foreign governments, stating that the goods for export, if products under the jurisdiction of the United States Food and Drug Administration (FDA), are acceptable for sale in the United States, i.e., that the products are sold freely without restriction. FDA will issue shippers a "letter of comment" to satisfy foreign requests or regulations.

certificate of inspection A document in which certification is made as to the good condition of the merchandise immediately prior to shipment. The buyer usually designates the inspecting organization, usually an independent inspection firm or governmental body.

certificate of manufacture A statement by a producer, sometimes notarized, that certifies that manufacture has been completed and that the goods are at the disposal of the buyer.

certificate of origin A document in which certification is made as to the country of origin of the merchandise.

C & F (cost and freight) A pricing term indicating that these costs are included in the quoted price. Same as c.i.f. (cost, insurance, and freight), except that insurance is covered by the buyer.

Chamber of Commerce An association of business people whose purpose is to promote commercial and industrial interests in the community.

charter party A written contract, usually on a special form, between the owner of a vessel and a charterer who rents use of the vessel or a part of its freight space. The contract generally includes the freight rates and the ports involved in the transportation.

C & I (cost and insurance) A pricing term indicating that these costs are included in the quoted price.

C.I.F. (cost, insurance, and freight) A pricing term under which the seller pays all expenses involved in the placing of merchandise on board a carrier and in addition prepays the freight and insures the goods to an agreed destination.

C.I.F. & C. (cost, insurance, freight, and commission) A pricing term indicating that these costs are included in the price.

C.I.F. & E. [cost, insurance, freight, and (currency) exchange] A pricing term indicating that these costs are included in the price.

Clayton Act A major U.S. antitrust law passed in 1914 to supplement the Sherman Act. The Clayton Act deals primarily with the prohibition of price discrimination among buyers by sellers in the sale of commodities and certain corporate mergers where the effect might be to substantially less encompetition or tend to create a monopoly.

clean bill of lading A bill of lading signed by the transportation company indicating that the shipment has been received in good condition with no irregularities in the packing or general condition of all or any part of the shipment. *See* **foul bill of lading**.

clean draft A draft to which no documents have been attached.

collection The procedure involved in a bank's collecting money for a seller against a draft drawn on a buyer abroad, usually through a correspondent bank.

collection papers All documents (invoices, bills of lading, etc.) submitted, usually with a draft or against a letter of credit, to a buyer for the purpose of receiving payment for a shipment.

commercial attache The commercial expert on the diplomatic staff of his or her country's embassy or large consulate in a foreign country.

commercial invoice A trade invoice.

commission agent *See* **purchasing agent** and **foreign sales representative**.

commission representative *See* **foreign sales representative**.

Commodity Credit Corporation A government corporation controlled by the Department of Agriculture to provide financing and stability to the marketing and exporting of agricultural commodities.

commodity groupings A numerical system used by the U.S. Bureau of the Census to group imports and exports in broader categories than are provided by the tariff schedules. Currently, Schedule A is used to categorize imports, Schedule E for exports. Schedule B was replaced by Schedule E in 1978. Compare **Standard Industrial Classification, tariff schedules of the United States**.

common carrier An individual, partnership, or corporation that transports persons or goods for compensation.

compensation A form of countertrade in which the seller agrees to take full or partial payment in goods or services generated from the sale.

conference line A member of a steamship conference. *See* **steamship conference**.

confirmed letter of credit Issued by a bank abroad whose validity and terms are confirmed to the beneficiary in the United States by a U.S. bank.

consignee The person, firm, or representative to whom a seller or shipper sends merchandise and who, upon presentation of the necessary documents, is recognized as the owner of the merchandise for the purpose of the payment of Customs duties. This term is also used as applying to one to whom goods are shipped, usually at the shipper's risk, when an outright sale has not been made. *See* **consignment**.

consignee marks *See* **marks**.

consignment Merchandise shipped to a consignee abroad when an actual purchase has not been made, under an agreement by which the consignee is obligated to sell the goods for the account of the consignor, and to remit proceeds as goods are sold.

consul   A government official residing in a foreign country who is charged with the representation of the interests of his or her country and its nationals.

consular declaration   A formal statement, made to the consul of a foreign country, describing goods to be shipped.

consular invoice   A detailed statement regarding the character of goods shipped, duly certified by the consul of the importing country at the port of shipment.

consulate   The official premises of a foreign government representative.

contingency insurance   Insurance taken out by the exporter complementary to insurance bought by the consignee abroad.

correspondent bank   A bank that is a depositor in another bank, accepting and collecting items for its bank.

counterpurchase   One of the most common forms of countertrade in which the seller receives cash but contractually agrees to buy local products or services as a percentage of cash received and over an agreed period of time.

countertrade   International trade in which the seller is required to accept goods or other instruments of trade, in partial or whole payment for his or her products.

countervailing duty   An extra duty imposed by the Secretary of Commerce to offset export grants, bounties, or subsidies paid to foreign suppliers in certain countries by the government of those countries as an incentive to export.

country of origin   The country in which a particular commodity is manufactured.

credit risk insurance   A form of insurance that covers the seller against loss due to nonpayment on the part of the buyer.

customhouse broker   An individual or firm licensed to enter and clear through customs.

customs   The duties levied by a country on imports and exports. The term also applies to the procedures and organization involved in such collection.

d/a   *See* **documents against acceptance**.

date draft   A draft drawn to mature on a specified number of days after the date it is issued, with or without regard to the date of acceptance.

delivery point   *See* **specific delivery point**.

demurrage   Excess time taken for loading or unloading a vessel as a result of a shipper. Charges are assessed by the shipping company.

Department of Commerce   An agency of government whose purpose is to promote commercial industrial interests in the country.

destination control statement   Any one of various statements that the U.S. government requires to be displayed on export shipments and that specify the destination for which export of the shipment has been authorized.

devaluation   The official lowering of the value of one country's currency in terms of one or more foreign currencies. Thus, if the U.S. dollar is devaluated in relation to the French franc, $1 will buy fewer francs than before.

developed countries   A term used to distinguish the more industrialized nations, including all OECD member countries as well as the Soviet Union and most of the socialist countries of Eastern Europe, from developing—or less developed—countries. The developed countries are sometimes collectively designated as the "North," because most of them are in the Northern Hemisphere.

developing countries (lcds)   A broad range of countries that generally lack a high degree of industrialization, infrastructure and other capital investment, sophisticated technology, widespread literacy, and advanced living standards among their populations as a whole. The developing countries are sometimes collectively designated as the "South," because a large number of them are in the Southern Hemisphere. All of the countries of Africa (except South Africa), Asia, and Oceania (except Australia, Japan and New Zealand), Latin America, and the Middle East are generally considered "developing countries," as are a few European countries (Cyprus, Malta, Turkey, and Yugoslavia, for example). Some experts differentiate four subcategories of developing countries as having different economic needs and interest:

1. A few relatively wealthy OPEC countries—sometimes referred to as oil exporting developing countries—share a particular interest in a financially sound international economy and open capital markets. **2.** Newly Industrializing Countries (NICs) have a growing stake in an open international trading system. **3.** A number of middle income countries—principally commodity exporters—have shown a particular interest in commodity stabilization schemes. **4.** More than 30 very poor countries ("least developed countries") are predominantly agricultural, have sharply limited development prospects during the near future, and tend to be heavily dependent on official development assistance. *See* **least developed countries**.

disc   *See* **Domestic International Sales Corporation**.

discount (financial)   A deduction from the face value of commercial paper in consideration of cash by the seller before a specified date.

discrepancy—letter of credit   When documents presented do not conform to the terms of the letter of credit, it is referred to as a discrepancy.

dispatch   An amount paid by a vessel's operator to a charterer if loading or unloading is completed in less time than stipulated in the charter party.

distributor   A firm that sells directly for a manufacturer, usually on an exclusive contract for a specified territory, and who maintains an inventory on hand.

dock receipt A receipt issued by an ocean carrier or its agent, acknowledging that the shipment has been delivered, or received at the dock or warehouse of the carrier.

documentary credit *See* **letter of credit (commercial)**.

documentary draft A draft to which documents are attached.

documentation/documents *See* **shippers documents**.

documents against acceptance (d/a) A type of payment for goods in which the documents transferring title to the goods are not given to the buyer until he has accepted the draft issued against him.

documents against payment (d/p) A type of payment for goods in which the documents transferring title to the goods are not given to the buyer until he or she has paid the value of a draft issued against them.

Domestic International Sales Corporation (DISC) An export sales corporation set up by a U.S. company under U.S. government authorization to promote exports from the United States by giving the exporter economic advantages not available outside such authorization.

domicile The place where draft or acceptance is made payable.

d/p *See* **documents against payment**.

draft The same as a bill of exchange. A written order for a certain sum of money to be transferred on a certain date from the person who owes the money or agrees to make the payment (the drawee) to the creditor to whom the money is owed (the drawer of the draft). *See* **date draft, documentary draft, sight draft, time draft**.

drawback (import) The repayment, up to 99%, of Customs duties paid on merchandise which later is exported, as part of a finished product, is known as a drawback. It refers also to a refund of a domestic tax that has been paid upon exportation of imported merchandise.

drawee One on whom a draft is drawn, and who owes the stated amount. *See* **draft**.

drawer One who draws a draft, and receives payment. *See* **draft**.

dumping Exporting merchandise into a country (e.g., the United States) at prices below the prices in the domestic market.

duty The tax imposed by a government on merchandise imported from another country.

Edge Act Corporation Banks that are subsidiaries to bank holding companies or other banks established to engage in foreign business transactions. They were established by an Act of Congress in 1919.

eurodollars U.S. dollars placed on deposit in banks outside the United States (primarily in Europe).

exchange permit   A governmental permit sometimes required of an importer to enable him or her to convert his or her own country's currency into foreign currency with which to pay a seller in another country.

exchange rate   The price of one currency in terms of another, i.e., the number of units of one currency that may be exchanged for one unit of another currency.

exchange regulations/restrictions   Restrictions imposed by an importing country to protect its foreign exchange reserves. *See* **exchange permit**.

excise tax   A domestic tax assessed on the manufacture, sale, or use of a commodity within a country. Usually refundable if the product is exported.

EX "from" (point of origin)   A pricing term (EX Factory, EX Warehouse, etc) under which the seller agrees to place the goods at the buyer's disposal at the agreed place, with costs from that point being paid by the buyer.

Eximbank   The Export/Import Bank of the United States in Washington, DC.

expiration date   The final date upon which the presentation of documents and drawing of drafts under a letter of credit may be made.

export   To send goods to a foreign country or overseas territory.

export broker   One who brings together the exporter and importer for a fee and then withdraws from the transaction.

export declaration   *See* **Shippers Export Declaration**.

export license   A governmental permit required to export certain products to certain destinations.

Export Management Company (EMC)   A firm that acts as local export sales agent for several noncompeting manufacturers. (Term synonymous with "Manufacturer's Export Agent.")

export merchant   A producer or merchant who sells directly to a foreign purchaser without going through an intermediate such as an export broker.

export trading company   An ETC, as envisioned by the ETC Act, is a company doing business in the United States principally to export goods or services produced in the United States or to facilitate such exports by unaffiliated persons. It can be owned by foreigners and can import, barter, and arrange sales between third countries, as well as export.

Export Trading Company Act   This act was passed on October 8, 1982 and was designed to encourage the formation of Export Trading Companies. It establishes an Office of Export Trading Company Affairs in Commerce, permits bankers' banks and holding companies to invest in ETCs, reduces the restrictions on export financing provided by financial institutions, and modifies the application of the antitrust laws to certain export trade.

factoring   A method used by businesses, including trading companies, to obtain cash for discounted accounts receivables or other assets.

F.A.S.—free along side, as in fas (vessel)   A pricing term under which the seller must deliver the goods to a pier and place them within reach of the ship's loading equipment.

FCIA   Foreign Credit Insurance Association.

F.I.—free in   A pricing term indicating that the charterer of a vessel is responsible for the cost of loading goods into the vessel.

F.O.B.—free on board, as in f.o.b. (vessel)   A pricing term under which the seller must deliver the goods on board the ship at the point named at his own expense. Similar terms are "f.o.b. (destination)" and "f.o.b. (named point of exportation)."

F.O.—free out   A pricing term indicating that the charterer of a vessel is responsible for the cost of loading goods from the vessel.

force majeure   The title of a standard clause in marine contracts exempting the parties for nonfulfillment of their obligations as a result of conditions beyond their control, such as earthquakes, floods, or war.

Foreign Credit Insurance Association (FCIA)   An association of 50 insurance companies that operate in conjunction with the Eximbank to provide comprehensive insurance for exporters against nonpayment. FCIA underwrites the commercial credit risks. Eximbank covers the political risk and any excessive commercial risks.

foreign distribution   *See* **distributor**.

foreign exchange   A currency or credit instrument of a foreign country. Also, transactions involving purchase and/or sale of currencies.

foreign freight forwarder   *See* **freight forwarder**.

foreign sales agent   An individual or firm that serves as the foreign representative of a domestic supplier and seeks sales abroad for the supplier.

foreign sales representative   A representative or agent residing in a foreign country who acts as a salesman for a U.S. manufacturer, usually for a commission. Sometimes referred to as a "sales agent" or "commission agent." *See* **representative**.

foreign trade zone   An area where goods of foreign origin may be brought in for reexport or transshipment without the payment of Customs duty.

foul bill of lading   A receipt for goods issued by a carrier bearing a notation that the outward containers or goods have been damaged. *See* **clean bill of lading**.

F.P.A.—free of particular average   The title of a clause used in marine insurance, indicating that partial loss or damage to a foreign shipment is not covered. (Note: Loss resulting from certain conditions, such as the sinking or burning of the ship, may be specifically exempted from the effect of the clause.) Compare **WPA**.

FSC—foreign sales corporation The Foreign Sales Corporation (FSC) replaces the DISC. To qualify for special tax treatment, an FSC must be a foreign corporation, maintain a summary of its permanent books of accounting at the foreign office, and have at least one director resident outside of the United States. A portion of the foreign sales corporation's income (generally corresponding to the tax deferred income of the DISC) would be exempt from U.S. tax at both the FSC and the U.S. corporate parent levels. This exemption is achieved by allowing a domestic corporation that is an FSC shareholder a 100% deduction for a portion of dividends received from an FSC attributable to economic activity actually conducted outside the U.S. Customs territory. Interest, dividends, royalties, or other investment income of an FSC would be subject to U.S. tax.

free port An area generally encompassing a port and its surrounding locality into which goods may enter duty-free or subject only to minimal revenue tariffs.

free sale *See* **certificate of free sale**.

free trade zone *See* **foreign trade zone**.

freight forwarder An agent who assists his or her exporter client in moving cargo to a foreign destination.

General Agreement on Tariffs and Trade (GATT) GATT is a multilateral trade treaty among governments, embodying rights and obligations. The detailed rules set out in the agreement constitute a code which the parties to the agreement have agreed upon to govern their trading relationships.

general license (export) Government authorization to export without specific documentary approval.

gross weight Total weight of goods, packing, and container, ready for shipment.

handling charges The forwarder's fee to his or her shipper client.

import To bring merchandise into a country from another country or overseas territory.

import license A governmental document that permits the importation of a product or material into a country where such licenses are necessary.

in bond A term applied to the status of merchandise admitted provisionally into a country without payment of duties. *See* **bonded warehouse**.

inconvertibility The inability to exchange the currency of one country for the currency of another.

inherent vice Defects or characteristics of a product that could lead to deterioration without outside influence. An insurance term. *See* **all risks clause**.

inland bill of lading A bill of lading used in transporting goods overland to the exporter's international carrier. Although a through bill of lading sometimes can be used, it is usually necessary to prepare both an inland bill of lading and an ocean bill of lading for export shipments. Compare **airway bill, ocean bill of lading, through bill of lading**.

inland carrier   A transportation line that handles export or import cargo between the port and inland points.

insurance certificate   A document issued by an insurance company, usually to order of shipper under a marine policy, and insuring a particular shipment of merchandise.

international freight forwarder   *See* **freight forwarder**.

International Trade Administration (ITA)   The ITA is a division of the Department of Commerce designed to promote world trade and to strengthen the international trade and investment position of the United States.

invoice   *See* **commercial invoice**.

irrevocable   Applied to letters of credit. An irrevocable letter of credit is one that cannot be altered or cancelled once it has been negotiated between the buyer and his bank.

joint venture   A commercial or industrial arrangement in which principals of one company share control and ownership with principals of another.

least developed countries (ldcs)   Some 36 of the world's poorest countries, considered by the United Nations to be the least developed of the less developed countries. Most of them are small in terms of area and population, and some are land-locked or small island countries. They generally are characterized by low per capita incomes, literacy levels, and medical standards, subsistence agriculture, and a lack of exploitable minerals and competitive industries. Many suffer from aridity, floods, hurricanes, and excessive animal and plant pests, and most are situated in the zone 10 to 30 degrees north latitude. These countries have little prospect of rapid economic development in the foreseeable future and are likely to remain heavily dependent upon official development assistance for many years. Most are in Africa, but a few, such as Bangladesh, Afghanistan, Laos, and Nepal, are in Asia. Haiti is the only country in the Western Hemisphere classified by the United Nations as "least developed."

legal weight   The weight of the goods plus immediate wrappings that go along with the goods, e.g., contents of a tin can together with its can. *See* **net weight**.

letter of credit (commercial)   Abbreviated "L/C." A document issued by a bank at buyer's request in favor of a seller, promising an agreed amount of money on receipt by the bank of certain documents within a specified time.

license   *See* **export license, import license, validated license**.

licensing   The grant or technical assistance service and or the use of product rights, such as a trademark in return for royalty payments.

lighter   An open or covered barge towed by a tugboat and used mainly in harbors and inland waterways.

lighterage   The loading or unloading of a ship by means of a barge, or lighter which because of shallow water permits the ship from coming to shore.

manufacturer's export agent   *See* **Export Management Company**.

marine insurance   An insurance that will compensate the owner of goods transported on the seas in the event of loss which cannot be legally recovered from the carrier. Also covers air shipments.

marks   A set of letters, numbers, and/or geometric symbols, generally followed by the name of the port of destination, placed on packages for export for identification purposes.

maturity date   The date upon which a draft or acceptance becomes due for payment.

most-favored-nation status   All countries having this designation receive equal treatment with respect to customs and tariffs.

named point   *See* **specific delivery point**.

net weight   Weight of the goods alone without any immediate wrapping, e.g., the weight of the contents of a tin can without the weight of the can. *See* **legal weight**.

Nomenclature of the Customs Cooperation Council   This term was known as the Brussels Classification Nomenclature prior to January 1, 1975. It is the customs tariff adhered to by most European countries and many other countries throughout the world, and only recently by the United States.

ocean bill of lading   A bill of lading (B/L) indicating that the exporter consigns a shipment to an international carrier for transportation to a specified foreign market. Unlike an inland B/L, the ocean B/L also serves as a collection document. If it is a straight B/L, the foreign buyer can obtain the shipment from the carrier by simply showing proof of identity. If a negotiable B/L is used, the buyer must first pay for the goods, post a bond, or meet other conditions agreeable to the seller. Compare **air waybill, inland bill of lading, through bill of lading**.

offset   A variation of countertrade in which the seller is required to assist in or arrange for the marketing of locally-produced goods.

on board bill of lading   A bill of lading in which a carrier acknowledges that goods have been placed on board a certain vessel.

open account   A trade arrangement in which goods are shipped to a foreign buyer without guarantee of payment. The obvious risk this method poses to the supplier makes it essential that the buyer's integrity be unquestionable.

open cargo policy   Synonymous with **floating policy**. An insurance policy which binds the insurer automatically to protect with insurance all shipments made by the insured from the moment the shipment leaves the initial shipping point until delivered at destination. The insuring conditions include clauses naming such risks insured against as "perils of the sea"—fire, jettison, forcible theft, and barratry. *See* **perils of the sea, barratry, all risks clause**.

open insurance policy   A marine insurance policy that applies to all shipments made by an exporter over a period of time rather than to one shipment only.

OPIC (Overseas Private Investment Corporation)   A wholly-owned government corporation designed to promote private U.S. investment in developing countries by promoting political risk insurance and some financing assistance.

order bill of lading   A negotiable bill of lading made out to the order of the shipper.

packing list   A list that shows number and kinds of packages being shipped, totals of gross, legal, and net weights of the packages, and marks and numbers on the packages. The list might be requested by an importer or might be required by an importing country to facilitate the clearance of goods through customs.

parcel post receipt   The postal authorities' signed acknowledgement of delivery to them of a shipment made by parcel post.

perils of the sea   A marine insurance term used to designate heavy weather, straining, lightning, collision, and seawater damage.

phytosanitary inspection certificate   A certificate, issued by the U.S. Department of Agriculture, to satisfy import regulations of foreign countries, indicating that a U.S. shipment has been inspected and is free from harmful pests and plant diseases.

piggybacking   The assigning of export marketing and distribution functions by one manufacturer to another.

port marks   *See* **marks**.

procuring agent   *See* **purchasing agent**.

pro forma invoice   An invoice forwarded by the seller of goods prior to shipment to advise the buyer of the weight and value of the goods.

purchasing agent   An agent who purchases goods in his or her own country on behalf of large foreign buyers such as government agencies and large private concerns.

quota   The total quantity of a product or commodity that may be imported into a country without restriction or the penalty of additional duties or taxes.

quotation   An offer to sell goods at a stated price and under stated terms.

rate of exchange   The basis upon which money of one country will be exchanged for that of another. Rates of exchange are established and quoted for foreign currencies on the basis of the demand, supply, and stability of the individual currencies. *See* **exchange rate**.

representative The word representative is preferred to the word agent in writing, since agent, in an exact legal sense, connotes more binding powers and responsibilities than representative. *See* **foreign sales representative**.

revocable Applies to letters of credit. A revocable letter of credit is one which can be altered or cancelled by the buyer after he or she has opened it through his bank. *See* **irrevocable**.

royalty payment The share of the product or profit paid by a licensee to his or her licensor. *See* **licensing**.

sales agent *See* **foreign sales representative**.

sales representative *See* **foreign sales representative**.

sanitary certificate A certificate that attests to the purity or absence of disease or pests in the shipment of food products, plants, seeds, and live animals.

s.a. (societe anonyme) A French expression meaning a corporation.

Schedule B Refers to "Schedule B, Statistical Classification of Domestic and Foreign Commodities Exported from the United States."

s/d *See* **sight draft**.

Sherman Act This law bars contracts, combinations, or conspiracies in restraint of trade and makes it a violation of law to monopolize or attempt to, or conspire to monopolize any trade in interstate or foreign commerce. Jurisdiction requires a direct, substantial, and reasonably foreseeable effect on domestic trade or commerce or on the export commerce of a person engaged in such commerce in the United States.

shippers documents Commercial invoices, bills of lading, insurance certificates, consular invoices, and related documents.

Shippers Export Declaration A form required by the U.S. Department of Treasury and completed by a shipper showing the value, weight, consignee, destination, etc., of export shipments as well as Schedule B identification number.

ship's manifest A true list in writing of the individual shipments comprising the cargo of a vessel, signed by the captain.

SIC *See* **standard industrial classification**.

sight draft (s/d) A draft so drawn as to be payable upon presentation to the drawee or at a fixed or determinable date thereafter. *See* **documents against acceptance, documents against payment**.

SITC *See* **Standard International Trade Classification**.

specific delivery point A point in sales quotations that designates specifically where and within what geographical locale the goods will be delivered at the expense and responsibility of the seller; e.g., F.A.S. named vessel at named port of export.

spot exchange   The purpose or sale of foreign exchange for immediate delivery.

Standard Industrial Classification (SIC)   A numerical system developed by the U.S. government for the classification of commercial services and industrial products. Also classifies establishments by type of activity.

Standard International Trade Classification (SITC)   A numerical system developed by the United Nations to classify commodities used in international trade as an aid to reporting trade statistics.

state-controlled trading company   In a country with a state trading monopoly, a trading entity empowered by the country's government to conduct export business.

steamship conference   A group of vessel operators joined together for the purpose of establishing freight rates. A shipper might receive reduced rates if the shipper enters into a contract to ship on vessels of conference members only.

stocking distributor   A distributor who maintains an inventory of goods of a manufacturer.

straight bill of lading   A bill of lading, nonnegotiable, in which the goods are consigned directly to a named consignee.

swap arrangements   A form of countertrade in which the seller sells on credit and then transfers the credit to a third party.

switch arrangements   A form of countertrade in which the seller sells on credit and then transfers the credit to a third party.

tare weight   The weight of packing and containers without the goods to be shipped.

tariff   A schedule or system of duties imposed by a government on goods imported or exported, the rate of duty imposed in a tariff.

tariff schedules of the United States (tsus)   A standard numerical system used by the U.S. Customs Bureau to classify imports and exports. Compare **Standard Industrial Classification, Standard Industrial Trade Classification**.

TDP   *See* **Trade and Development Program**.

tenor   The time fixed or allowed for payment, as in "the tenor of a draft."

through bill of lading   A single bill of lading covering the domestic and international carriage of an export shipment. An air waybill, for instance, is essentially a through bill of lading used for air shipments. Ocean shipments, on the other hand, usually require two separate documents—an inland bill of lading for domestic carriage and an ocean bill of lading for international carriage. Through bills of lading, therefore, cannot be used. Compare **air waybill, inland bill of lading, ocean bill of lading**.

time draft A draft drawn so it matures at a certain fixed time after presentation or acceptance.

Trade Development Program (TDP) This program is designed to promote economic development in the Third World and the sale of U.S. goods and services to these developing countries. It operates as part of the International Development Cooperative Agency.

trade mission A mission to a foreign country organized to promote trade through the establishment of contracts and exposure to the commercial environment. They are frequently organized by federal, state, or local agencies.

tramp steamer A ship not operating on regular routes or schedules.

trust receipt Release of merchandise by a bank to a buyer in which the bank retains title to the merchandise. The buyer, who obtains the goods for manufacturing or sales purposes, is obligated to maintain the goods (or the proceeds from their sale) distinct from the remainder of his or her assets and to hold them ready for repossession by the bank.

turnkey A method of construction whereby the contractor assumes total responsibility from design through completion of the task.

United States standard master A single business form with correctable stencil which includes space for information required on many different export forms. Use of this form enables multiple typing.

validated license A government document authorizing the export of commodities within limitations set forth in the document.

vertical ETC An ETC that integrates a range of functions taking products from suppliers to consumers.

visa A signature of formal approval on an entree document. Obtained from a consulate.

warehouse receipt A receipt issued by a warehouse listing goods received for storage.

w.a.—with average A marine insurance term meaning that a shipment is protected from partial damage whenever the damage exceeds 3% (or some other percentage).

Webb-Pomerene Association Institutions engaged in exporting that combine the products of similar producers for overseas sales. These associations have partial exemption from U.S. antitrust laws but may not engage in third country trade or combine to export services.

wharfage Charge assessed by carrier for the handling of incoming or outgoing ocean cargo.

without reserve A term indicating that a shipper's agent or representative is empowered to make definitive decisions and adjustments abroad without approval of the group individual represented. Compare **advisory capacity**.

Index

Illustration page numbers are in **boldface**.

About the Author

Carl Nelson is a recognized global trade strategist. In addition to this book, he's published *Your Own Import-Export Business: Winning the Trade Game, Global Business Trade Communications*; *Global Success: International Business Tactics for the 1990s*, McGraw-Hill; and *Managing Globally: A Complete Guide to Competing Worldwide*, Irwin Professional Publishing.

Dr. Nelson is a former chief executive of five organizations and is currently president of Global Business and Trade, an international business consulting and training company. He is a decorated former naval captain who held many demanding command and staff positions in strategy, planning, and logistics. Dr. Nelson is listed in Who's Who in California and in the World.

Dr. Nelson is an adjunct professor at several San Diego universities and has conducted worldwide workshops and seminars about global strategy, international development, Mexican Maquiladora operations, and economic integration (NAFTA) and the European Union (EU).

Dr. Nelson earned his Doctorate in Business Administration, Finance, (emphasis on international trade) from the United States International University (USIU) in San Diego, California where his research focused on U.S. small business export problems. He was recognized by USIU with its 1989 outstanding alumni award. Dr. Nelson is also a graduate of the Naval War College, holds a Master of Science degree in Management (Economics/Systems Analysis) from the Naval Post Graduate School in Monterey, California, and an engineering degree from the U.S. Naval Academy at Annapolis, Maryland.